Elliot Yale Neaman

Selected Writings

A Journey in Intellectual History (1988–2025)

With a foreword by Martin Woessner

The Best of Scholars and Scholarship in the Humanities

Edited by:
Elliot Y. Neaman, Matthew Feldman, and Karim Mamdani

ISSN (print): 3054-0488 ISSN (digital): 3054-0496

1 Elliot Neaman
Selected Writings
A Journey in Intellectual History (1988–2025)
With a foreword by Martin Woessner
ISBN 978-3-8382-2000-0

Elliot Yale Neaman

SELECTED WRITINGS

A Journey in Intellectual History (1988–2025)

With a foreword by Martin Woessner

ibidem
Verlag

Bibliographic information published by the Deutsche Nationalbibliothek

Die Deutsche Nationalbibliothek lists this publication in the Deutsche Nationalbibliografie; detailed bibliographic data are available on the Internet at http://dnb.d-nb.de.

Bibliografische Information der Deutschen Nationalbibliothek

Die Deutsche Nationalbibliothek verzeichnet diese Publikation in der Deutschen Nationalbibliografie; detaillierte bibliografische Daten sind im Internet über http://dnb.d-nb.de abrufbar.

Cover picture: Martin Jay (left) and the author (right) at graduation ceremonies, University of California, Berkeley, May 1993.

ISBN (Print): 978-3-8382-2000-0

ISBN (E-Book [PDF]): 978-3-8382-8000-4

Printed in the United States of America

For Nina,
who saw from far away what I could not see up close

Table of Contents

Acknowledgments 9
Introduction 11
Foreword 19

Part One: Collective Memory and Geopolitics 29
I. Politics of Life and Death: Globalism's Conceptual Roots in German Military Strategy 33
II. Towards a Critical Hermeneutics of the Enemy: A Whigless Reflection on Collective Memory 47

Part Two: World and Ideas of Ernst Jünger 71
I. Unfinished Business: Ernst Jünger's Legacy 73
II. Intimité: Ernst Jünger's French Connections 93
III. Hiding in Plain Sight: Ernst Jünger's Own Inner Emigration 115
IV. A Crononaut in Swabia: Ernst Jünger and Postwar German Conservatism 123
V. L'Ernst Jünger in the Sky with Diamonds: A Visit to Godenholm 145
VI. Mutiny on Board Modernity: Heidegger, Sorel and Soft Fascism 151

Part Three: Leftwing Radicalism in Postwar Germany 187
I. Ideas of and About 1968 189
II. West German Generations and the *Gewaltfrage*: The Conflict of the Sixty-Eighters and the Forty-Fivers 213

Part Four: The Book Matters 245
I. Avihu Zakai: *The Pen Confronts the Sword: Exiled German Scholars Confront Nazism* 247
II. Johannes Fritsche: *Historical Destiny and National Socialism in Heidegger's Being and Time* 255
III. Ben Mercer: *Student Revolt in 1968; France, Italy, and West Germany* 263

Part Five: Interview with Martin Woessner 269

Acknowledgments

I aim to keep my expression of gratitude short and sweet. I have been unwittingly lucky to have met and kept so many friends in my life. I must have done something right, and lucky to have received their trust and affection, deserved or not. To list them all here would run the risk of offending someone who I never should have left out. I wrote an exhaustive list in the acknowledgements section of my last book, *Free Radicals*. Things have not changed much, so I am grateful to you all, and will remain so to my last breath. I thank my family, my mother Leah, my sister Evelyn, my brother Noah, and my beautiful and wise daughter, Rebba Estie Spike-Neaman. I would like to express deep gratitude for this book to Columbia University Press and the ibidem Verlag in Germany, in particular the chief editor Christian Schön, as well as Karim Mamdani and the man who came up with the idea of this book in the first place, my new close friend Matthew Feldman. I thank my mentor and friend Martin Jay, for many years of dedication and support. His influence and inspiration can be found, it goes without saying, on every page of this book. I would also like to express deep thanks to the people around me who helped me through my recent, most involuntary medical leave. First and foremost, my step-daughter Kristin Joly, who saved my life, and the friends who were first responders and helped me get through the crisis, Nicholas Ballard, Liam Collins, Heath Pearson, Lars Trägårdh, Brett Green, Chris Hart, David Philpott, Tony Fels, Brian Weiner, Joe Wertman, Jeff Kahn, Jono Schrode, Carl Oddo, and last, but definitely not least, with deep gratitude and love, Nina Joly, the beautiful and smart woman, to whom the rest of my life and this book are dedicated.

Introduction

This book brings together a selection of my writings from 1988 to 2025 that trace what I have come to think of as my "journey through intellectual history." I began my teaching career at the University of San Francisco in the immediate aftermath of the Cold War, when "the end of history" and the apparent triumph of liberal democracy framed much of our public conversation. I have written and taught through the unipolar moment, the Balkan wars, German reunification, the "long 1960s" in retrospect, the global war on terror, the return of hard geopolitics, and the present crisis of the liberal-democratic order. Throughout these tumultuous times, I have been preoccupied by a fairly constant set of questions: How do ideas travel between the pages of scholarly books (now also screens) and the mentalities of people in their daily lives? What is the connection between ideas and actions, in both the real and the now equally consequential digital world? How do states and movements use memory and myth to define enemies and justify violence? Can a Whigless, genuinely critical intellectual history contribute to both scholarship and public debate in an age that oscillates between technocratic complacency and apocalyptic panic? If we concede that history does not proceed in any kind of arc—that progress is not only non-linear, but also often regressive and impossible to predict—then how do we adjust our understanding of history accordingly?

The pieces collected here do not present a system or a definitive theory. The age of system-builders is long behind us. Theory is suspect. They are snapshots taken at different moments as I tried to make sense of the "subterranean forces" at work in our political and intellectual life. Read together, they trace an arc from geopolitics and collective memory through the world of Ernst Jünger and the Conservative Revolution, to left-wing radicalism in postwar Germany, and finally to extended engagements with other historians and philosophers whose books, in my view, still "matter" for how we understand the past we inhabit.

My most talented former student Martin Woessner, who is a distinguished scholar today in New York City, was kind enough to write a foreword for this book, "Intellectual History, San Francisco Style," which situates this book in a very particular time and place: the University of San Francisco in the mid-1990s, where he encountered intellectual history in a city still haunted by the ghosts of the Beats, the Summer of Love, and, increasingly, the first visible tremors of Silicon Valley. He tells the story of arriving as an undergraduate in his parents' footsteps, missing his own era's transformations—email, Amazon, the "Silicon Valley-ification" of everything—for the same reason they missed the Grateful Dead on Haight Street: we were all too busy in the library.

In the foreword he describes how two teachers—a philosopher, Eduardo Mendieta, and a historian, myself—gave him complementary tools: slow, generous, hermeneutic reading on the one hand, and a stubborn insistence on context, reception, and the messy entanglement of ideas with politics on the other. He recalls a joke I made in a lecture on Heidegger—reducing Aristotle to "he was born, he wrote, he died"—only to then spend the rest of the hour doing exactly what Heidegger refused to do for Aristotle: reconstructing the philosophical and historical worlds in which such a thinker becomes possible. That movement, from close textual analysis out to the wider archipelago of institutions, events, and afterlives, is what Martin calls "intellectual history, San Francisco style."

Martin also evokes the atmosphere of those years: the book-a-week Honors seminar on "Intellectuals and Crisis," where we read everything from Stephen Kern and Peter Gay to Tony Judt, Greil Marcus, James Miller, and Richard Rorty; a second semester devoted entirely to Martin Jay's *Downcast Eyes* and its French precursors and interlocutors; visits by Jürgen Habermas and Richard Rorty to our little hilltop campus; and his first encounters with my own work on Ernst Jünger and, later, on Germany's "Red Decade." For him, and for many students like him, these courses were not just about mastering content; they were rehearsals in how to think like an intellectual historian—how to follow ideas wherever they lead, without losing your sense of humor or your ethical bearings. Martin went on to publish a brilliant and witty book, *Heidegger in America* (Cambridge, 2010), in which he dazzled readers with all his learning and innate talent.

By framing this collection against that backdrop, Martin reminds readers that these essays came out of very concrete institutional and generational contexts: from Vancouver and Berlin to Berkeley and San Francisco, to New York and now back, in a way, to Columbia. He presents intellectual history not as a sterile subfield but as "the best kind of conversation-starter," a way of connecting past, present, and future in a single, if sometimes vertiginous, field of vision. His foreword is, among other things, a testimony to what—if a teacher is lucky to have students like Martin—can be set in motion: intellectual trajectories that bend forward for decades. It is a reminder that the issues treated in this volume (fascism and antifascism, globalism and protest, youth revolt and terrorism, memory and enmity) have always been discussed, for better or worse, in particular rooms, with particular people, in particular cities.

If there is a single thread that ties these disparate pieces together, it is a suspicion of comforting stories—whether Whig tales of inevitable progress or romantic laments about lost communities and "ancient hatreds." I have tried instead to practice a form of intellectual history that takes ideas seriously, follows them across borders and generations, and remains alert to the ways in which they can be weaponized as selective memory, or honest enlightenment. Whether this stance can help us navigate our own anxious moment is for the reader to judge. My hope is that these selected writings, read together with Martin Woessner's foreword and an interview we did at my home in the spring of 2025, will at least show how I have tried to think with—and sometimes against—the history that has shaped us.

Part One: Collective Memory and Geopolitics

The opening essays in Part I go back to conference papers I wrote early in my career, but have revised and expanded here. They grew out of two debates that defined the 1990s: the "end of history" discussion sparked by Francis Fukuyama, and the revival of geopolitics in the wake of the Balkan wars and the so-called unipolar moment of American power.

In "Politics of Life and Death: Globalism's Conceptual Roots in German Military Strategy," I track how notions like Lebensraum, sea power, and Großraum—elaborated by figures such as Ratzel, Mahan, Haushofer, and others—reappeared in the late-twentieth-century language of globalization and "globalism." I argue that the apparent dematerialization of power in the age of the electronic herd and geo-economics never in fact displaced classical questions of territory, resources, and strategic position; it merely obscured them. The essay ends by contrasting Weimar geopolitics with today's anti-globalization movements and populist revanchism, and by suggesting that any serious analysis of our world still has to think in terms of competing spatial orders and the necro- and biopolitics they entail.

"Towards a Critical Hermeneutics of the Enemy: A Whigless Reflection on Collective Memory" turns from space to time. Starting with Halbwachs and Warburg, and moving through Nietzsche, the Frankfurt School, Foucault, Lyotard, Rorty, and contemporary memory politics, I ask what happens when "collective memory" displaces older notions of historical inquiry. Through case studies ranging from Hindu nationalism and the Balkan wars to critical race theory, African-American storytelling, and Vladimir Putin's fantasy of "historical unity" with Ukraine, I argue that collective memories are less organic inheritances, than deliberate, often cynical constructions. They divide the world into "our" memory and "theirs," sacralize victimhood, and easily slide into a politics of enmity. Here I introduce an idea that runs through much of this volume: the need for a "hermeneutics of the enemy," a non-Schmittian way (more on that later) of reading that exposes how we imagine and manufacture enemies, and how those imaginaries can become deadly when they fuse with state power, media, and new technologies.

Part Two: The World and Ideas of Ernst Jünger

My long engagement with Ernst Jünger is the subject of Part II. I stumbled upon *On the Marble Cliffs* in a Berlin used bookstore in 1983 and have been trying to understand Jünger—and what his reception tells us about Germany and Europe—ever since. My book

A Dubious Past (California, 1999) examined his role in Weimar and the politics of his post WWII canonization. The essays collected here pick up that story and push it forward.

"Unfinished Business" sketches Jünger's life from Wilhelmine soldier to Weimar dandy, inner emigrant under National Socialism, Paris diarist, Swabian hermit, LSD experimenter, and ultimately national icon and "centenarian sage." I am less interested in hagiography or denunciation than in showing how Jünger's work—on war, technology, the Worker, drugs, insects, diaries—became a screen onto which successive generations projected their own longings and fears. "Intimité" explores his complex French reception, where he was long hailed as le plus grand écrivain allemand and embraced by intellectuals whose own entanglements with Vichy, collaboration, and postwar amnesia are part of the story. "Hiding in Plain Sight" revisits *On the Marble Cliffs* through the lens of "inner emigration," asking what kind of opposition is possible inside a dictatorship, and whether aestheticized allegory can substitute for political courage.

"A Chrononaut in Swabia" situates Jünger in postwar German conservatism and *post-histoire* debates. "L'Ernst Jünger in the Sky with Diamonds" reads Visit to Godenholm as a psychedelic *Vexierbild* that fuses esotericism, drugs, prehistory, and a search for transcendence beyond both fascism and technocratic modernity. "Mutiny on Board Modernity, Sorel, Heidegger and Soft Fascism" then widens the frame again, engaging the work of Zeev Sternhell and Hans Sluga to ask how fascism emerged from serious attempts to "correct" Marxism and transcend liberal modernity—and what it might mean today to speak of "soft fascism" in illiberal democracies that tolerate a certain amount of dissent while hollowing out liberal institutions from within.

Part Three: Left-Wing Radicalism in Postwar Germany

My work on Jünger and the conservative revolution eventually pushed me to ask a parallel question on the other side of the spectrum: how should we understand the German student movement and the radical left of the 1960s and 1970s? For the generation of '68, 1945 was the caesura for the right; 1968 became the putative turning point for democracy. Much of the literature written by the 68ers themselves cast them as heroic agents who dragged a fascist-remnant society into liberal modernity.

In "Ideas of and About 1968," I argue that this self-image badly distorts causality. Democratization, anchoring in the Atlantic alliance, and the legal reckoning with National Socialism were largely the work of the two older generations of classical liberals who had lived through the Weimar collapse and the Third Reich. The student movement, by contrast, was the first major challenge to the consolidation of a stable democracy in the Federal Republic. Its most utopian, quasi-revolutionary strands—steeped in misreading Weimar's significance, Lenin, Mao, and decolonization—had to be defeated or domesticated for liberal norms and practices to take root.

At the same time, the "long 1960s" did bring genuine emancipation in civil rights, women's rights, sexual mores, education, and youth culture. My contention is that these changes were driven more by global structural shifts and American cultural influence than by the often-provincial antics of the German student Left. The second essay in this section, co-authored with Dirk Moses, takes up the *Gewaltfrage*, the question of political violence, and the generational conflict between the "Forty-Fivers" and the "Sixty-Eighters." We employ of his unique concept of the "Weimar Syndrome" to explain why so many debates in the Bonn Republic—from emergency laws to the Red Army Faction—were conducted under the shadow of 1933, with each side accusing the other of replaying the fatal script of Weimar. Here again, the theme of "melancholic repetition" and the dangers of analogical thinking in politics connects back to the essays on memory and the hermeneutics of the enemy.

Part Four ("The Book Matters") and Part Five

The section I have called "The Book Matters" collects three substantial review-essays on works by intellectual historians Avihu Zakai, Johannes Fritsche, and Ben Mercer. They may look, at first glance, like conventional book reviews; in reality they are mini-essays in their own right, using these texts to revisit questions that animate the volume as a whole: exiled German scholars facing Nazism, Heidegger's *Being and Time* and National Socialism, student revolts across France, Italy, and West Germany. I have kept them here because I still believe in the book as a political intervention, and in close reading as a form of intellectual history that can illuminate, and sometimes correct, our grand narratives.

The volume closes with the extended interview conducted by Martin Woessner. It is the most personal document in the book and offers readers who have followed me through Sils Maria, German trenches, Paris salons, Upper Swabia, Balkan villages, Berlin communes, Baader-Meinhof, ending in the faculty lounge, a different kind of entry into my work. In that conversation, I try to connect the abstract arguments of the preceding essays to the contingencies of my own life: how I came from Vancouver to Switzerland, then Germany, then Berkeley, to questions of fascism and anti-fascism, to 1968, to Ernst Jünger to the contemporary debates that now preoccupy us.

If there is a single thread that ties these disparate pieces together, it is a suspicion of comforting stories—whether Whig tales of inevitable progress or romantic laments about lost communities and "ancient hatreds." I have tried instead to practice a form of intellectual history that takes ideas seriously, follows them across borders and generations, and remains alert to the ways in which they can be weaponized in the name of memory, identity, or salvation. Whether this stance can help us navigate our own anxious moment is for the reader to judge. My hope is that these selected writings, read together, will at least show how I have tried to think with—and sometimes against—the history that has shaped us.

Foreword

by Martin Woessner

Intellectual History, San Francisco Style

I arrived at the University of San Francisco in the late summer of 1995, some thirty years or so after my parents had matriculated at the very same institution. The first in their families to go to college, Mom and Dad were diligent students: they spent more time hitting the books than exploring the countercultural ferment that would culminate in the famous Summer of Love, a happening my parents missed by just a few months, having already met, graduated, married, and moved down to Southern California by September, 1967. The family joke has always been that my parents were too busy studying in the library, or attending mass over in Saint Ignatius, to catch the Grateful Dead jamming, or the hippies dancing, just a few blocks away.

Traces of the psychedelic sixties still lingered when I got to the city by the bay three decades later, enticed to USF as much by an academic scholarship that promised to pay three-quarters of my tuition as by my parents' fond memories of the place. Tie-dye everything could be found in the shops over on Haight Street, even if it was only a modest mix of tourists and students—the ones committed to a nostalgic, role-playing aesthetic built largely around the florals, patchouli, and shoelessness then in vogue—who seemed interested in buying any of it. City Lights, the famous Beat bookstore, was still going strong, as it is today, thankfully. And bands worth seeing still played the Fillmore, though the name of the concert promoter who made it famous, Bill Graham, now adorned the much larger Civic Auditorium where I saw Radiohead on their *OK Computer* tour. There was no way I was going to let *that* cultural milestone pass me by.

Every generation fancies itself wiser than the last, but it is only the retrospective gaze that makes sense of what is really going on. Back in the 1990s, I had no idea the small changes taking place all around me—personal computers, my first email account, the rise of a book-selling website called Amazon—would lead to yet another transformation of not just San Francisco or California or even the United States, but the whole world. The early signs of the gradual Silicon Valley-ification of everything were everywhere, bright and flashing, and yet I missed them completely. Just like my parents, I was too busy reading books—old-fashioned, analog ones, plucked from library stacks or bookstore shelves (Green Apple Books, also still going strong)—to notice.

My original plan was to be an English major. One pre-registration meeting with the history department chair, a formidable Renaissance scholar named Elisabeth Gleason, put an end to that. History it would be. I survived a couple of Professor Gleason's upper-level courses, but just barely. She returned my papers drenched in so much scarlet—I remember thinking to myself at the time—that she must have purchased her red pens in bulk. Still, if I looked closely enough, there was usually a hint or two of encouragement buried somewhere in her comments. It was tough love, but it was enough to keep me within the orbit of the history department until I stumbled upon topics more interesting than the social and cultural consequences of the Black Death.

My good fortune was to have stepped on campus in the middle of what was, in retrospect, a pretty remarkable hiring spree at USF. The professors who became my mentors would not be old Jesuits, I quickly realized, but rather, young, hip intellectuals who seemed to have their fingers on the pulse of every meaningful debate in contemporary arts and letters. Studying with them opened up a whole new world for me, one built around strange, magical names—Michel Foucault, Jürgen Habermas, Richard Rorty—that I began slipping into conversation whenever and wherever I could. Those conversations usually took place at the local coffee shop or the dingy but delightfully named *Would You Believe? Cocktails*, an unassuming corner bar on Geary Boulevard without an ID-checking doorman that just happened to be two flights below the first off-campus apartment I shared with two other classmates. I'm pretty sure the second-wave coffee shops are long gone now, replaced by inevitable third- or even fourth-wave variants, but last time I checked, *Would You Believe?* is still there.

In those heady days of theory, ideas mattered, and my friends and I debated them vigorously, mostly because we had teachers who took them seriously. I ended up studying with professors who were committed to their research, but also to their students. They seemed eager and willing to introduce us to the life of the mind. Even better, they did not correct papers in red pen. Two of them, in particular, became my guides: a philosopher, born in Colombia but raised in New Jersey, who had trained at The New School and taught everything from Boethius to Habermas; and an historian from across the bay at Berkeley, though originally from Canada by way of Berlin, who introduced me to the subject I would one day call my own—though I had no way of knowing it back then, of course—the history of ideas.

From Eduardo Mendieta I learned to read slowly, carefully, and critically, all while remaining as hermeneutically generous to an author as I possibly could. But first I had to learn what the word hermeneutics meant. In no time I was immersed in more German philosophy than I ever dreamed existed, all of it seemingly pointing backward toward, or forward from, a philosopher whose first name, at least, I had no trouble pronouncing: Martin Heidegger.

Serendipitously, Elliot Neaman, the history professor who rescued me from the Renaissance, also knew a whole lot about German philosophy. And he knew a thing or two about Heidegger, too. Not only that, but he had lived in Berlin, which was as far away as one could get from San Francisco. If Eduardo, the philosopher, taught me to study texts closely, Elliot, the intellectual historian, reminded me not to lose sight of their contexts: the ones in which they first appeared, but also, and perhaps more importantly, the ones into which they were eventually disseminated and received. No philosophical treatise, text, or idea was an island, or, if it was, it was part of an archipelago that deserved surveying as a whole, not just as so many individual landmasses. Everything, I started to learn, was connected.

You had to be willing to put in the work to understand all this, though. It helped to have a sense of humor about things, too. "As good intellectual historians, in order to make sense of Heidegger," Elliot told us in History 327, Modern European Intellectual History, "we would have to situate his thought in both philosophical and historical context." This Elliot did brilliantly, summarizing all the relevant philosophical, historical, political, religious, and cultural contexts one needed to know to make sense of the Magician from Messkirch. But he did this in just two breathless paragraphs, before settling into his punch line. "If we had time, we could do all this," he said, but we didn't, so instead we would "have to be content with the description that Heidegger himself gave when he lectured on Aristotle: 'he was born, he wrote, he died.'"[1]

The joke, of course, was that Elliot would not do to Heidegger what Heidegger had done to Aristotle. The rest of his lecture was a deep dive into Heidegger's philosophical lexicon, covering everything from *Dasein* to *Seinsvergessenheit*, because, as Elliot told us, "giving a lecture on Heidegger" meant "giving a lecture on the German language, the peculiar and very idiosyncratic German of Martin Heidegger." It's that attention to detail, and that willingness to zoom in on a text one minute, and carefully back out to a larger context the next, that made me decide intellectual history was the subject for me. I may have lost out on the chance to be an English major, but I had gained something much better in the process, the chance to think like an historian and a philosopher at the same time—in other words, to pretend like I was an historian of ideas.

While telling somebody at a dinner party that you earn your living as an intellectual historian is often something of a conversation-stopper—"Is there such a thing as *unintellectual history*?" they always ask—I am thankful I learned, early on, that it is just the opposite, actually. Especially when it is done in the right spirit, intellectual history is the best kind of conversation-starter. It helps us understand not just the thoughts of the past but also, and perhaps more importantly, the beliefs, concepts, and discourses that have shaped our present. It even helps us to look ahead, into the world of tomorrow. While respecting the pastness of the past and the foreignness of the future, intellectual history reminds us that our lives are inescapably connected to both, that our world bends both backward and forward, sometimes at the very same time.

Thanks to the energy and initiative of the young scholars who had flocked to USF around the time I studied there, our little liberal

1 Elliot Y. Neaman, "History 327 Lecture: Heidegger" (Spring 1997), 2-3.

arts campus on the hill became, somewhat improbably, a beacon of intellectual debate, one that stretched from the seemingly far-off past into a future very few of us could have imagined at the time. The most famous contemporary German philosopher, Jürgen Habermas, visited once to lecture about the moral legacy of the cold war, a subject less distant than it appeared, maybe, in the rearview mirror of the day.[2] Richard Rorty, perhaps the most famous American thinker of the era, came up from Palo Alto to talk about the philosophy of history, only to be heckled in the Q&A by philosophy students who took issue with his easy-going relativism. Little did we know then that Rorty's oft-repeated warnings—in books such as *Achieving Our Country: Leftist Thought in Twentieth-Century America* (1998)—about the demise of what he called the old left would be resuscitated one day as prescient, though largely unheeded, predictions about the rise of a political phenomenon like Trumpism.[3] Maybe Rorty was right: we should have been worrying less about philosophical objectivity—the stuff the grad students obsessed over—and more about political freedom and economic inequality.

I first came across Rorty's work in a seminar I took my sophomore year, Honors 339: Intellectuals and Crisis in the Twentieth Century. I still remember how heavy my shopping basket was when I purchased the required texts for the course at the campus bookstore. The class, as Elliot had designed it, was a book a week for fifteen weeks. We didn't get to Rorty's *Contingency, Irony, and Solidarity* (1989) until almost the end, week thirteen.[4] By then, my classmates and I had already made our way through Stephen Kern's *The Culture of Time and Space* (week 2); Peter Gay's *Weimar Culture* (week 5) H. Stuart Hughes's *The Obstructed Path* (week 3) and *The Sea Change* (week 8), Tony Judt's *Past Imperfect* (week 10), Greil Marcus's *Lipstick Traces* (week 11), and James Miller's *The Passion*

2 For more on this event, see Martin Woessner, "Habermas: Up from Heidegger," *Los Angeles Review of Books* August 11, 2019.

3 Richard Rorty, *Achieving Our Country: Leftist Thought in Twentieth-Century America* (Cambridge, Massachusetts: Harvard UP, 1998). See also, Martin Woessner, "Rorty and Social Hope," *Los Angeles Review of Books*, July 22, 2017.

4 Rorty, *Contingency, Irony, and Solidarity* (Cambridge: Cambridge UP, 1989).

of Michel Foucault (week 12).[5] I don't know how any of us survived such a syllabus, but, to this day, the conversations we had in that bookcase-lined room in the back corner of Lone Mountain, with foghorns bellowing off in the distance, are some of my fondest memories of college.

No wonder I decided to do it all over again just two years later. Elliot taught Honors 339 again in the fall of 1998, the beginning of my senior year. On paper, it was a class I had already completed. But the syllabus was totally different this time around: a whole course devoted to just one big book, Martin Jay's *Downcast Eyes: The Denigration of Vision in Twentieth-Century French Thought* (1993), which would be complimented with primary source materials stretching from Diderot to Guy Debord and Jacques Derrida.[6] I had read Jay's book on the Frankfurt School in the previous iteration of Honors 339—*The Dialectical Imagination* (week 9)—but I knew this would be something else entirely. And it was. I was thrilled I got to take the class as an independent study, especially because it culminated in the kind of reader-meet-author moment one remembers for a long time to come. After spending a whole semester parsing his sweeping intellectual and cultural history of ocularcentrism and its critics, my classmates and I got the chance to pepper Jay with more questions about Georges Bataille's *The Story of the Eye* than he probably cared to answer.[7] Still, the conversation continued amiably enough over Chinese food in the Outer Richmond, after which I made sure to get my copy of *Downcast Eyes*

5 Stephen Kern, *The Culture of Time and Space, 1880-1918* (Cambridge, Massachusetts: Harvard UP, 1983); Peter Gay, *Weimar Culture: The Outsider as Insider* (New York: Harper, 1970); H. Stuart Hughes, *Between Commitment and Disillusion: The Obstructed Path & The Sea Change, 1930-1965*, with a new introduction (Middletown, Connecticut: Wesleyan UP, 1987); Tony Judt, *Past Imperfect: French Intellectuals, 1944-1956* (Berkeley: University of California Press, 1992); Greil Marcus, *Lipstick Traces: A Secret History of the 20th Century* (Cambridge, Massachusetts: Harvard UP, 1989); James Miller, *The Passion of Michel Foucault* (New York: Simon & Schuster, 1993).

6 Martin Jay, *Downcast Eyes: The Denigration of Vision in Twentieth-Century French Thought* (Berkeley: University of California Press, 1993).

7 Georges Bataille, *The Story of the Eye*, trans. Joachim Neugroschel (San Francisco: City Lights, 1987).

signed. The inscription was a good one: "From one Martin to another."

It was while studying with Elliot—and eventually working as his research assistant—that I got a sneak peek into the life of the intellectual historian, a craft he had learned from Jay, his *Doktorvater* (though it was one of his professors back in Vancouver, Edward Hundert, an expert on Bernard Mandeville, who first introduced him to the guild, I later came to learn).[8] When I first started taking Elliot's classes, he was busy revising the manuscript, based on his Berkeley dissertation, of what would become his first book, *A Dubious Past: Ernst Jünger and the Politics of Literature after Nazism* (1999).[9] Reading it alongside *The Dialectical Imagination* and *Downcast Eyes*, I could see how Elliot stayed true to Jay's influence, while still charting his own unique path forward.

And what an ambitious path it was. Combining biography, literary reception, cultural analysis, and political history, all while offering keen close readings of one of Germany's most mercurial writers, *A Dubious Past* showed me just how important it was to read widely but also critically, to argue carefully but also to appreciate paradox and uncertainty, too. How else could one make sense of a career—and a legacy—as complex and seemingly so all-over-the-place as Jünger's? After all, his was a life that stretched past the century mark, included service in two world wars, globetrotting travel, extensive experimentation with drugs, and a perennial refusal to be fitted into any of the usual political, philosophical, or literary categories. Jünger was an "anarch" but not an anarchist; a militant nationalist, but never a Nazi; a self-taught entomologist but also a fantasist, somebody who maintained that "the real is just as magical as the magical is real."[10] It takes a kind of double-mindedness, Elliot argued, to take it all in, both "the ambiguity of Jünger's

8 E. J. Hundert, *The Enlightenment's Fable: Bernard Mandeville and the Discovery of Society* (Cambridge: Cambridge UP, 1994).

9 Elliot Y. Neaman, *A Dubious Past: Ernst Jünger and the Politics of Literature after Nazism* (Berkeley: University of California Press, 1999).

10 Ernst Jünger, *The Adventurous Heart: Figures and Capriccios*, trans. Thomas Friese, ed. Russell A. Berman, with an introduction by Eliah Bures and Elliot Neaman (Candor, New York: Telos Press, 2012), 130. On the figure of the "anarch," see Jünger, *The Forest Passage*, trans.

authorship and the sharp contrasts of opinion manifested by the history of his works' reception."[11]

Regular historians could get away with just a recitation of the facts, maybe, but intellectual historians, I learned from Elliot, are held to a higher calling, if only by their choice of subject matter. We have to be willing to go wherever our subjects—be they novelists, philosophers, or artists; politicians, professors, or agitators—take us. And they can take us to some pretty far-off places. Part Two of the book you have in your hands proves as much, with essays ranging widely across Jünger's life and various legacies. But parts One, Three, and Four—on the subjects of collective memory and geopolitics; leftwing radicalism in postwar Germany; and contemporary scholarship in European Intellectual History—offer ample proof of this fact as well. In them you'll find fascinating accounts of ideas and concepts that, for better or worse, still shape our world: globalism and globalization, protest and revolution, fascism and antifascism.

Many of these essays stem from the research Elliot undertook after publishing *A Dubious Past*, research that eventually led to another wide-ranging book, *Free Radicals: Agitators, Hippies, Urban Guerillas, and Germany's Youth Revolt of the 1960s and 1970s* (2016).[12] If tackling Jünger meant taking a deep dive into conversative, even reactionary thought on the right, then narrating the various twists and turns of West Germany's so-called Red Decade, spanning from 1967 to 1977, meant a deep dive into the rhetoric of the left. It meant balancing, as Elliot puts it in the opening pages of the work, "the authenticity of the rebellion with the disingenuousness with which the revolt was expressed."[13]

Free Radicals shows how "the spirit and the mystique of 1968 did not fade away noiselessly," but went on to inform everything

---

Thomas Friese, ed. with an introduction by Russell A. Berman (Candor, New York: Telos Press, 2013).

11 Neaman, *A Dubious Past*, 271.

12 Elliot Y. Neaman, *Free Radicals: Agitators, Hippies, Urban Guerillas, and Germany's Youth Revolt of the 1960s and 1970s* (Candor, New York: Telos Press, 2016).

13 Ibid., 2.

from human rights activism to environmentalism in Germany, forming the backbone of the Green Party along the way. But *Free Radicals* also shows how utopian energies went in the other directions, too, sometimes ending up as decidedly dystopian realities: bank robberies, kidnappings, assassinations. "While the majority of the students came to accept the fact that their goals could only be achieved in small and unglamorous steps," Elliot writes, "a small minority refused to accept the inevitable grayness of life and braced for the final contest between good and evil."[14] The end result was, as we well know, political violence, but of a particularly spectacular kind, a made-to-be-watched-on-television-or-at-the-movies kind, one that was one-part Alain Delon in a trench coat and two-parts *The Battle of Algiers.*[15] Anybody who has seen Paul Thomas Anderson's recent film *One Battle After Another* (2025)—a loose adaptation of *Vineland*, Thomas Pynchon's 1990 novel of 1960s-era countercultural burnout—will recognize the aesthetic.[16]

Back in the 1990s, when I was first reading Pynchon (though never in an English class), the 1960s seemed impossibly distant to me—the stuff of my parents' generation, not mine. But the 2020s seemed impossibly faraway, too. I never thought I'd end up here, doing this. I never thought I, too, would get the chance to follow in my mentor's footsteps, just as he had followed in his. What good fortune, I continue telling myself. I'm very grateful Elliot's intellectual journey, which took him from Vancouver to Berlin to the Bay Area, intersected with mine in San Francisco, that beautiful city by the bay, all those years ago. I think you'll be glad it has intersected with yours in the shape of this book.

Martin Woessner
The City College of New York, CUNY, Center for Worker Education.

New York City
December 3, 2025

---

14 Ibid., 134.
15 Ibid., 169, 173.
16 Thomas Pynchon, *Vineland* (New York: Penguin, 1991).

Part One: Collective Memory and Geopolitics

To set the stage, or the table, if you prefer, to my selected writings, I have chosen two pieces that I wrote early on in my career as conference papers, never published. I have revised and updated them to present here as an indication in my early career interest in two academic debates, one on geopolitics, the other on collective memory. Both had to do with the politics of the 1990s, in particular the notion of the End of History, made famous by Francis Fukuyama, the other geopolitics, both of which had to do with the Balkan Wars and the so-called Unipolar Moment, when the United States seemed to possess unique power to shape history since the Soviet Union no longer posed a threat, and shaping a new liberal international order seemed a worthy goal, but more importantly, eminently doable. These two essays, written decades apart, belong together. Both ask how concepts forged in earlier crises—geopolitics and collective memory—continue to shape the ways we imagine the world, define enemies, and justify violence in the present.

"Politics of Life and Death: Globalism's Conceptual Roots in German Military Strategy" reconstructs the intellectual genealogy of geopolitics from late-nineteenth-century political geography and naval strategy through Weimar and Nazi Germany, the Cold War, and the post-1990 era of globalization. It shows how seemingly technical ideas—Lebensraum, sea power, Großraum—became "necropolitical" doctrines that helped legitimate imperial expansion and, later, total war. The essay then tracks how these older notions re-emerge after 1989 in debates about globalization, "globalism," and the unipolar moment: in Gulf War geo-economics, the porousness of borders under digital capitalism, the backlash against the "electronic herd," and contemporary populist revolts against liberal internationalism. The main argument is that we cannot understand current conflicts—from the rise of right-wing populism to new forms of great-power rivalry—without recognizing how deeply our strategic thinking is still structured by earlier, often discredited, geographical and spatial imaginaries. In an era of renewed territorial wars, energy insecurity, and techno-nationalist competition, that historicization is more urgent than ever.

"Towards a Critical Hermeneutics of the Enemy: A Whigless Reflection on Collective Memory" turns to the question of the construction of the enemy. I could have called this essay a "Non-Schmittian Hermeneutics of the Enemy," but that would have required a very different exegesis. Here I treat "the enemy," not as the foundation of politics (as in Nazi jurist Schmitt's legal theories), but as an object of inquiry—something to be explained, historicized, and morally constrained.

Schmitt treats the friend/enemy distinction as existential and inescapable; politics becomes the possibility of destroying the enemy. A critical alternative is to view enmity as historically and socially constructed, not ontological. Ask who defines the enemy, by which narratives, and for whose interests. I suggest we treat images of the enemy as diagnostic of a society's fears, myths, and power structures, rather than as descriptions of some natural opposition

This essay begins with Halbwachs, Warburg, and the "memoriologists" of the late twentieth century, then moves through Nietzsche, the Frankfurt School, poststructuralism, and critical race theory to ask what we mean when we speak of "collective memory." Against romanticized views of memory as an organic inheritance, the essay insists on its constructed, selective, and often instrumental character. Through case studies—from Hindu nationalism and the Macedonian question to the Balkan wars, Black storytelling in the United States, and Vladimir Putin's fabricated history of a triune "Russian people"—it shows how elites manufacture narratives of victimhood and antiquity to mobilize communities, harden friend–enemy distinctions, and legitimize violence. The second half sketches what I call a "hermeneutics of the enemy": a way of reading that exposes how collective memories are made, how they travel, and when they turn deadly.

At a moment when politics across the globe is saturated with memory talk—statues toppled or defended, school curricula weaponized, genocides invoked and denied, algorithmically amplified resentments circulating at high speed—these essays offer tools for thinking critically about both the spatial and temporal frameworks that underwrite such conflicts. They argue, in different registers, that if we want to understand our contemporary disorders, we have to take seriously the long, often uncomfortable histories of the concepts with which we describe them, and to remain vigilant about how those concepts can be turned into justifications for new rounds of exclusion and war.

I.
Politics of Life and Death:
Globalism's Conceptual Roots in German Military Strategy

Isolationism and globalization are two sides of the same coin. Or to use a different metaphor from physics, isolationism and globalization are two related but opposite gravitational vectors on a geopolitical field line. To understand how geopolitics explains political ideology and policy, it is important to go back to the origins of geopolitics as a scholarly discipline, in order to understand the gravitational fields that have determined politics at a distance from World War I until today. The following attempts to a provide framework for that kind of paradigm.

At the beginning of America's short-lived Unipolar Moment after the end of the Cold War, Francis Fukuyama published a provocative thesis in 1989, the auspicious year as the Berlin Wall fell, called *The End of History*. The text set the tone for a series of debates on the future of liberalism as a set of economic and political doctrines that would, as he argued, be the only remaining ideological alternative in a world in which no nation could afford to isolate itself from the march of history into its final phase.[1] More people dismissed the phrase "end of history" than had actually read his rich and complex argument. In many ways, Fukuyama's main intuition has withstood the test of time, especially the ignored Nietzschean description of the "Last Man." My argument in the following is, however, about something else, namely that several years earlier, a sin-

1 First published as an essay in *The National Interest* in 1989, and then in an expanded book, *The End of History and the Last Man* (New York: The Free Press, 1992). In my view, Fukuyama has won the argument over Samuel Huntington, whose "clash of civilizations" excluded America (North, South, and Central), all Eastern Orthodox nations, and the entire Africa. There are more differences, in any case, inside so-called civilizations than between them. The long-lasting Fukuyama-Huntington divide, though, has still been far from settled.

gle term emerged as shorthand for what Fukuyama described: globalization, which transformed itself into a negative political term for activists: *globalism.*[2] Globalism was not a new term. *Globalismus* was first used in a book, *The War for Man's Soul* (1943), by a German diplomat, Ernst Jäckh, who was an internationalist, alarmed by the expansionist policies of Hitler. He emigrated to the United States in 1940 and taught at the University of Columbia's School of International Affairs.[3] The word globalism of the 1990s was similarly used, in a different context, to oppose the internationalization and global expansion of finance capital and corporate power.

Globalization and globalism are, in terms of international relations, versions of what was once called "geopolitics," a school of political geography that emerged as an intellectual discipline, movement, and fashion in Germany in the 1920s and 1930s. I wish to point out certain parallels and differences between that analysis of world politics and the contemporary re-ordering of trade and power relations, or what I would call post-Atlanticist geopolitics, in the wake of the end of the Cold War and the concomitant fundamental change in the status of territorial boundaries, made porous by electronic commerce, environmental pressures, mass immigration, and new communication technology. One purpose is to better understand the rise of rightwing populism across many countries today, but at a deeper level to articulate the subterranean forces at work in how geography affects international relations in many ways, that go far beyond physical features of the earth and the usual activities of populations studied by geographers.

The original impetus for geopolitics was developed by nineteenth-century political geographers, in particular Friedrich Ratzel (1844-1904) and Rudolf Kjellen (1864-1922), on the basis of Darwinian biology and vitalist ideas about the origins and development of modern states. Ratzel coined the phrase "*Lebensraum*" (Living

2 The term "globalization" was coined by an economist, Theodore Levitt, in an article, "The Globalization of Markets," in the *Harvard Business Review*, (May-June, 1983), 93-94. But the concept can be traced back much further to the age of industrialization.

3 See Peter Weber, "Ernst Jäckh and the National Internationalism of Interwar Germany." *Central European History* 52, no. 3 (2019).

Space) in his book *The Earth and Life*, published in 1901.[4] The treatise was an attempt to provide a comprehensive description of the earth as an organic whole. The first part of the exposition described the watery surface of the globe, the rivers, oceans, and glaciers, in other words, the hydrosphere, while the second covered the atmosphere, that is, climate, light, heat, rain, and pressure, what we would call today simply weather patterns. In the third part, on the life of the earth, he employed a new term, "biogeography," the nomadic patterns of animals and peoples as an endless fight for nourishment. On pages 590-600, he introduces the ill-fated term *Lebensraum*, in a chapter that dealt with the "origins and mixing and meeting of the races. According to Ratzel, the oft-misused phrase "struggle for existence" actually meant "struggle for space."[5] When space grows quadratically, the periphery only expands arithmetically; that is, the larger the territory, the less the possibility of contact and mixing with the neighbor. All plants and animals, according to Ratzel, fight for space—otherwise there would be constant population explosions. Ratzel did not accept race as a scientific category, because all humans can breed with one another, but like most nineteenth-century ethnographers, he accepted the term "race" to describe the different phenotypical characteristics of Blacks, Asians, and Whites. The white race, according to Ratzel, can be recognized by its fine hair, white skin, more noble facial construction, and higher intelligence.

Ratzel's publications coincided with the high point of European imperialism and provided a pseudo-scientific, "necropolitical" underpinning for the doctrine of geopolitics.[6] Geopolitics went be-

---

4 Friedrich Ratzel, *Die Erde und das Leben; eine Vergleichende Erdkunde* (Leipzig, 1901), https://archive.org/details/dieerdeunddasleb02ratz.

5 Ratzel, *Earth and Life*, 598.

6 Necropolitical refers to how social and political power determines decisions over the life and death of people, derived from Cameroonian philosopher Achille Mbembe, who inverted Michel Foucault's concept of Biopower. See Achille Mbembe, *Necropolitics* (Durham, NC: Duke University Press, 2019). See also, Ian Klinke, *Life, Earth, Colony, Friedrich Ratzel's Necropolitical Geography* (Ann Arbor: University of Michigan Press, 2023.)

yond a Darwinian framework and encompassed military, racial, demographic, and historical ideas that justified territorial expansion and the conquest of subject non-European peoples. Franz Neumann argued in *Behemoth*, a book published during WWII, that geopolitics was unscientific, but dangerous, since, from a Marxist perspective, "in the final analysis, geopolitics (was) nothing but the ideology of imperialist expansion."[7] One need not take the side of this Leninist view to concede that the Great Powers clash before 1914 was driven by a geopolitically-informed strategy. After 1897, when Admiral Tirpitz was Secretary of State of the Imperial War Office, he set Germany on a course of rebuilding the navy that could be likened to the U.S. Star War Program of the 1980s: in other words, it was not just a plan to build heavy battleships (instead of lighter cruisers), but rather a visionary program to challenge the hegemonic position of England. Tirpitz's main influence in this thinking was the American theorist of geopolitics Alfred Mahan, who wrote in his classic *The Influence of Sea Power in History* (1890), that neither commercial raiding nor a defensive army would determine the relative military positions of the Great Powers, but rather control of the seas. Geopolitics was not just a hobby for armchair strategists, but rather played a real-world role in fracturing the relationship between Great Britain and Germany that led to World War I.

By ignoring the English overtures for an Anglo-German naval agreement in the late 1890s, Tirpitz's naval program had the effect of prodding Great Britain and France to resolve their colonial differences and work together to isolate Germany. In the case of Russia, Tirpitz insisted on taking Kia-Chow Bay, which interfered with Russia's plans for Northern China. Geopolitical calculations were also present in the growing investment, both military and economic, in the Ottoman Empire, the result of which was Russian anger and suspicion of German intentions in the Balkans, forcing Russia to turn to France and Great Britain in the alliance that eventually went to war against Germany. Germany was left with only one reliable ally, so the German government, backed by the generals, supported the adventurous Austrians to the hilt when the fateful steps were

7 Franz Neumann, *Behemoth: The Structure and Practice of National Socialism, 1933–1944*. (New York: Harper & Row, 1944), 164.

taken to declare war on Serbia. An even more sinister turning point for geopolitics came in the wake of the German defeat in 1918, when a geopolitical school emerged under the leadership of Karl Haushofer and his *Zeitschrift für Geopolitik*. This school transformed geopolitics from a set of military doctrines into a populist program. Geopolitics played a public role in fanning the widespread resentment in Germany against the harsh dictates of the Versailles Treaty.

Germany had lost its colonies and its territorial ambitions in the East, realized for a short time by the crushing dictate imposed on the Bolsheviks with the Treaty of Brest-Litovsk in the late winter of 1918. With a declining birthrate and the other social and economic crises of Weimar Germany as a backdrop, geopolitics provided the intellectual stimulus for a program of an aggressive foreign policy aimed at overturning Versailles. *Geopolitik* had an ambiguous relationship to National Socialism. On the one hand, the geopolitical version of German homogeneity did not stress race, but rather culture (Haushofer was married to a "half-Jewess, by Nazi terms). Hitler viewed colonies, the subject of the famous polemical novel *People Without Space*, as a distraction from his goal to build a vast continental empire to the east. On the other hand, with the political success of National Socialism in the 1930s, some geopoliticians began to support the expansive and aggressive foreign policy of the Nazis in accordance with what they considered to be pragmatic, "Realpolitik" considerations. Haushofer himself was a more complicated case. Rudolf Hess had been a student of his in the 1920s, and the 14th chapter of *Mein Kampf* concerning *Ostpolitik* is strongly influenced by geopolitical conceptions of space and the struggle for existence. Hitler's basic principle for conducting foreign policy was encapsulated in the dictum that "only a large enough space on this earth assures a people the freedom of existence."[8] In Hitler's so-called *Second Book*, from 1928, Hitler elaborated on Germany's new foreign policy direction and quite openly declared that after the defeat of France, Germany would need to secure living space in Russia and other Eastern Territories, so that Germany would be existentially assured for the next hundred years.[9]

---

8 *Mein Kampf* (1937, Vol. II, 728).

9 *Hitlers Zweites Buch*, 1961, 163.

Haushofer, on the other hand, believed that Germany's best chance to secure hegemony on the Eurasian continent would be to enter into a tactical alliance with Russia and create a German-dominated federation of middle-European states as a bulwark against England and American capitalism. Haushofer was extremely skeptical of what he considered to be Hitler's foreign policy adventurism in the late 1930s, and as a result, he became *persona non grata* for the Nazi leadership. The question of the conceptual ties between geopolitics and National Socialism has long been debated among scholars, and cannot be addressed here, except to note that abstractly, geopolitics was clearly part of the National Socialist *Weltanschauung*, while its application as strategy was contested.

The Cold War that followed Hitler's defeat, caused primarily by a power vacuum in central Europe, obscured the importance of geopolitics in the rebuilding of Europe after 1945 for two reasons. First, it was discredited by the perceived association between geopolitics and the foreign policy disaster of the Third Reich. Second, the binary logic of superpower domination of the globe obscured the relevance of resources, borders, technology, and cultural/historical differences between nation-states. The Atlantic alliance was founded to "keep the Americans in, the Germans down and the Russians out," according to Lord Ismay, the first secretary-general of NATO. Smaller nations attached themselves to one of the two military blocs and could gain access to economic rewards and strategic protection through fidelity to one side or by playing one side off against the other. Geography could elevate a nation's strategic value. The second half of the twentieth century supposedly belonged to the realists, those theorists of international relations who believed, like Thucydides, that all nations are driven to compete with each other through honor, fear, or interests, and not much else. But with the defeat of fascism, the competition between the two remaining twentieth-century world systems created a fervent ideological struggle that resembled more the sixteenth-century European religious wars than either classical or modern wars of strategic advantage. Geopolitics during the Cold War was dominated by the "domino theory" in the West, the fear that communism was like an infectious disease that had to be contained, and the notion of Revolution/Counter-Revolution in the Soviet Union, best expressed in the Brezhnev Doctrine, which stated that all questions of legality and autonomy must be subordinated to the "laws of class struggle." Both doctrines justified intervention in the affairs of foreign countries in the name of protecting higher abstract principles, democracy, and communism. While many people think of geopolitics and Cold War realism as synonymous, the influence of the physical environment (location, resources, territory, and so forth) was vastly underemphasized by the foreign policy establishment.

The writings of Kennan, Gray, Luttwack, Kissinger, and Brzezinski, and many lesser-known thinkers, as well as journals and think-tank literature of the Cold War, all display a marked aversion to thinking about grand strategy as based in geography. With the fall of the Berlin Wall in 1989 and a decade of ever faster global integration (the fall of economic and technological walls between all nations that wish to participate in the world economy), geopolitics then came back to influence the discussion of foreign policy, economic development, technological progress, and global integration. According to globalization boosters, the world was no longer a closed system of limited resources, but rather reflected a new kind of decentralized synchronic system of production and distribution that shifts the emphasis from fixed boundaries and limited resources to information technology and its non-spatial (or cyber-spatial) structure. The Internet, accordingly, supposedly made individuals more powerful, corporations more mobile, governments weaker, and markets more sensitive to changing circumstances. By the late 1990s, globalization led to a backlash among people who resented the anonymous nature of powerful and volatile global markets and the apparent ability to cause havoc and dislocations as much as creating enormous and unprecedented wealth, the struggle between the 99% and the elites. In 1994, Robert D. Kaplan described the post-Cold War world as facing encroaching chaos driven by demographic pressures, environmental scarcity (like water shortages), urbanization, and resource depletion, leading to failed states, tribalism, and criminal anarchy, particularly in West Africa, as a new form of geopolitical instability replacing superpower conflict. He argued this would erode the nation-state, empower non-state actors like warlords, and shift conflicts from ideological to struggles for survival, challenging both the era's end of history optimism and clash of civilizations pessimism.[10] The debates on geopolitics in the early twenty-first century revolved around the question of how much culture, geography, ideology, and religion play in an age when political and economic success was measured by increasingly global and homogenization.

With the breakup of the Soviet Union in 1990, to put it another way, forty-five years of national security thinking in the United States and the containment principles of NATO became obsolete. The fixed markers of the Cold War suddenly evaporated with the dissolution of the Warsaw Pact in 1991 by the liberated, formerly communist states of Eastern Europe. When Saddam Hussein invaded Kuwait on August 2, 1990, and the United States assembled a coalition of thirty states which succeeded in pushing Iraq out of Kuwait in a 100-hour war, the contours for a New World Order emerged, in which so-called "rogue states" (now called "states of concern") would be held in check by the collective acts of a world policeman and international organizations.

The eruption of so-called ethnic wars in the 1990s, in the former Yugoslavia, Rwanda, the states of the former Soviet Union, and elsewhere tragically disclosed the limits of collective action by the international community. In terms of geopolitics, the New World Order disclosed the extent to which global strategy had changed drastically with the end of the Cold War. First, the world is no longer a chessboard, on which every space represents a potential win or loss for two competitors. During the Cold War, every international crisis represented either a threat or a potential advantage to the Western states or the Soviet Union. It was essentially a zero-sum game. After 1990, the rules for intervention changed. Nobody could come up with an ethical reason why a huge international coalition was assembled to force Hussein out of an undemocratic, half-feudal state run by the oil-rich rulers of Kuwait, the Al-Sabah family, but why the "West" stood by helplessly as Tutsis killed Hutus in Rwanda, or Serbs killed Muslims in Bosnia. But in terms of geopolitics, the relative inaction of the international community can be explained quite

10 Robert D. Kaplan, "The Coming Anarchy, " *Atlantic Monthly* (February, 1994), 44-46. Later expanded into a book in 2001.

easily, since there was no Cold War pressure to force one side to act for fear that by not doing so, the other side would gain an advantage. Quite the contrary, when Albania broke out into a civil war in 1997, all Western governments scrambled to get their citizens out of the crisis area as soon as possible. When civil war broke out in Sierra Leone in the early part of 2000, no Western states were prepared to send troops to restore order, despite the pleas of the United Nations' leadership.

A second, less noticed geopolitical reality was disclosed by the Gulf War. By the time Hussein's troops had captured Kuwait City and were able to loot the city of its gold faucets, Rolls-Royces, and airplanes, most of Kuwait's real wealth had already been transferred electronically to safe havens in Saudi Arabia, Western Europe, and North America. That was because oil wealth had for decades been converted into stocks, global real estate holdings, and other nonlocal assets. Although the Al-Sabah family nominally ruled over the physical borders of Kuwait, in fact, the annual 18-billion-dollar oil revenues were the foundation of a global investment strategy that had a net value of around 100 billion dollars in 1990. The consequences of ignoring Hussein would have been the disruption of the transnational machinery of global energy markets and a threat to major global capital. The Kuwait example led to the much larger question of economic globalization, or what may be better labelled geo-economics. Geopolitics in the era of globalization referred to the fall of economic walls around nations and the rise of what the neo-Liberal Thomas Friedman called the "electronic herd" into almost every aspect of the economic life of nominally autonomous nations. A series of economic panics in the late 1990s, from Mexico to South Asia, poignantly displayed the power of international flows of capital to create ripple effects across international boundaries, joining all nations together in moments of crisis. Globalism created unknown opportunities for wealth creation, as well as the undermining of living standards the biopower of the working class. in the old dominant centers of capitalist production. After China was admitted to the WTO by the Ministerial Conference in December 2001, so-called "management experts" began talking about vertical and horizontal integration, in which climate and geography suddenly played a large role.

Horizontal societies, almost all of which are in cold and temperate zones, according to the model, tend to have a more egalitarian distribution of wealth, allow technological change, educate youth to know more than their parents, have decentralized and representative political systems, and obey the rule of law. In vertical cultures, many of which are located in tropical Africa, power is located in traditional elites so that change can only occur through coups and revolutions. Education tends to reinforce ancient traditions and magical superstition rather than practical knowledge, and the strongman, rather than the law, rules. Whereas in horizontal societies, uncertainty is tamed by technology, jurisprudence, and religion, in vertical societies, an immutable divine order is presupposed that stifles innovation and leads to fatalism. At first, China fit into neither of these patterns, with the hope that its society and economy would begin to adopt the horizontal model. Instead, what emerged as the Chinese economy grew more powerful, and left behind its undeveloped status was a hybrid state of political authoritarianism and economic dynamism. Massive government investments, a form of infrastructure and military Keynesianism, shuffled the cards for the horizontal-vertical differentiation calculus.

Let me conclude by offering several points of contrast and comparison between the epoch of classical geopolitics and globalization. Weimar geopolitics was *zivilizatonskritish* (that is, reflected despair about the loss of culture), as well as being anti-American, anti-capitalist, and ultra-nationalist. It also encompassed a broad spectrum from left to right in its fight against Versailles. Opponents of globalization come from across the political spectrum and paint a bleak picture of global trends as hostile to human culture. The left, including a new global youth revolt, demonstrated against the IMF and the World Bank in the late 1990s, continues to view capitalism as a system tilted against the young, while the protectionist right rails against the global institutions, opposes U.S. military interventions, humanitarian or otherwise, in a redux of isolationism and 1930s-style isolationism. Anti-globalization is the return of revanchism in a form that re-conceptualizes geopolitics of the dispossessed.

Geopolitics never proposed itself as a "*Wissenschaft*"; that is, it was always a mixture of geography, politics, and publicity. Geopolitics didn't want to just describe politics, but shape it. The current debates about globalization are also not purely academic discourses, but rather reflect deep political and ideological divisions. Geoeconomics displays the darker side of the victory of liberal capitalism, manifest in the example above of the Gulf War: the spread of Western "values" is touted as universalism, but actually obeys the dictates of the market. A universal ethical imperative is belied by the selective enforcement of those values. In the 1930s, Carl Schmitt defended the notion of a German-dominated Middle Europe as spatial protection against the liberal victors in World War I. The anti-globalization forces in Europe today follows the same logic. No wonder Schmitt's *Grossraum* ideas have been enthusiastically received on the left.[11]

Weimar Geopolitics was based on resentment of the perceived hegemonic powers and the encirclement of Germany by hostile adversaries. Haushofer's idea of a "New order" was supposed to appeal to the "younger" powers, Italy, Japan, and Germany. Germany's *Mittellage* was both expansionist and defensive, to protect Germany from further interference by the victors in World War I. Coined by then-French Foreign Minister Hubert Védrine in the late 1990s, the French idea of "hyper-puissance" is comparable to Haushofer's opposition to the power of the allies, as is the desire by many Europeans to convert the European Union into a bulwark against American military and cultural imperialism in the Age of Trump. The massive cultural critique in France against neo-liberalism is an example of

11 For a good overview, see David Dyzenhaus (ed.) *Law as Politics; Carl Schmitt's Critique of Liberalism* (Durham: Duke University Press, 1998). As an example of the Left's use of Schmitt, see Chantal Mouffe (ed.) *The Challenge of Carl Schmitt* (London: Verso, 1999). See also the writings of the Italian iconoclast Heideggerian Giorgio Agamben, the postmodern writer Slavoj Žižek and the neo-Marxist Mario Tronti, who redefined class struggle in the 1960s along Schmitt's friend/foe distinction. The Frankfurt School jurist Otto Kirchheimer has been labelled a forerunner of "Left-Schmittianism," but this is a skewed perspective. See Martin Jay, "Reconciling the Irreconcilable?" *Telos* 71 (spring 1987); and Jeffrey Herf's contribution to "Reading and Misreading Schmitt: An Exchange," Telos 74 (winter 1987-8). 14.

the European intellectuals' revolt in a global age that mirrors the Weimar experience.

Technology is a key component of geopolitical currents. In contemporary Germany, the debate between the anti-globalization forces of the AfD against the modernizer, pro-business, Atlanticist strategy of the current Friedrich Merz government,[12] reminds one of similar struggles within the SPD and smaller liberal parties of the Weimar period over the issue of free trade, labor relations, and the fight against the rise of an authoritarian, populist movement. Both Weimar's geopolitical discourse and today's globalization debates are informed by the unsettling development of transformative technologies like radio in the interwar period and the internet today. Without radio, it is unlikely that Hitler would have succeeded in spreading his ideology so far and deep into the minds of German voters. Without social media today, it is unlikely that the Trump backlash against the so-called elites in established institutions and economic populism would have had the same valence as in the pre-internet era.

Modern communications technology has created new spatial issues of competition in "virtual" and real space, of which the Weimar geographers, of course, could have no conception. But what made geopolitics so interesting and new in the 1920s was its stress on the impact of aviation, radio, and other modern technologies on geopolitical questions. One could argue that the synthesis between politics, geography, technology, economics, and military strategy is still a stimulating but no less controversial method for analyzing global issues. Contemporary geopolitical thinkers treat the problems of neo-colonialism, economic development, free trade, state sovereignty, federalism, universal human rights, and crimes against humanity all with the same valency of Necro vs. Biopower. Like geopoliticians in the 1920s, today's proponents of the globalization imperative insist that all nations are subject to the same forces of

---

12 See Phyllis Berry, "Chancellor Merz's Key Choices on Foreign and Security Policy," American German Institute, https://americangerman.institute/2025/09/chancellor-merzs-key-choices-on-german-foreign-and-security-policy/#:~:text=The%20Role%20of%20the%20European%20Union&text=On%20migration%2C%20Germany%20has%20followed,approach%20to%20relations%20with%20China.

competition and struggle for survival that will determine success in the twenty-first century.

From the late nineteenth century until World War II, the idea that nations were locked in a Darwinian struggle for space and resources was understood by most educated observers of politics to be incontrovertible. In the highly contentious Wilhelmine period, political parties across the middle spectrum, including the Social Democrats, disagreed on just about everything, except for the necessity of a strong defense and colonial expansion. The rise of fascism required the combined powers of an unlikely alliance of east and west, to create a stable but dangerous peace based on mutually assured destruction. The peace dividend at the end of the Cold War lasted only a short time. Globalization tore the old alliances apart. Today, the struggle over new rules for the global order seems to be an unavoidable reality. Only the perspective of time will tell us whether we are trapped in a shared cognitive model that was as limited in its horizon as the geopolitics of previous eras, or whether a proper understanding of the past, which previous generations lacked, can give us the tools to prevent future wars between the major powers.

II.
Towards a Critical Hermeneutics of the Enemy:
A Whigless Reflection on Collective Memory

All profound changes in consciousness, by their very nature, bring with them characteristic amnesias. Out of such oblivions, in specific historical circumstances, spring narratives.
—Benedict Anderson, Imagined Communities[1]

All reification is a forgetting[2]
—Letter from Adorno to Benjamin

The concept of collective memory was first systematically developed by Maurice Halbwachs—a student of both Bergson and Durkheim—and by the cultural historian Aby Warburg in the 1930s as an alternative to racial and biological notions of collective consciousness, such as Carl Gustav Jung's "archetypes." For Warburg, certain cultural figures, from everyday objects to high art, possess surplus meaning, a kind of "mnemonic energy" which transcends their own age and can be studied as an "organum of remembrance" or a "cultural memory" (*kulturelle Erinnerung*).[3] By contrast, Halbwachs situated collective memory sociologically and ontogenetically in the everyday communicative acts of cultural and social groups, families, associations, classes, estates, and in the historical development of the nation.[4] In this model, language, rather than individual consciousness, is the social carrier of memory, and functions by contemporaneously transmitting culturally relevant information

1 Benedict Anderson, *Imagined Communities: Reflections on the Origin and Spread of Nationalism*, rev. ed., (London: Verso, 1991), 204.

2 Henri Lonitz ed., *Adorno Benjamin Briefwechsel* 1928-1940 (Frankfurt: Suhrkamp, 1940/1994), 417.

3 Michael Diers, "Warburg and the Warburgian Tradition of Cultural History," *New German Critique* 65 (Spring/Summer, 1995), 59-73.

4 Maurice Halbwachs, *The Collective Memory*, trans. Francis J. Ditter Jr & Vida Yazdi Ditter (New York: Harper, 1980).

from generation to generation. The "place" of memory, in Pierre Nora's phrase, is to be found in the physical topography of cultural objects, like buildings, museums, monuments, and the symbolic topography of art, texts, emblems, and landscapes. In these τόπο, *memoires* become transformed into *histoire*.[5]

From Halbwachs to contemporary "memoirologists" like Pierre Nora and Jacques Le Goff, history, as a science of verification of evidence and adjudication between conflicting interpretations of events, should be replaced by holistic representations of the fusion of memory and history as collective cultural and social experiences. In the place of linear, universal time, the "new" history would accommodate Henri Bergson's notion of "duration," which contains the possibilities of multiple, incommensurate and polycentric experiences of time.[6] By locating the object of history in de-personalized and collective structures, the individual becomes absorbed and subsumed by social power. Like many post-structuralist theorists, the memoirologists would replace the concept of the self- conscious individual with the notion of the person as a "space" determined by language, economics, biology, demography and other collective powers of differentiation.

The effacement of individual consciousness has elicited some hand-wringing among historians who are nervous about the abandonment of any distinction between personal and collective memories.[7] Like many post-structuralist theorists, the memoirologists would replace the concept of the self-conscious individual with the notion of the person as a "space" determined by language, economics, biology, demography and other collective powers of differentiation. Michael Foucault called this space a "discourse," which is "not the majestically unfolding manifestation of a thinking, knowing,

5 Pierre Nora, ed., *Les Lieux de Mèmoire*, 3 vols. (Paris: Gallimard: 1984-1986).

6 Halbwachs objected to the alleged "subjectivism" in Bergson's description of individual consciousness, but he nevertheless retained the most important features of "duration" as a subjective perception of time. See Halbwachs, *The Collective Memory*, ibid., 90-98.

7 See Jacques LeGoff, History and Memory, tran. Steven Rendall and Elizabeth Claman (New York: Columbia University Press, 1992), esp. 51-99.

speaking subject, but, on the contrary, a totality, in which the dispersion of the subject and his discontinuity with himself may be determined."[8]

Many years ago, F.C. Bartlett criticized Halbwach for not distinguishing properly between memory in the group and memory of the group.[9] Bartlett detected in the idea of collective memory a dubious importation of Durkheim's hypostatization of the psychological unity of the group. Amos Funkenstein offered a similar critique, arguing that Halbwachs ascribed independent existence to collective entities, similar to the romantic idea of a "spirit of the nation." "Remembering," Funkenstein observed, "is a mental act, and therefore it is absolutely and completely personal."[10] Instead of rejecting the notion of collective memory, Funkenstein argued that the concept can be saved as a heuristic device, denoting the emergence in Western culture of "historical consciousness," a means of forging collective identity and understanding the past on its own terms. In this way, Funkenstein hoped to strike a balance between the integrity of o memory and the collective totalization of remembrance. Jan Assmann has also argued that the hypostatization of the two realms (the personal, the group) as phenomenologically distinct was non-dialectical.[11] Assman's more integrative approach would locate a dynamic interaction between the two spheres at particular nodal points of past experience that focus cultural memory as history. Assman's understanding of cultural memory would tie together objective culture with personal and group memory, out of which emerges a "concretion of identity."[12]

---

8 Michel Foucault, *The Archaeology of Knowledge*. Trans. A.M. Sheridan Smith. (London and New York: Routledge), 2002. 50

9 Frederick C. Bartlett, *Remembering: A Study in Experimental and Social Psychology* (Cambridge: Cambridge University Press, 1932/ rep.1954), 294-296.

10 Amos Funkenstein, "Collective Memory and Historical Consciousness," *History and Memory* 1 (Spring/Summer, 1989), 6.
Ibid., pp. 11-12.

11 See Jan Assman, "Collective Memory and Cultural Identity," *New German Critique*, 65 (Spring/Summer, 1995), 125-133.

12 See A. Assmann and D. Harth, eds., *Mnemosyne: Formen und Funktionen der kulturellen Erinnerung*, (Frankfurt/Main: Suhrkamp, 1991).

One problem that both Assman and Funkenstein elide, even with the more dialectical approach, is that instead of leading to a richer notion of historical memory, in practice, social memory necessarily involves a decontextualization of history, a narrowing, rather than an enlargement of the focus, and a fabrication of the past to make sense of the present. For whatever purpose, social memory often establishes a group-specific appropriation of the past, between a positive (our memory) and a negative (their memory) field of contested identity. Out of an entire horizon of possible interpretations of the past, history becomes reduced to a normative act of identity-creation in the present.

This "abuse" of history has already been described by Nietzsche in his famous essay in which he differentiated between a "monumental," "antiquarian," and "critical" type of history.[13] Both monumental and antiquarian history narrow the focus: the latter conjures up a panorama of powerful heroes, while antiquarian history adulates, preserves, and romanticizes the past, transforming history into a sentimentalized practice of self-immersion in the past of the ancestors. "The antiquarian," writes Nietzsche, "recognizes his own soul in the soul of his people, across the wide, obscure and confused centuries."[14] By contrast, Nietzsche counterintuitively describes "critical" history as a kind of forgetting, enabling the individual to break out of the chains of remembering and have history serve life, rather than the reverse.

In the *Genealogy of Morals*, Nietzsche offered his most systematic explanation of the development of human consciousness as a consequence of a certain kind of reflective forgetting. In the famous fable, Nietzsche posited a state of nature in which certain human beings developed a superior sense of power over others, becoming a warrior class of men who live out an instinctual desire for cruelty and take pleasure in punishment. The "slave revolt" against morality brought about a renunciation of violence at the cost of repressing the cruel instincts and internalizing them in a soul, a conscience,

13 Friedrich Nietzsche, "Vom Nutzen und Nachteil der Historie für das Leben," *Unzeitgemäße Betrachtungen* (Stuttgart: Kroener, 1976), 112.

14 "...begrüsst, aber weite verdunkelnde und verwirrende Jahrhunderte hinweg die Seele," Ibid. 120.

and ultimately passing on the "self-mutilation" in the form of the Jewish and Christian religions. The human psyche, according to Nietzsche, is formed as the result of a burning into consciousness the memory of the cruelest forms of past sacrificial rites. This process he calls mnemotechnics: "only that which doesn't stop causing pain remains in memory.[15] Nietzsche's theory locates the traumatic function of repression, sublimation, and ultimately a diachrony of selective collective memories over time, which probably influenced Freud.[16] The *Übermensch* achieves autonomy by successfully escaping the straightjacket of memory, of group morality, and resists the social system of rules.

It is unclear whether the contemporary renunciation of "grand narratives," the postmodern skepticism in regard to the possibilities of social emancipation and the eclectic style of pastiche and quotation would qualify as the kind of vitalist forgetting Nietzsche recommends. Postmodernity plausibly follows Nietzsche in celebrating the inevitability of multiple perspectives in locating history as an arbitrary assemblage of narrative strategies based on a shifting and endlessly variable foundation of empirical facts.

In *The Postmodern Condition*, a foundational text of French poststructuralism, Jean-François Lyotard privileged storytelling, or the "narrative form" as a more authentic kind of knowledge than empirical science, because the community of listeners and the narrator bond together to legitimize and recognize their own past, whereas scientific knowledge places the narrator outside the community.[17] In a similar vein, Richard Rorty's reading of Nietzsche and Wittgenstein led him to suggest that we replace any teleological view of history with new language games undergirded by non-directional metaphors for describing historical events. One jettisons the idea of

15 Friedrich Nietzsche, *Zur Archeology der Moral*, Part II. Section 3 (Stuttgart: Kroener, 1976), 289.

16 See Ernest Gellner, *The Psychoanalytic Movement; The Cunning of Unreason* (Evanston: Northwestern University Press, 1996).

17 Jean-François Lyotard, *The Postmodern Condition: A Report on Knowledge*, trans. Geoff Bennington & Brian Massumi (Minneapolis: University of Minnesota Press, 1984), esp. pp. 14-31.

an integrated "history of humanity," to be replaced by contingent, individually situated dramatic narratives.[18]

In contrast to providential history, no preexistent goal can be triumphantly reached in the postmodern space, neither as a post-capitalist era, as with Marx or decline, as with Spengler; nor by triumphant reason, as cumulative in the inexorable march of science as in Comte or Hegel. In a history without teleology, neither the drama of an individual life nor the history of humanity as a whole is at stake. Neither external reality in the form of events, nor an unfailing interior source of inspiration in the form of heroes, forms the background of human drama. Instead, to see one's life, or the life of one's community, as a dramatic narrative is to see it as a process of Nietzschean self-overcoming. The postmodern embrace of heterogeneous "language games," the "genealogical" method, and the "pragmatics of narrative knowledge," on the one side, and the concomitant renunciation of any Ur-meanings, innate natures or essences, valorizes the contingency of collective memory over the facticity of history, the latter being caricatured as hopelessly positivist, "essentialist" or shallowly empirical. Collective memories become poetic, an interstitial set of metaphors, in Rorty's sense. In another context (not made explicit by Rorty, but taken up by other scholars), the stress on the self-creative function of memory can lead to a radical questioning of a supposedly dogmatic and dominant discourse about the past ("history," which needs to be deconstructed and delegitimized in order to give back to oppressed people a past which has been denied.

Note in this context a relatively contemporary example, an observation on the legacy of Malcolm X by Michael Eric Dyson. According to Dyson, from slavery until the present, African-American heroes have been instrumental in preserving the collective memory of black culture against the detrimental consequences of racial amnesia while fighting racism in American public culture.[19] The idea of a "collective memory of Black culture" constitutes, however, a

---

18 Richard Rorty, *Contingency, Irony and Solidarity* (Cambridge: Cambridge University Press, 1989), 29.

19 Michael Eric Dyson, *Making Malcolm: The Myth and Meaning of Malcolm X* (New York: Oxford University Press, 1995), p.148.

double-edged sword. Does it imply that Caucasian Americans or Asian Americans have a collective memory that cannot be integrated into a simple "American collective memory?" When Blacks feel their collective memory is not being respected, which form should the "fight against racism" take? For example, a violent turn? There exists a large shaded area between the benign cultivation of selective memory and the aggressive instrumentalization of memory for violent ends. In his other writings, Dyson has attempted to counteract the rage elicited by the memory of past oppression with a careful analysis of the "subtext," "pretext," and "context" of race, and a call for transcending the "prison of race." Other intellectuals, sometimes identified under the rubric of Critical Race Theory, (of late under specific attack by the political right), explicitly invoke the collective memories of Blacks as an alternative narrative to the supposedly racist constructions of white historians.[20] Collective memories in this account are embodied in what is called "storytelling," a method of recollecting the past that not only provides alternative narratives but also "voices of color" that are said to be more emotional than analytic, less descriptive, but more genuine. "Storytelling" denigrates the conventional academic notions of logic, objectivity, evidence and rational argument and replaces the critical apparatus with edifying narratives designed to bolster the identity of a particular community of listeners, in effect, to confirm its prejudices.

Beyond the ethereal confines of academic theory, critical race theory contributed in the United States, after the O.J. Simpson trial, to a growing number of Black juries acquitting Black defendants, in spite of overwhelming evidence in support of a guilty verdict, with

20 Critical Race Theory can be traced to legal scholars of the 1970s such as Derrick Bell, Kimberlé Crenshaw, and Richard Delgado. See Derrick Bell, *Faces from the Bottom of the Well: the Permanence of Racism* (New York: Basic Books, 1992); See also A. Leon Higginbotham, Jr. *Shades of Freedom: Racial Politics and Presumptions of the American Legal Process* (Oxford: Oxford University Press, 1996; On storytelling see Peter Brooks & Paul Gewirtz eds., *Law's Stories: Narrative and Rhetoric in the Law* (New Haven: Yale University Press, 1996), esp. 24-59. Hans Ibram X Kendi is a good example of a contemporary exponent. On the attack by the right, see "Critical Race Theory Is a Convenient Target for Conservatives," *Slate* (June 12, 2021).

the justification that the history of past racism legitimizes the nullification of sentences to counteract current racism[21]. Jury nullification recapitulates the racist practice of white southern juries that acquitted whites who murdered Blacks.[22] As recently as the riots that erupted after the police murder of George Floyd, a new type of historical consciousness emerged in popular form, which used history as a repository of past victimization, and the new vocation of the "storyteller" to be the keeper of the sacred memories of injustice.[23]

This new configuration of collective memory in the public sphere had partly to do with the resorting of global power after the end of the Cold War. In that period of the "unilateral moment" of hegemonic American power, Hans Magnus Enzensberger counterintuitively connected the resurgence of cultural civil wars, whether they took place with the Rodney King Los Angeles riots of 1992, or the bloody altercations in the Bosnian wars—all sides had their tribal gods demanding tribute of one form or another.[24] Enzensberger was accused of falling back on the tropes of conservative cultural pessimism, but Derrida, hardly a "conservative," described tribal conflict in similar terms in his polemic against Francis Fukuyama's version of *posthistoire*. Contemporary ethnic wars are driven, wrote Derrida, "by the primitive conceptual phantasm of community, the nation state, sovereignty, borders, native soil and blood..."[25] Derrida argued further that the drive for stability, order and a coherent national narrative is always "rooted first of all in the memory or the anxiety of a displaced—or displaceable—population." In other words, the strength of the politics of cultural particularism

21 Paul Butler, "Racially Based Jury Nullification: Black Power in the Criminal Justice System," *Yale Law Journal* (105, 3, Dec. 1995), 677-725.

22 See Jeffrey Rosen, "The Blood and the Crits," *The New Republic*, December 9, 1996, 27-42.

23 See Thomas Chatterton Williams, *The Summer of Our Discontent* (New York: Knopf, 2025).

24 Magnus Enzensberger, *Civil Wars From LA to Bosnia* (New York: New Press, 1994).

25 Jacques Derrida, *Specters of Marx: The State of the Debt, the Work of Mourning and the New International*, trans. Peggy Kampf (New York: Routledge, 1994), 82.

often increases or decreases in an inverted relationship to the "displacement" of national or religious traditions: the more displaced the identity, or as Benedict Anderson puts it in the epigram above, the deeper the oblivion, the stronger the narrative of cohesion.[26]

The Politics of Collective Memory

I would like to offer empirical underpinning to the argument that collective memories should be conceived theoretically as imaginary redefinitions of the past to suit contemporary political exigencies, as an alternative to Halbwachs's notion of organic and natural anamnestic links between generations within a community. The question posed is whether these "primitive conceptual phantasms" are invented by intellectuals and then exploited by politicians, in order to mobilize social groups one against the other, or whether the imaginary re-definitions can be traced to authentic traumas of displacement, that call forth a new kind of political and religious leadership. Much of the evidence speaks for the former thesis, that supposed deep religious or political hatreds need to be called up, carved out of the past and made usable for the present. One should not, however, conclude that just because deep religious or political hatreds are conjured up artificially, they are therefore harmless. In *The Elementary Forms of Religious Life*, Emile Durkheim used the term "collective effervescence" to point to the phenomenon of delirium in the psychology of religious and political movements.[27] In this context, Durkheim analyzed the psychology of threatened groups, who band together and create sacred myths and rituals, while shutting down internal dissent in the name of collective security. The

26 For an overview of the debates within the historical profession, see Joyce Appleby & Lynn Hunt, *Telling the Truth About History* (New York: Norton, 1994). See an enlightening discussion of four case studies by Alan B. Spitzer, *Historical Truth and Lies About the Past* (Chapel Hill: University of North Carolina Press, 1996). Spitzer argues that when the political stakes are high, participants in historical debates, regardless of their theoretical biases, tend to favor traditional rules of rationality and evidence-based argument.

27 Emile Durkheim, *The Elementary Forms of Religious Life*, trans. Jospeh Ward Swain (London: George Allen & Unwin, 1915), 227 ff.

collective effervescence can easily lead to "excesses, and cause men to lose sight of the distinction separating the licit from the illicit."[28]

Case Study 1: Bahratyia Janata (BJP) in India

The outbreak of religious violence in India since the early the early 1980s provides a case in point. In December 1992, after three years of political agitation by the Hindu nationalist party Bharatiya Janata, (one of two major parties in India, along with the Indian National Congress), Hindu fanatics destroyed a Mosque in the city of Ayodhya because it was supposedly built by the Mughal ruler Babur on a holy site where the Hindu God Rama was born. As a result of violent clashes between Hindus and Muslims, over 2,500 people were killed. The goal of the Hindus was to build a new temple to Lord Rama where the mosque had stood. These revisionist ideas were put into the heads of the Hindu fanatics like the Hindu mystical nationalist Gawal Kar (1906-1973), or public influencers like the political cartoonist Bal Thackeary (1926-2012), who abetted the platform of neo-fascist parties, such as the Shiva Sena and Jana Sangh by stirring up resentment and fundamentalist passions. Many of these conflicts have to do with current political struggles and are not, as western observers too readily conclude, the result of "age-old" animosities. Up until the nineteenth century, for example, few people in India ever dreamed of claiming that Lord Rama's birthplace was located at Babur's Mosque. These "ancient hatreds," observed Susanne and Lloyd Rudolph, were invented as much as they were inherited. To call them ancient is to pretend they are derived from primordial forces, outside of history and human agency, when often they were merely synthetic antiques. Intellectuals, writers, artists and politicians "make" hatreds. Films, videos, texts and textbooks, certify stories about the past, the collective memories that shape perceptions and attitudes.[29]

---

28 Ibid. 383.

29 See Susanne Hoeber Rudolph and Llyod I. Rudolph, "Modern Hate: How Ancient Animosities get Invented," *The New Republic* (March 22, 1993), 24-29. See also Atul Kohli, *Democracy and Discontent: India's Growing Crisis of Governability* (New York: Cambridge University Press, 1990). On Gawaltar, see Thomas Blom Hansen, *The Saffron Wave; Democracy*

Case Study 2: Greece and Macedonia

To take another example, in Greece, nationalists since the late nineteenth century have rattled their swords over the issue of control of Ottoman Macedonia, in the build-up to the World War I and then again in the wake of the Balkan Wars of the 1990s, when Greece claimed that the tiny newly independent Balkan state of former Yugoslavia had no right to use the name Macedonia because the area is situated in the antique boundaries of the empire of Alexander the Great. Angry denunciations of the Macedonians and long historical articles could be found regularly in Greek newspapers, laying forth these kinds of claims. As Eric Hobsbawm pointed out at the time, the Greek national state never existed in the fourth century and, if anything, the Athenians of the day considered the Macedonians to be frightening barbarians, not ethnic brothers.[30] Bulgaria, Serbia and Albania claim, for similar reasons, and for reasons related to the Macedonian dialect, that Macedonia and its language were created artificially during the Yugoslav era.

Case Study 3: The Balkan Wars "Ancient Hatreds" Justification

In the case of the wider Balkans Wars of the 1990s, Both the Europeans and the Americans justified their inaction in the face of genocide by arguing that the events in Bosnia could be traced to ancient hostilities and that military engagement in these civil wars would just make things worse. Elizabeth Drew, who published a book about the first eighteen months of Bill Clinton's presidency, described the conflicting advice the President received from his foreign policy advisors and how he came to a wrenching decision on May 1, 1993 to lift the arms embargo against the Bosnian Muslims and conduct limited air strikes against the Serbs if they continued to take advantage of the situation on the ground. The French, British,

and Hindu Nationalism in Modern India (Princeton: Princeton University Press, 1999).

30 Eric Hobsbawm, "Die Erfindung der Vergangenheit," *Die Zeit*, 37, (Sept. 9, 1994) 49-50.

Germans and Russians all immediately opposed the plan, but according to Drew, the event that persuaded Clinton to back off from the "life and strike" policy was his reading of geopolitical theorist Robert Kaplan's book *Balkan Ghosts*.[31] Clinton and Powell (who apparently read part of the book) were impressed by Kaplan's depiction of Bosnian history as a long litany of war, determined by the living memory of historical events, such as the Battle of Kosovo. Kaplan was particularly shocked by the way in which almost every people in this region perceives itself as a victim of historical injustices and blamed its neighbor for the many economic and social problems.[32] Timothy Garten Ash criticized Kaplan for exaggerating the role of memory in these conflicts and thereby causing Clinton and Colin Powell to refrain from intervening at the beginning of the Balkan Wars when American military presence could have held back Serbian aggression.[33] It is true that one can read *Balkan Ghosts* as a confirmation of the power of "organic" memories, in Halbwach's sense. But the book also demonstrates the process whereby historical memories are arbitrarily invented. Kaplan articulates how each ethnic group made claims to huge areas of territory by isolating those periods in which the geographical boundaries of a particular people were most extended. He tells horrifying tales of Romanian and Hungarian intellectuals who lack even an inkling of detached objectivity and mobilize history, it seems, only to substantiate their hatred of each other, and their deep anti-Semitism, while lamenting their nation's decline from some long past idealized greatness. Kaplan doesn't stress enough, however, the role of the elites in manufacturing these memories, and their motives for doing so, as the American ambassador Warren Zimmerman, an eye-witness in Bosnia, has poignantly observed.[34]

The breakup of Yugoslavia is a classic example of nationalism from the top down—a manipulated nationalism in a region where

31 Elizabeth Drew, *On the Edge: The Clinton Presidency* (New York: Simon & Schuster, 1994). 156-7.

32 Robert D. Kaplan, *Balkan Ghosts* (New York: Vintage, 1994).

33 See Brendan Simms, "The Battle Over the Balkans—And America's Role in the World," *Wall Street Journal* (August 3, 1999).

34 Michael T. Kaufmann, "The Dangers of Letting a President Read," *New York Times* (May 22, 1999).

peace has historically prevailed more than war and in which a quarter of the population were in mixed marriages. The manipulators condoned and even provoked local ethnic violence in order to engender animosities that could then be magnified by the press, leading to further violence. Fouad Ajami, in his reading of national histories of various Balkan countries, pointed out that many Serbian historians had portrayed their development into a nation as one long and tragic battle to retain a Christian identity in the face of repeated foreign oppression and intervention. First, their lands were destroyed by the infidel Turks, then they were tricked and maligned by a long list of foreigners, including Magyars, Austrians, Nazis and Croats. The final insult was when Germany recognized Croatia's independence in 1991, on the same date as the Battle of Kosovo in 1389, thereby enforcing the belief that Serbia had once more been betrayed by outside powers. All this history, Ajami wrote, is an invention, spun out of vanity and need for consolation: "The Serbs love the legend of themselves standing at the ramparts defending Christendom. However, the truth is far more complex. After Kosovo, Serbs fought on behalf of the Turks as their vassals and allies in intermittent campaigns that stretched nearly two centuries. Serbs made their way into the Ottoman court and imperial army, and found a niche for themselves in the polyglot Ottoman world."[35]

How Collective Memories Become Deadly

The stories people tell themselves may be myths, inventions and reconstructions, yet the consequences of telling and re-telling them can be very real and very deadly. The most startling aspect of the Balkan wars of the 1990s was the sudden transformation of a multicultural, multi-religious and multi-ethnic nation, which had lived together more often in harmony than at war for a thousand years, into a genocidal blood-bath, pitting neighbor against neighbor, sometimes husband against wife. The eye-witness observers' accounts of this transformation seem to agree on two points: First, there existed a large reservoir of discontent and resentments buried underneath Tito's more or less successful imposition of a federalist

---

35 Fouad Ajami, "In Europe's Shadows," *The New Republic* (November 21, 1994), 30.

structure on a bewilderingly complex ethnic patchwork. Second, Serbs, Croats, Albanians, Slovenians, Macedonians and other groups had to learn to see themselves, through the mirror of history, and through the mirror of religion, as victims of enormous past discrimination. Through gradual stages the leadership on all sides manipulated the narrative of victimization into an apocalyptic battle for ethnic purification.

Nowhere was this process more self-consciously enacted as public drama than in the early stages of the conflict when the Serbian leader Slobodan Milosevic, organized an elaborate celebration for the 600th anniversary of the Battle of Kosovo, on June 28, 1989, in Phrishtina, in the majority-Albanian region of Kosovo. Although the defeat of the Serbs by the Ottomans in 1389, on the Field of Blackbirds (Kosovo Polje), is annually commemorated as the origin of the struggle for an independent Serbian nation, the 600th anniversary event had ominous and poignant political overtones. In attendance were Serbs from Bosnia, Voljvodina and from as far away as Toronto and Melbourne. As an officially Yugoslavian celebration, the Slovenian President Janez Drnovsek and the Croatian Prime Minister Ante Markovic were in attendance. They cannot have failed to register, with alarm, the significance of Milosevic's carefully orchestrated speech, offered six centuries (after Kosovo Polje), the "ancient' battles were re-enacted.[36]

A few short years later, the war that Milosevic prepared and hoped for, had become a reality. The combatants by now had magically assimilated the collective social perceptions of why the war was being waged. No better example of this can be given than the following encounter by David Rieff with drunken Serbian soldiers in a tavern in Banja Luka in October 1992.[37] The dialogue is worth quoting at length because it is a perfect example of what Halbwachs describes as the reconstruction of individual memory by the group:

> The fighter leaned across the table toward me. "You know, he said, "before the Second World War, Banja Luka was a Serbian town. If

36 Cited by Misha Glenny, *The Fall of Yugoslavia: The Third Balkan War* (London: Penguin, 1992), 35.

37 David Rieff, *Slaughterhouse, Bosnia and the Failure of the West* (New York, Simon & Schuster, 1995), 86

> there hadn't been so many massacres, if the Muslims and the Ustasha hadn't tried to exterminate the Serb people in Bosnia, we would still be in the majority here, instead of having to always defend ourselves against them every fifty years." The fighter leaned across the table toward me. "You know, he said, "before the Second World War, Banja Luka was a Serbian town. If there hadn't been so many massacres, if the Muslims and the Ustasha hadn't tried to exterminate the Serb people in Bosnia, we would still be in the majority here, instead of having to always defend ourselves against them every fifty years." His comrade interrupted. "Why do you Americans hate the Serb people now? We were allies in two world wars, fighting together. Why do you side with the fascists? It is bad. We should be friends. He paused. "Many of my comrades say America has become a bad country. I do not think so. I think you do not understand what has happened here. Do you know about the battle of Kosovo in 1389?" I must have grimaced, for he shook his head and grabbed my wrist. "No, really it is important. You Americans care nothing for history, but you should care. Serbs only have history. For five hundred years we Serbs have been defending Western civilization against the Turks. Vuk Karadzic did it in the nineteenth century, our leader Radovan Karadzic, does it now. We all do. All!

Whereas Halbwachs's description of the social experience of the "affective community," conveys the mental representation of a cozy harbor of familiarity, Rieff's example puts in sharp relief the image of the opposite: a collective social image of the enemy.

Case Study 4: Putin's Invented Memory

The break-up of the Soviet Union and the end of its political and military dominance in Eastern Europe led to a resurgence of civil wars, both in areas where religious or political minorities wished to assert independence against the remaining center of Soviet power, or where the centralization imposed by communist dictatorship could no longer contain ethnic conflict. Unresolved border disputes, religious hatreds, and historical feuds, rooted deeply in European memory, thawed out and determined the course of political events in a manner inconceivable during the Cold War. The breakup of the Soviet Union and the end of its political and military dominance in Eastern Europe led to a resurgence of civil wars, both in areas where religious or political minorities wished to assert independence against the remaining center of Soviet power, or where the centralization imposed by communist dictatorship could no longer contain ethnic conflict. Unresolved border disputes, religious hatreds, and historical feuds, rooted deeply in European memory, determined the course of political events in a manner that allowed Vladimir Putin later to reassert central control from Moscow by claiming that Russia's identity and national security were undermined by forces unleashed by westernization. Putin has taken it upon himself as his life mission to unify Russia along the lines of imperial maps and to reconstitute collective memory for Russians living today, in the aftermath of what he considers the tragedy of the fall of the Russian Empire, even though he harbors little affection for, indeed outright hostility to, Soviet-style communism.[38] On July 21, 2021, Putin published a speech, now infamous, titled "On the Historical Unity of Russians and Ukrainians," in which he argues, using twisted historical sources, that Ukrainians, Russians, and Belarusians are historically one people, part of a *triune* or pan-Russian nation.[39] Putin denies that Ukrainians have a distinct culture and history; he falsely draws a straight line from Kievan Rus' to the modern Russian state and claims that Ukrainians have no agency, but rather serve as puppets of Western interests. None of this stands up to historical scrutiny.[40]

Memory as Experience of the Enemy

One of the reasons why we have been lulled into valorizing collective memories as somehow more authentic representations of history is that it has increasingly seemed important to battle against forgetting in the face of modern culture's tendency to erase the past as quickly as possible. The battle against forgetting was one of the recurring themes of those German thinkers whom we associate with

38 Andre Kolesnikov, "How the Putin Regime Subverted the Soviet Legacy," *Carnegie Politika* (June 11, 2024). https://carnegieendowment.org/russia eura-sia/politika/2024/05/putin-anti-soviet-russia?lang=en

39 https://web.archive.org/web/20220125053520/http://en.kremlin.ru/en.kremlin.ru/events/president/news/66181.

40 See Peter Dickinson, "Putin's New Ukraine Essay Reveals Imperial Ambitions," *Atlantic Council*, https://www.atlanticcouncil.org/blogs/ukrainealert/putins-new-ukraine-essay-reflects-imperial-ambitions/.

the "Frankfurt School," and "critical theory." In concluding, I turn to this body of work in order to highlight the fact that the theoretical problems I have tried to point out so far are not necessarily tied to the particular methodological constructions of French social history or the influence of anti-positivist thinkers like Bergson, but might be placed in the broader context of postmodernism, as a tension between the desires, memories and displacements of the individual and the collective.

The Frankfurt School, recapitulating the French tradition, did not differentiate sharply enough between memory as an individual and as a collective phenomenon. Herbert Marcuse, for example, argued consistently for the positive function of memory as a means of emancipation from the one-dimensional, constricted present; in particular he viewed art as a reservoir of past, unrealized possibilities that look to a different future.[41] Memory functions here as a means of turning toward the world, engaged in what Stendhal called a *promesse de bonheur*,

Since art preserves, with the promise of happiness, the memory of the goals that failed, it can enter, as a "regulative idea," the desperate struggle for changing the world.[42] Against all fetishism of the productive forces, against the continued enslavement of individuals by the objective conditions (which remain those of domination), art represents the ultimate goal of all revolutions: the freedom and happiness of the individual. As Martin Jay points out, "memory, in fact, played a key role in the Frankfurt School's understanding of the crisis of modern civilization."[43] While it is possible

41 Herbert Marcuse, *The Aesthetic Dimension: Toward a Critique of Marxist Aesthetics*, trans. Erica Sherover & Herbert Marcuse (Boston: Beacon Press, 1978). 69.

42 "Modernity" may indeed be defined as the inexorable replacement of the memory of the past by the present, creating what David Frisby calls the "eternal present," see Frisby, Frag*ments of Modernity* (Cambridge: MIT Press, 1986), 38-108.

43 Martin Jay, *The Dialectical Imagination* (Boston: Little, Brown & Co., 1973), 267.

Walter Benjamin, "On Some Motifs in Baudelaire," in Hannah Arendt, ed., *Illuminations*, trans. Harry Zohn (New York: Harcourt, Brace & World, 1968), 161.

that Marcuse's desire to break away from a bad present was more utopian or more romantic than the philosophical position of Adorno, Horkheimer, Benjamin and others, it can nevertheless be stated without contradiction that the memory of injustice and enslavement in the past, captured in Marcuse's aesthetic of redemption, served the Frankfurt School as a justification to sustain a consistent critique of the present, and to hope for emancipation in the future

The idea that anamnestic solidarity with past generations may lead to alienation from and hostility to the heirs of the alleged perpetrators of past crimes never seems to have been countenanced by the proponents of Critical Theory. This omission can be clearly shown in Benjamin's otherwise admirable attempts to articulate a philosophy of history that eschews a totalized view of the past and valorizes the fragmentary nature of memory. In commenting on Proust's concept of "involuntary memory," Benjamin distinguished between the unconnected snippets of information that "paralyze" the modern newspaper reader and the more organic, connected mode of the storyteller, which connects the individual to a collective past.[44] But does Benjamin's distinction really allow us to separate shallow and momentary experiences (*Erlebnisse*) from genuine ones (*Erfahrungen*), those in which a true convergence of the experiences of the individual and the collective appears? Haven't we shown above that the storyteller's narratives are often manipulated fabrications? The abuse of collective memory through the kind of politicization described in this essay occurs through the reconstruction of fragments of historical images into powerful, agonistic narratives.

"Wouldn't it be the task," Adorno wrote to Benjamin in a letter, "to connect the entire antithesis between *Erlebniss* and *Erfahrung* to a dialectic theory of forgetting? One could also say, to a theory of reification, for all reification is a forgetting." Adorno goes on to ask whether or not there is forgetting, per se, and a kind of "reflective" forgetting, which may also be described as a "good" and "bad" form of reification. An investigation of these categories would take us beyond the scope of this essay. See Henri Lonitz ed., Adorno Benjamin *Briefwechsel* 1928-1940 (Frankfurt: Suhrkamp, 1994), 417-18

44 Walter Benjamin, 'The Storyteller: Reflections on the Works of Nikolai Leskov' (1936). First printed in *Orient und Okzident*, 1936; rep. in *Illuminations*, op. cit. 83-108.

Since the decline of any kind of shared collective experience of mediated events on television and the loss of dramatic stories that created common rituals and experiences, at least around an electronic town square, social media today "paralyzes" the viewer beyond what Benjamin could have imagined, with unconnected fragments of information, at an ever-increasing speed, disassociated from any collective experience of the present or past. The prospects of an hallucinatory past, invented by AI, portends an even more disconnected future. The reified nature of fragmented experiences comes about, not only because the past has been cut up into disjointed memes, but because the link between past and present has also been forgotten, or to put it another way, the storyteller is also a story-forgetter, as Adorno suggested in a letter to Benjamin.[45]

Articulating the relationship between forgetting and remembering is what Ernst Bloch had in mind when he distinguished between "anamnesis" and "anagnorisis.[46] The first refers to the Greek understanding of knowledge as passive, possibly unconscious memories which are called up into consciousness, while the latter constitutes a more active form of subjective knowledge as a conscious meeting between the past and the future in the present. The former conceives of the past as a totality, a secure repository of remembrance, while the latter recognizes the ephemeral nature of the act of remembering and does not overvalue the traditions of the dead generations which weigh, as Marx said, like a nightmare on the brains of the living.

A Non-Schmittian Hermeneutics of the Enemy

An understanding of collective memory that takes seriously the "nightmares" left by the memory of the dead must also grapple with the problem of the enemy. In 1932, Carl Schmitt famously argued that the political realm is defined by the most intense degree of as-

45 Henri Lonitz ed., *Adorno Benjamin Briefwechsel* 1928-1940 (Frankfurt: Suhrkamp, 1994, (February 29, 1940), 417.

46 Michael Landmann, "Talking with Ernst Bloch: Korcula, 1968," cited by Martin Jay, *Marxism and Totality* (Berkeley: UC Press, 1984), 238.

sociation and dissociation, ultimately resting on the capacity to distinguish between friend and enemy.[47] This distinction, for Schmitt, is not metaphorical but refers to the concrete possibility of mortal combat between collectivities.

A non-Schmittian approach begins by refusing to make this friend–enemy distinction the essence of politics. Instead, we can distinguish "enemy" from "opponent" or "adversary." Democratic and liberal traditions insist on precisely the categorical differences that Schmitt collapses. An adversary, in this sense, may be a person, a party, or an institutionalized force (even an abstract entity such as a state) whose views or interests we contest, but who's right to exist and to participate we nonetheless recognize. An enemy in the strict sense would be a party to armed conflict, subject to the law of war and, ideally, to jus in bello constraints.

On this view, the health of a constitutional order can be measured by the extent to which it can contain conflict at the level of opponents—through parliamentary struggle, protest, litigation—without upgrading domestic rivals into "enemies of the people." Politics ought not to be defined by enmity, but by the institutions and norms that prevent enmity from redefining adversaries as objects of elimination. Rather than glorifying existential friend/enemy confrontation, we can treat the enemy as a tightly bounded juridical category (for example, in just war theory or international humanitarian law), subject to rules about discrimination, proportionality, and non-combatant immunity. In domestic politics, an "enemy" in Schmitt's sense has no legitimate place at all.

The ultimate goal, then, is to reduce the space in which human beings appear to one another as enemies, by strengthening law, diplomacy, and shared institutions. The central question is not "Who is the enemy?" but "Under what strictly limited conditions, if any, may we legitimately treat anyone as an enemy in Schmitt's existential sense?" Whereas Schmitt grounds politics in the killable enemy, the default stance toward foreign strangers and domestic rivals in a liberal order is ethical recognition, not pre-emptive hostility.

47 Carl Schmitt, The Concept of the Political, trans. George Schwab (Chicago: University of Chicago Press, 1996), 26–37; originally published as Der Begriff des Politischen (Berlin: Duncker & Humblot, 1932).

A "hermeneutics of the enemy" would ask: What has to happen—conceptually, institutionally, emotionally—for a particular Other to be stripped of that ethical claim and recoded as an enemy? Every act of naming an enemy should trigger questions about our own interests, fears, and fantasies. Such a critique must also be turned back on Western intellectuals themselves, who are not immune to uncritical assimilation of dominant cultural stereotypes. Edward Said, for one, long labored to expose the nationalistic prejudices embedded in Western representations of the enemy as the cultural Other. In his 1993 Reith Lectures, he argued that because intellectuals write and think in particular, not universal, languages, the division between "us" and "them," with all the attendant oversimplifications and generalizations about other peoples, remains a hidden and unexamined dimension of collective identity formation around the enemy.[48] To feel, as many Americans are encouraged to feel, that "the Russians are coming," or that a Chinese "economic invasion" is underway, or that militant Islam will impose sharia on the West—or that Islam as such is incompatible with Western pluralism—is not merely to experience collective alarm. It is also to consolidate "our" identity as beleaguered and at risk.

Followers of Trump's MAGA movement, for instance, ground their primary cultural self-identity in an antagonistic view of the enemy as the Other, and imagine a retrieval of a past homogeneity of a primarily white and Christian America. Within this paradigm, Muslims in particular are treated as non-assimilable—not only because they are not Christian, but because they are framed as fundamentally outside the civilizational community (with secular non-Muslims and Jews only provisionally tolerated inside the artificial construct "civilization").[49]

For Said, the "West" often appeared as unipolar, one-dimensional, and incapable of transcending its self-created prejudices. "Westernism" thus became the mirror image of the cultural-conservative notion of "the West" as a self-contained, synthetic set of values and ideas. More problematic than crude stereotyping alone,

48 Edward W. Said, Representations of the Intellectual: The 1993 Reith Lectures (New York: Vintage, 1996), 32.

49 See Yuri Sleskine, "Why the West?" New York Review of Books, (December, 2025), 52-58

however, was the difficulty many Western intellectuals—despite their universalist claims—had in explaining the precise links between linguistic and cultural identities, on the one hand, and various forms of intra- and inter-group animosity on the other. The uncanny experience of recognizing cultural familiarity in contrast to the strangeness of others seems to be universal; what varies is how that strangeness is coded and politicized.

One starting point for a social science of the enemy is a psychology of hostility anticipated by Freud in his theory of narcissism, which explains how human beings create libidinal attachments to some persons while exhibiting enormous cruelty toward others.[50] James Aho and Elaine Pagels have both undertaken pioneering work on the historical and sociological link between memory and the construction of the enemy.[51] Primo Levi cut to the core of the problem when he wrote in Survival in Auschwitz that the conviction "the foreigner is the enemy" lies deep down "like some latent infection" in the human mind.[52] The task of a comparative sociology of collective memory, then, is to investigate when and how this latent infection erupts into plagues of hate.

After the attacks by Hamas on Israel on October 7, 2023, and the subsequent Israeli response that devastated Gaza, the international cascade of blame and counter-blame revealed—if further evidence were needed—the deep necessity of a sociology of enmities. Participants in wars have, from ancient times, believed that the killing of their enemies was justified. The image of the enemy is likely inscribed both in what we call "human nature" and in cultural memory, then passed on to the social body as part of the "civilizing process." Collective memories are often anchored in primordial myths of conquest and violence. The historian's task should be to trace how this transformative process works and to assess both the

50 Sigmund Freud, "The Libido Theory and Narcissism," Lecture XXVI in James Strachey, ed., The Complete Introductory Lectures on Psychoanalysis (New York: Norton, 1966).

51 Elaine Pagels, The Origins of Satan (New York: Random House, 1995); James Aho, This Thing of Darkness (Seattle: University of Washington Press, 1994).

52 Primo Levi, Survival in Auschwitz, trans. Stuart Woolf (New York: Collier, 1961), 5.

destructive and the lyrical impact of these mythologies upon civilization.

A truly critical practice of collective memory would identify and expose the cultural-nativist impulses embedded in these narratives by applying a disciplined hermeneutics. Rather than pursuing a Nietzschean "overcoming of the past," a more modest and realistic goal would be for intellectuals to recognize that we are always already part of communities whose values and historical constructions we share, perhaps inextricably—but that we can and must, as citizens, learn to stand partially outside these hermeneutic circles.

A hermeneutics of the enemy would thus be one of the tools available to critical observers to warn against collective effervescence when systems of identity lose their substance as connective tissue and are transformed instead into metaphorical allergens that the social body uses to attack itself. Political theory in the Western tradition has always begun with questions about human nature and about whether, and how, the use of force—political violence—can and should be constrained. All rules are enforced; the question is how. Theories of collective memory have not yet adequately incorporated that primary dimension of human experience into their analyses of how we remember—and how, in remembering, we make enemies.

Part Two: World and Ideas of Ernst Jünger

My fascination with Ernst Jünger spans more than four decades. I came across a copy of Ernst Jünger's *On the Marble Cliffs* in a dusty used book store in Berlin in 1983, and haven't looked back. The five selections on Jünger printed here represent various aspects of the scholarly conversations and debates about Jünger, which were written after the publication of *A Dubious Past*, (1999), my reception history and intellectual biography of Jünger. I will let the pieces speak for themselves, only to note that they were written in response to the need I felt to clarify certain aspects of Jünger's work, or to respond to debates that had arisen after 1999, in which I took part. I have revised and updated all five selections. The sixth entry is a revised article I wrote for *Critical Review* in 1995. I updated the argument below to include recent debates about Heidegger, which have intensified, among other reasons, with the publication of his controversial *Black Notebooks*, first published in 2014 (in English 2016). The essay contains a discussion of changing theories of fascism, especially in light of the rise of populist authoritarianism across the globe.

I.

Unfinished Business:
Ernst Jünger's Legacy

Ernst Jünger was born at the height of the Wilhelmine Empire, in 1895 and died on the cusp of the next millennium in the spring of 1998. He became a celebrity overnight in late September 1918, being the youngest soldier ever to receive the Pour le Merite, Germany's highest military honor, at a ceremony attended by the Kaiser himself. He published his war diaries, *In Storms of Steel*, in six different editions during the 1920s, each reflecting the changing literary fashions of the day and becoming more truculently nationalistic as the war veterans organizations' resistance to the Weimar Republic grew.

Jünger wrote for a number of rightwing journals during the mid-twenties and was heavily involved in the debates over what form of German socialism should be embraced once the capitalist republic of Weimar collapsed. That the republic would eventually be superseded by some kind of authoritarian government was simply assumed by the intellectual right, but the hotly debated question remained, how state and society would be re-shaped. Like other representatives of the so-called Conservative Revolution, Jünger believed that Marxism was a false path for Germany because it was simply a negative form of capitalism, based on the primacy of economics in which the proletariat took over and redesigned the capitalist system. The radical conservatives wanted instead an anti-materialist, corporatist state based on the primacy of politics, that is, a fusing of the realms of state and society into a larger, homogeneous, "spiritual" entity in which economic activities were subordinated to the dictates of national self-interest and molded by German traditions.[1] Jünger's version of this type of National Socialism was

1 On the Conservative Revolution in general, see Roger Woods, *The Conservative Revolution in the Weimar Republic* (New York: St. Martin's Press, 1996); on the distinction between politics and economics, see Dick Pels, "Fascism and the Primacy of the Political," Telos, 110 (Winter, 1998), 39-70.

laid out in a murky, rambling, obtuse treatise called *The Worker*, published in late 1932.

Already at this time, Jünger was considered persona non grata with the real existing National Socialists who were about to come to power. In the mid-twenties, Goebbels had courted the talented writer, only to be rebuffed. He disdained the Nazis for being a movement that pandered to the mob and thus seemed to represent a typical product of modern mass democracy. Jünger retreated into the so-called inner emigration. In 1932 it would not have been hard to predict the demise of the first German republic, but the author of *The Worker* nevertheless saw no connection between his "radical utopia" and the reality of the Nazi state. In 1933, he left Berlin for Goslar, moved again to live near his brother in Überlingen in 1936, and moved again, just before the outbreak of the World War II to Kirchhorst, near Hannover. Jünger kept his distance from politics during this period, and apart from one house search by the Gestapo in 1933, he was left in peace by the Nazis. He also didn't entirely disapprove of Hitler's foreign policy in the 1930s. He later admitted to being "fully in accord" with the occupation of the Sudetenland and the Austrian Anschluss, an action "Hitler succeeded in where our grandfathers had failed."[2] Not until after 1938 did Jünger perceive the Hitler regime as "obviously unjust" (*offenbares Unrecht*). In 1936 he published *Afrikanische Spiele*, a novel about his short adventure in the French Foreign Legion in North Africa. Perhaps the novel was not coincidentally about a failed escape. As the mass emigration of intellectual exiles continued, Jünger viewed flight from Germany as a fruitless response.

In Überlingen, in February, he began writing the famous novel *On the Marble Cliffs*. Six miles to the west of Überlingen the Nazis had established a work camp, where political prisoners were constructing a munitions factory. Since the prisoners were paraded out of the city every morning, causing uneasiness among the townsfolk and even outspoken criticism, it is not unjustifiable speculation to

2 "Ein Bruderschaftstrinken mit dem Tod," *Der Spiegel* 33, Aug. 16, 1982, 159.

suppose that Jünger incorporated these images into his book.[3] When published, the story was immediately interpreted as a *roman à clef* about National Socialism, complete with caricatures of Nazi leaders. It took the Nazi censors a few months to catch on to the fact that the book had subversive undertones; Goebbels became furious and eventually had the book taken out of print in 1941.[4] Though unavailable, the work continued to be publicly discussed. In occupied Belgium and France, reviews of the work even passed the military censor as late as the summer of 1942, including a positive critique written by Paul de Man for the Belgian *Le Soir*.[5]

After Hitler launched the World War II, Jünger was conscripted to train a regiment for front duty during the "phony war" of the winter of 1940. In May and June, he commanded his company during the six-week invasion of France. Following the armistice, the occupied zone was administered by the Military Command, whose offices were established at the Parisian Hotel Majestic, on Avenue de Kleber. In June 1940, he took a post here under Colonel Hans Speidel, who had the dubious honor of taking Hitler on a whirlwind tour of Paris the first day of occupation and survived the war to become head of the Federal Republic's *Bundeswehr*. Jünger assisted Speidel in the administrative section that dealt with army security and military justice. He had to sift through the daily correspondence of German soldiers and their mail from home. During the war, Speidel had collected under his aegis a group of scientists and artists, an officer elite whom he hoped to protect from the threatening reach of the Gestapo. Himmler had managed to convince the *Wehrmacht* to allow his security forces a free hand in occupied Paris and the army and the SS lived in constant friction. In

---

3 See Peter Schünemann, "Das Entschwinden der Biographie: Beobachtungen zum Werk Ernst Jüngers," *Text und Kritik* 105/6, (Jan. 1990), 56.

4 According to Jünger, in his interview with Jean-Louis Foncine, *La Nouvelle Revue de Paris* (Monaco: Rocher, 1985), 18. There exist contradictory accounts about the availability of the book during the war in Germany.

5 Paul de Man, "Sur les falaises de marbre," *Le Soir* (March 31, 1942). See also Louis Fournel, "sur les falaises de marbre," *L'union françaises* (July 11, 1942); Henri Thomas, "sur les falaises de marbre," *La Nouvelle Revue française* (October, 1941) 509-511.

1941 Jünger was asked by Speidel to investigate and make a report on the power struggle, in the hope that interference by the Nazis could be limited, particularly in the question of taking French hostages.[6]

There remained, however, constant friction between the Military Command at Majestic and other services there that took orders directly from Berlin. Goebbels had established a propaganda section under Major Heinz Schmidtke and by the spring of 1942, Himmler had installed an SS apparatus of 5,000 men under Karl Oberg. Another important part of the machinery of occupation was the German Embassy, headed by Otto Abetz. His plan, to integrate French businessmen and intellectuals in a net of collaboration, enjoyed intermittent support from the Nazi hierarchy, but Hitler, in the end, wanted to crush France, not enlist its support.[7]

Speidel resided in the Hotel George V, where a group of high-ranking officers, led by General Karl Heinrich von Stülpnagel met regularly to discuss the military situation. They spoke openly of their opposition to Hitler's execution of the war, particularly after the disastrous battles of Stalingrad and Kursk in 1943. The group had contact with Field Marshall Erwin Rommel and General von Falkenhausen, who hoped to negotiate a secret armistice with Eisenhower.[8] Under this plan, Hitler would be arrested, the entire Nazi apparatus dismembered and harsh peace terms accepted. In return, the bombing of Germany would end and the war against the

6 French civilians were arrested as a response to a wave of attacks by the French Resistance on German soldiers. In August, 1941, Hitler ordered the execution of these hostages. Speidel and the other commanders at Majestic opposed the executions on the grounds that deepening the resentment of the French population made the duties for the occupier more difficult. See Hans Speidel, *Aus Unserer Zeit: Erinnerungen* (Frankfurt: Propyläen, 1977), 110.

7 Philippe Burin, *France Under the Germans*, trans. Janet Lloyd (New York: New Press, 1993), 89-97. See also Eberhard Jäckel, *Frankreich in Hitlers Europa; Die deutsche Frankreichpolitik im 2. Weltkrieg*, (Stuttgart: Deutsche Verlags-Anstalt, 1966).

8 See Constantine Fitzgibbon, *To Kill Hitler; The Officers' Plot July 1944* (Stevenage: Bath Press, 1956/1994), 137-143.

Soviet Union continued. Jünger was part of this circle, but remained on its periphery.[9] Rommel's ultimate aim was a United States of Europe as outlined in Jünger's secret treatise, *Der Friede* (*The Peace*).

Rommel's plan never materialized because Hitler cut short his visit to the Atlantic Wall in May, 1944, when the conspirators had planned to strike. In a separate incident, Colonel Claus Schenk Graf von Stauffenberg planted a bomb in Hitler's bunker in East Prussia, but failed to kill the Führer on July 20, 1944. After news that Hitler had survived the attack reached Paris, the Nazis quickly flushed out the military command and made numerous arrests. Jünger escaped with his life because there was no proof that he had been involved. The end of the war found him back in Kirchhorst, as a commander of the so-called *Volkssturm*, the last "people's defense" of the Third Reich. His only military command was apparently to clear away the useless tank barricades as the U.S. army approached.[10]

Jünger's journal shows how indignant he was that Germany was being occupied by Americans, whose culture he considered inferior. "On the street, an endless row of trucks rolls by, driven by Negroes," he observed, with barely concealed contempt, as if Europe were being overrun by African bushmen.[11] He was also concerned about rumors that young girls were being raped by black soldiers.[12] When the Allied questionnaire arrived, Jünger refused to fill it out. By now Lower Saxony was in the British zone. Jünger was put on the blacklist and forbidden to publish. In 1948 he moved to Ravensburg, in the French zone, where the restrictions were laxer.

In 1950 Jünger was invited by Count Stuffenberg's cousin to take up residence in Wilflingen-Langenslingen, a tiny town in the hilly, isolated Schwäbische Alb, just northeast of Stuttgart. He moved into the former house of the forester who took care of the large Stauffenberg property. Coincidentally, Pierre Laval had been quartered in the same house after feuding with Pétain, who headed

9 See Walter Bargatzky, *Hotel Majestic: Ein Deutscher in besetzten Frankreich* (Basel & Vienna: Herder, 1987).

10 Karl O. Paetel, *Ernst Jünger in Selbstzeugnissen* (Hamburg: Rowohlt, 1962), 114.

11 Jünger, *Strahlungen II*, April 11, 1945, 405.

12 Ibid., 410.

the exiled collaborationist government in the Sigmaringen Castle (near Wilfslingen) in the fall of 1944. Laval fled to Franco's Spain after the liberation before the French troops could find him.[13] That Jünger took up domicile in the Chief Ranger's house where the arch-collaborationist Laval had lived, is an example of the many ironic interplays between life and literature occasioned by the war. That Jünger's eldest son was killed on the marble cliffs of Carrara was another.

Jünger remained in the same house in Wilflingen until his death. He was thus near his friend Martin Heidegger, whom he often visited in Todnauberg on the way to see his brother Friedrich Georg at Konstanz on the Bodensee. The now forgotten "literary pope" Friedrich Sieburg also lived in the area, and Jünger visited him often, or the two writers met in Stuttgart. A large number of ex-military figures and followers of the conservative revolution eventually settled in the area around Stuttgart. The conservative Ernst Klett publisher is located in Stuttgart, so that one can speak of this part of southwest Germany as being a center of traditional German conservatism: Baden and Wurttemberg were the areas least susceptible to Nazism in the interwar period or to neo-Nazism after the war.[14]

After the war, Jünger's books found a particularly positive echo among conservatives, theologians and religious writers.[15] Both the novels, *The Marble Cliffs* and *Heliopolis* (1949), provided explanations, in the form of allegories, for the purported civil war that had marked the Nazi period. In both novels, the easily swayed masses were the victims while Nietzschean Supermen heroes who withstood tyranny and reestablished stability. The proto-fascist language of higher/lower, ethical purity, and natural social rank still dominates these texts, while the discourse of order spoke to an omnipresent desire for getting on with rebuilding Germany.

---

13 L. Noguères, *La dernière etape: Sigmaringen* (Paris: Gallimard, 1956); "Franzosen fanden das Schloss der Verräter leer," *Ludwigsburger Kreiszeitung*, 93 (April 22, 1985), 9.

14 Fitzgibbon, 107.

15 See for example Robert Morel, "Ni pour, ni contre, mais avec—ou les quartre bonnes voluntés de Robert Harcourt, Karl Barth, Ernst Jünger, Werner Bergengruen," *Temoignage chrétien* (December 27, 1946).

Since most of Germany's important authors remained in exile, Jünger became one of the few voices of authority in German literature in the postwar period. He was respected as a figure who had survived the brown terror with dignity intact. Jünger's books also found a sympathetic audience among the surviving soldiers who could identify with the battle experiences of an officer-author. One ex-soldier wrote, "When we could steal away a moment from the horror of the bombs flying overhead and read a few pages of *The Marble Cliffs*, suddenly we knew what we were experiencing."[16] For most, it was the experience of reading *The Marble Cliffs* that many found emancipating. Heinrich Böll, who didn't like the mysticism and symbolism of Jünger's "heavy German," nevertheless had to acknowledge the personal courage of the author of *The Marble Cliffs*, a book that "was a sensation, regarded as a book of the opposition."[17] Others were less equivocal. Joachim Besser wrote, "This book (*The Marble Cliffs*) was unforgettable, because we, as soldiers at the front, took it up as the gospel."[18] Literary critic Jürgen Peter Wallmann remembered, "In the Third Reich one read *The Marble Cliffs*—the book was never forbidden, though strongly attacked—as a *roman à clef*, an allegory of Nazi barbarism."[19]

As impressive as these testimonies to the power of the novel appear, it must also be remembered that readers in the Third Reich were starved of political literature not slavishly echoing fascist language. *The Marble Cliffs* might have appeared more oppositional on a political plane than it really was simply because readers were desperate for a narrative that did not conform to the hollow heroism of the party literature. It is in any case unlikely that the book would have gone through so many printings in the first two years of the war had the censors detected an obvious oppositional stance. The

---

16 Egon Mayer, "Zweideutig, ästhetisch und verkannt," *Vorwärts* (March 27, 1975).

17 Heinrich Böll, "Das meiste ist mir fremd geblieben," *FAZ*, 74 (March 29, 1975).

18 Joachim Besser, "Ernst Jüngers Sanduhren," *Welt am Sonntag* (Jan. 21, 1955).

19 Jürgen P. Wallmann, "Der Erzähler Ernst Jünger," *Kölner Rundschau*, March 30, 1975.

book was finally censored in 1942 because the Gestapo learned that the book was widely perceived as non-conformist.

In the 1950s, Jünger published a series of political essays designed to take stock of the new political configuration of still foreign-controlled Germany. He dealt with the Cold War, and then turned to a contemporary philosophical debate on nihilism, reflecting not only contemporary existentialist debates in France, but also with a subplot of what he saw as a specific loss of meaning in American-influenced West German society. He attempted to recapture the high ground of the 1920s and early 1930s, when both supporters and opponents read his books and essays as a register of the contemporary *Zeitgeist*. But the chastened middle classes, their spirits dour, did not now take well to the metaphysical lectures of the Oracle from Wilflingen.

In the early 1950's Jünger had discussed the Cold War with Ernst Niekisch and wrote of his great distrust of both the United States and the USSR, in contrast to his friend who still thought, as a National Bolshevist, that the Germans should throw in their lot with the Russians. Jünger saw the loss of former German territory in Poland as an injustice as great as the Versailles Treaty and predicted that "millions of refugees from the east will build a silent army which will mean disaster."[20] Surprisingly, the tenor of this letter was more conciliatory than his published essays of the period, above all *Der Gordische Knoten*, which was strongly anti-Communist. Jünger there expressed great admiration for the Russian people, if not for their government, and admitted,

> We have paid the price for our actions .... I won't even dwell on the horrible things that happened when the Russians marched in and in the months afterward .... that is their revenge, which is not to be approved, but it is understandable. Somewhere the hatred has got to stop, and it would be good if we began.[21]

In the 1950s, Jünger embraced his status as a public intellectual, speaking for the "we" for perhaps the last time. The lack of an echo

20 Ernst Jünger to Ernst Niekisch, April 3, 1950, *German Literature Archive, Marbach*, Sammlung des Coudres (unsorted box).

21 Ibid.

comparable to the 1920s disappointed him, and perhaps his aristocratic sense of being an individual elevated above the masses, led to a later distaste for public life. For whatever reason, after a series of highly publicized lectures put on by the Bavarian Academy of the Arts from 1953 to 1957—a series which included contributions by Heidegger, Werner Heisenberg, Carl Friedrich von Weizsäcker, Friedrich Georg Jünger and Carl J. Burckhardt[22]—Jünger retreated from the public arena. Not until the controversy over the Goethe Prize in 1982 would he emerge, reluctantly, again as a public persona.

After writing the *Zeitmauer* in 1959, a book that was supposed to bring *The Worker* up to date but was all but ignored, Jünger turned inward. He became preoccupied with his butterfly and beetle collection, later the subject of a book, *Subtile Jagden* (1967). He romped around the world seeking out the last patches of pristine nature and isolated tribal communities, publishing small pieces now and then from his travel diaries. In the 1950s he took LSD trips under medical supervision with Albert Hoffman, the Swiss scientist who discovered the drug, and wrote about his experiences in *Annäherungen, Drogen und Rausch* (1970). These books were read by a relatively small circle. Jünger refused to become involved in the polemics that still surrounded his work, or take part in congresses and other writers' activities.[23] As the reading public discovered the books of Heinrich Böll, Günter Grass, Hans Magnus Enzensberger, Siegfried Lenz, and other young writers of the 1960s, Jünger seemed to have disappeared though his own time wall.

But he hadn't retreated or changed his position toward the public sphere; as always, he cultivated the image of the quintessential outsider, the lone wolf. He tried to recreate, in his provincial

---

22 See Hugo Ott, *Martin Heidegger: A Political Life*, trans. Allan Blunden (New York: Basic Books, 1993), 366.

23 There was one important exception. Jünger celebrated his 75th birthday with Martin Heidegger and Clemens Graf Podewil in Amriswil, a small town near St. Gallen in eastern Switzerland. There Dino and Franz Larese organized a cultural meeting of German poets and philosophers whose politics were reactionary, according to Heinz Saueressig, "Deutscher Geist im schweizerischen Amriswil," *Schwäbische Zeitung*, Aug. 28, 1965.

surroundings, the ambiance of the life of the eighteenth-century man of letters. In the course of collecting stranded objects from Europe's cultural past, he hoped to reconstitute lost worlds. He bought many first editions of precious books by Hamann and Goethe, autographs, and other curiosities, like the carpenter's bill for Friedrich Schiller's casket. In these years of relative obscurity, Jünger's favored literary genre was his journal. Ironically, the diary is supposed to be the most intimate of all literary forms. But in Jünger's later journals, *Siebzig Verweht* (1980-1998) and *Zwei Mal Halley* (1987), the author conducted interior monologues devoid of any personal revelations or emotional expression. His way of describing the world with ultimate detachment might be called a phenomenology without a subject. At a minimum, the diary genre allowed Jünger to place armor around his feelings, and keep himself protected from the activities of the larger world. This predisposition can be traced back to the battles of the World War I. During the long pauses between fighting, while other soldiers played cards in the trenches, Jünger jotted down copious notes which his father urged him to organize and publish after the war. Later, the diary form allowed a retreat from the controversies and literary publicity that he so despised. The diary was also congenial to the writing of aphorisms, penetrating, but sharply focused observations that reflected in style and form Jünger's entomological training. He perceived the modern world as deeply fragmented, and the diary form the most accurate mirror of that condition. Finally, the diary granted Jünger the most freedom of individual expression and stylistic idiosyncrasy, a good fit with his self-image as an aristocratic anarchist.

Well into old age, Jünger projected the appearance of, if not a dandy, at least a fashionable gentleman, as well as an other-worldly aesthete. His house in rural Swabia was 1950s Biedermeier, but it emanated the charm of a collector of esoterica and a man of fine tastes. He made France his spiritual home, cultivated friendships with French authors, and was rewarded with an appreciative reading audience and large following. In 1962, Salvador Dali, a Spaniard who nevertheless figured centrally in the French art world, invited Jünger to participate in the auratic charm of publishing in a single copy million-dollar book. Included were contributions from several

French artists and many of Jünger's friends, including Jean Cocteau, Jean Rostand, Bernard Buffet, and Leonor Fini. Jünger contributed a piece from his book *Fassungen*, calligraphing it in large letters on a piece of sheepskin. According to one critic, Jünger was a good choice, because he cut an appropriate figure in the group, in which "serious research came together with magical clowning, Catholic-and-Rosicrucian inspired mysticism, surrealism, and private mythologizing."[24]

By the 1970s, Jünger's aristocratic pose and haughty rejection of mass culture itself became a kind of market commodity. Starting with the stylized EJ signature branded into the covers of his books, Jünger's works took on the ambiance of a mass-produced luxury item, like a fine German car or a French perfume. By now it had become clear that Jünger followed fashions as much as any other writer. After all, the shrill tones of antibourgeois defiance in Weimar were followed by the religious introspection of *Strahlungen* in the 1940s, the science fiction of *Heliopolis* in 1949, and the hallucinogenic experiments described in *Annäherungen* in 1970.

Jünger's interest in drugs made his books somewhat of a secret tip among the psychedelic generation of the 1970s. But the beatniks and hippies didn't understand that the author was hardly advocating the drop-out-and-tune-in mood of the late 60s. In the 1920s, Jünger had already experimented with the classic drugs of that era—ether, hashish, opium, and cocaine.[25] In his opinion, the newfangled drug craze could be explained by the cultic search of youth for metaphysical crutches after the Enlightenment had destroyed religion, faith in the fatherland and "higher moral notions." If blaming drugs on the Enlightenment seemed far-fetched, even more questionable was the double standard by which Jünger accorded himself privileged access to the powers of drugs, the secrets to which his literary imagination held the key. "I only take drugs

---

24 Werner Helwig, "Eher zart als stählern: Besuch bei dem 75 jährigen Ernst Jünger," *Rheinischer Merkur*, April 3, 1975.

25 Rudolf Baucken, "Mit Ernst Jünger durch die Zeitmauer," *Welt am Sonntag*, Dec. 31, 1978. On the fashionable use of drugs in the 1920s, see Norman Ohler & Shaun Whiteside, *Blitzed: Drugs in the Third Reich* (London: Penguin, 2017), Chs. 1 & 2.

under medical supervision," he said, "as a literary experiment .... it all comes from my curiosity for transcendental spaces."[26]

After 1982 Jünger became a fixture on the right, then gradually evolved into a national icon. The mathematical accomplishment of very old age alone combined with unceasing productivity guaranteed him growing celebrity. As a writer who could still remember the Kaiserreich, his somewhat bizarre interests and eccentric style made him interesting as a cultural oddity. His ecological bent even attracted a reading public among the young, especially in New Age and esoteric circles. That young conservatives pillaged his writings for ideas went without saying.

In the wake of the Wende that, in 1982, ended the first Social-Democratic regime experiment in Germany, politicians discovered a Goethe-substitute living in the Swabian hills. But despite the lavish attention paid to Jünger by Franz Joseph Strauss, Helmut Kohl, and other members of the conservative establishment, he remained characteristically underwhelmed by the attempt to turn him into an Olympian symbol of democratic Germany. He once said to an interviewer, "My wife and I are loyal citizens of the Federal Republic, but not particularly enthusiastic—our reality is the German Empire."[27]

When asked about democracy, he registered his skepticism with the following bizarre examples:

> Question: Do we live in a pseudo-democracy?
> Jünger: The things which are allowed today are, compared to the baroque period, much reduced.
> Question: What for example?
> Jünger: For example, one cannot say today, "I am a fascist." Say that and you are considered to be the lowest of the low. Today you can't just drive on the left side of the road. That is a deep affront to the individual. Even our grandfathers were freer than us[28]

One wonders when he speaks of the freedom of the grandfathers, if he meant the majority of them who were poor peasants scraping by

26 Ben Witter, "Mit Ernst Jünger im Schlosspark," *Die Zeit* 8 (Feb. 23), 1968.

27 "Ein Brudershaftstrinken mit dem Tod," *Der Spiegel*, 33 (Aug. 16, 1982), 163.

28 Ibid., 160.

to make ends meet. But Jünger's language was always polemical and nostalgic at once. He refused to bend to the prevailing fashions or say what was politically correct. He naturally understood that people would be infuriated when arguing that one should be allowed to say, "I am a fascist." The provocations were meant to sting liberal sensibility and elicit responses that he ignored.

Jünger's hundredth birthday on March 29, 1995, was a European event followed closely by the media, particularly in France, Germany, and Italy. Whatever one thought of Jünger's qualities as a writer, even his detractors had to admit that his long life gave the centenarian a unique vantage point as a chronicler of the century. Mitterand took the high ground in an address, in which he situated Jünger in a line of thinkers from Goethe to Hölderlin and Nietzsche, as well as Stendhal, claiming that "Jünger's thought conjugates the riches of the Enlightenment with those of Romanticism, the rigor of the one with the generosity of the other.[29]

As Jünger pointed out in his response before assembled notables at a celebration in Saulgau, the long history of sharply differing opinions about his person and work had become part of his legacy as a writer; his friends and opponents "belonged," as he put it, "to my karma—without them no profile."[30] The Jünger controversy had lasted so long, one might argue, because the qualities his admirers highlighted—the premier of Baden-Württemberg, Erwin Teufel, spoke of Jünger as a thinker and seer who "seeks from the depth of time the timeless"[31]—were exactly the characteristics that critics found pseudo-profound and conceptually hollow.

Two writers from the same generation (of 1968), in commenting on a century of Jünger, illustrated well the last point. Nicolaus Sombart praised Jünger's outsider status, his "sovereign disregard for the mainstream," [32] while Heinz Ludwig Arnold lamented

---

29 Francois Mitterand, "Geburtstagsrede für for Ernst Jünger; Hier ist ein freier Mensch," *Frankfurter Allgemeine Zeitung*, March 29, 1995.

30 Alfred Behr, "Dank an meine Freunde und Gegner," *FAZ* (March 30, 1995).

31 Ibid.

32 Nicolaus Sombart, "Der Dandy im Forsthaus," *Der Tagesspiegel*, (March 29, 1995).

Jünger's stubbornness, his refusal to ever admit writing an offensive sentence or producing a misguided word.[33] What is sovereignty for one is pigheadedness for the other.

Elke Schmitter observed that the debates over Jünger tended to be carried out by men. Women appeared quite infrequently in his writings and, when they did, usually as objects of desire for men without women. Jünger's martial style and his war record seemed to provoke male intellectuals to take a stand on the author, either aggressively for or against, while women tended to remain indifferent. For every young man, Schmitter wrote sarcastically, Jünger offered a little something.

> For the peace-lover there is the convert with his little Königsberger world peace; for the confused young man in the third row there is the war author who mixes up freedom and service; and for the nationalist high school kid, there is the uncritical collected works, which function as a schoolbag edition of the century.[34]

Schmitter's emphasis on the male attraction to Jünger was born out by the flood of homages and tributes to his work published during 1995. Jünger's publisher, Michael Klett, put out a special birthday catalogue with essays by Frank Schirrmacher, Heiner Mueller, Bruce Chatwin, and Serge D. Mangin, the latter an artist shown at work on a bust of the writer which has an uncanny resemblance to Julius Caesar.[35] *Die Zeit* carried a critical essay by Christian Graf von Krockow who warned, with predictable liberal anxiety, about the continuing fascistic appeal of Jünger's war writings.[36] In *Der Stern*, Jünger was also portrayed as a "warrior and a dreamer," with photographs of him as a soldier in the foreign legion, as a German soldier on the roof of Hotel Raphael in occupied Paris, and as an the eighty-year-old showing off his bullet-ridden helmet from the World

33 Jürgen Berger, "Ideal Deutsch—Ein Gespräch mit Heinz Ludwig Arnold," *tageszeitung* (March 29, 1995).

34 Elke Schwitter, "Deutschland Glückwunsch," *Die Zeit*, 13 (March 24, 1995), 65-66.

35 Michael Klett, Hundert Jahre und: Jünger (Stuttgart: Klett, 1995).

36 Chistian Graf von Krockow, "Grübler, Deuter, Wegbereiter," *Die Zeit* 12 (March 17, 1995), 20-26.

War I.[37] In *Der Spiegel*, Rudolf Augstein lauded Jünger's sinewy prose—"John Wayne, Clausewitz, and Rimbaud all in one person."[38] The satirical journal *Titanic* spoofed Jünger's machismo, showing an inebriated Mitterand, Kohl, and Herzog at a rowdy birthday party at Wilflingen.[39]

Jünger's friends in France, all male, concerned themselves with somber masculine themes. Frederic de Towarnicki wrote about "the patriarch of Wilflingen," Julien Hervier on the "active militarism" of Jünger's early work, Jean-Michel Palmier on Jünger's obsession with beetles and other insects, Dominique Saatdjan on Heidegger and *The Worker*, and Lou Bruder on Jünger's relation to Luther, Goethe, Hölderlin, and Nietzsche.[40]

The year 1995 also saw a ballet, based on Jünger's war diaries. see a premier in the *Berliner Volksbuehne*, once a mecca of socialist-realist drama. The East German director Johann Kresnik conceived of the twenty-six scenes as a pacifist critique of war. The dancers were supposed to communicate the brutality of soldiers, raping innocent girls and destroying villages. But Kresnick's fascination with the pure aesthetics of horror revealed a much more ambivalent relationship to Jünger and the violent allure of his writings.[41] Earlier in the year, Kresnick's superior, Frank Castorf, revealed in an interview that in the dying days of the East German regime, he had yearned for new "storms of steel," but had been disappointed with the failure of a more thorough revolution after communism collapsed.[42] In light of that remark, Kresnick's ballet seemed to echo the resentment of artists in East Germany to the new conditions of capitalist culture after 1989. Jünger became an interesting object

37 Siegfried Schober, "Krieger und Träumer," *Stern* 12 (March 25, 1995), 40-54.

38 Rudolf Augstein, "Der Ton der Bratsche," *Der Spiegel* 12 (March 20, 1995), 216.

39 "Drogengott Ernst Jünger feiert 100 Jahre Ecstasy," *Titanic* 186 (April 1995).

40 "Ernst Jünger: Cent ans d'Histoire," *magazine littéraire* 326 (November, 1994), 16-50.

41 See Susanne Heyden, "Bilderwucht aus Biedersinn und Brutalitaet," *Rheinische Post* (May 18, 1995).

42 *Der Spiegel*, 12 (March 20, 1995), 214.

of cultural appropriation, one could speculate, precisely because he was treated with such suspicion in the West.[43]

To broaden this thesis, one might argue that Jünger's books could be used in a provocative way in the 1990s wherever resistance was sought to what were seen as establishment values in German society. In East Germany that may have meant the widespread feeling of resentment against the arrogant and sometimes patronizing manner of West Germany's attempt to rebuild a ruined economy. In the West, these resentments could take the form of a youth culture reacting against boredom and malaise in what is perceived as a materialistic and empty consumer culture. In 1994, The young conservative newspaper *Junge Freiheit*, for example, interviewed a twenty-one year old techno-rave fan who liked the music because of its militance—war is positive, he claims, because it gets rid of "decadence and the yearning for security," and "it can't go on like this forever," he muses, because "war is an inner experience, as Jünger once said..."[44] A similar theme was echoed in a short television film made by the twenty-six year old director Martin Weinhart the same year. In the film a skinhead was presented reading passages from *Storms of Steel* and later seen courting death as he takes a thrill ride on top of a Berlin underground subway train.[45]

Even Jünger's older conservative admirers wanted a naughty hero, a *poèt maudit*, or at least a Nietzschean out-of-season rebel. Two substantial collections of essays in honor of Jünger's hundredth birthday- contributed by almost entirely male authors—valorized Jünger both as representative of his age and as offering an alternative vision to a culture of empty and bloodless passions.

---

43 This author directly encountered this phenomenon while in Berlin on September 4, 1994, when I give the keynote address to a colloquium on Jünger at the Berlin Forum, the formerly East German cultural center and Brecht archive. After my talk, which was fairly critical of Jünger's politics, several East Germans in the audience pointed out that their interest in Jünger was piqued because he is so roundly criticized in the west—this fact alone made them more receptive and sympathetic to the author.

44 Roland Bubik, "Endlich mal den Kick 'ham," *Junge Freiheit* 7 (Feb. 11, 1994) 20.

45 Martin Weinhart, "Das Abenteuerliche Herz: Eine Annäherung an Ernst Jünger, *Bayerischer Rundfunk*, June 13-14, 1994.

Jünger's work reflects the "character of the epoch"[46] and possess a "key to the century,"[47] but also holds out an alternative to the eclectic and disoriented postmodern period, a higher form of modernity, or "Übermoderne," in Richard Herzinger's phrase.[48] Most striking about the centennial was the attempt to domesticate Jünger's political marginality that fitted his life into a usable past. An outcast and rebel in life, like a romantic hero of collective memory, Jünger had been transformed into a solitary warrior for German self-consciousness.

In the early hours of February 17, 1998, Ernst Jünger died peacefully in his sleep in the regional hospital at Riedlingen, near Wilflingen. He had been healthy and active down to the last few days. He was buried the following Saturday afternoon next to his first wife and two sons in the local graveyard.[49] Over a thousand guests listened to the funeral service on loudspeakers from the overflowing baroque St. Johannes-Nepomuk church. The casket was carried to the final resting place by civic guards who had marched in from all over the southwest, dressed in bright uniforms with tassels, flags, swords, cockades and hats from the Napoleonic era. A bright early spring sun shone. A few very elderly gentlemen tagged along, iron crosses visible underneath their dark suits. Tourists with backpacks and binoculars, serious-looking young men in black suits, two- and three-star generals, camera teams, policemen, townspeople and dignitaries followed the provincial, strictly orchestrated final procession. In front of the casket, the words "Knights of the Order Pour Le Merit" hung from a blue and gold tasseled banner. The deceased had ordered the military decorations himself years ago when the second-to-last last knight of the order had died.

46 Hans-Harald Müller & Harro Segeberg, *Ernst Jünger im 20. Jahrhundert* (Munich: Fink, 1995), 10.

47 Gunter Figal & Heimo Schwilk, *Magie der Heiterkeit* (Stuttgart: Klett-Cotta, 1995), 7.

48 See Richard Herzinger, "Werden wir alle Jünger?" *Kursbuch* 122 (December 1995), 93-117.

49 The following information taken from Frank Schirrmacher, "Besuche in der Dämmerung," *FAZ*, Feb, 23, 1998; Johnannes Wilms, "Von Käfern, Unifomern und Menschen," *Süddeutsche Zeitung*, Feb. 23, 1998; "Ernst Jünger beigesetzt: *Die Welt*, Feb. 23, 1998.

Official Germany was not in attendance. Helmut Kohl was on a government visit in Poland and sent Anton Pfeiffer, a state minister, to represent the republic. François Mitterand was already in Valhalla. Kohl published a memorial in the *Weltwoche* recalling the meeting with Mitterrand and Jünger at Douaumont in 1984. In a letter of condolence to Liselotte Jünger, he called her late husband "one of the greatest author personalities of the twentieth century."[50] The Minister of Baden-Wurttemberg, Erwin Teufel, gave the funeral oration. The only writer in attendance was the dramatist Rolf Hochhuth, who spoke at the funeral service, as did Michael Klett, his publisher. Jünger's granddaughter Irina gave a solo performance of the "Ave Maria" from Charles Gounod.

Feuilliton editors, authors and journalists across the country were sent quickly to their desks to write one last meditation. Everyone had carefully prepared a piece for the hundredth birthday; now at 102, the commentaries were an afterthought. Best not to speak evil of the dead. The characterizations of Jünger's life were recounted one more time, recited with the familiarity of grandfather's well-worn tales: war hero, Weimar dandy, fiery nationalist, non-Nazi, Latin esthete, hermit, recluse, LSD tripper, world traveler, insect collector, controversial Goethe Prize winner, rightwing symbol, Olympian sage, witness of the century.

The only original component of the obituaries was the canvassing of cultural figures for their thoughts on the departed writer. My unscientific sample counted over one hundred short responses, the majority expressing admiration and respect for Jünger, while only a few reflected hostility or contempt. Green politician Jutta Ditfurth alone dragged out the same selective, inflammatory quotes that the Frankfurt leftists had used in 1982 to fight Jünger's nomination for the Goethe Prize.[51] The improbable accomplishment of dying at such a ripe age with all faculties intact seemed to impress even the traditional anti-Jüngerites. The once president of the East German Writer's Union Hermann Kant was a good example. Nothing good comes to his mind when he thinks of Jünger, he wrote, and what should he add to the insincerities of the day? But in his long life,

---

50 "Ernst Jünger starb im Alter von 102 Jahren," *Die Welt*, Feb. 18, 1998.
51 Jutta Ditfurth, "Der veredelte Faschist," *Jungle World* 9, Feb. 26, 1998.

Jünger was at least consistent.[52] Klaus Theweleit, who pilloried Jünger as a misogynist of the first order in his famous book *Male Fantasies*, conceded that the very old Jünger shone as an artist. His death was unexpected, "I thought he would last until 107!"[53]

Praise was effluent.[54] Hans Georg Gadamer, himself having reached Biblical age, lauded Jünger as a thinker whose work influenced every turn of intellectual history in the twentieth century. Michel Tournier compared him to Gide, Hugo, Rousseau and Goethe. Felipe González characterized Jünger's diaries as the most important reflections on the tragedies of the century. Oscar Lafontaine said that Germany had lost one of the most important writers of the twentieth century. Ernst Nolte pronounced him simply the "most representative figure of the German twentieth century." Wolf Lepenies called him the last diagnostician of the modern. Frank Schirrmacher compared Jünger's work to an illuminated aquarium of the twentieth century. Even eminent historian Hans Mommsen, who noted that Jünger's writings from the 1920s helped prepare the ground for the NSDAP to become a mass movement, argued that his writings also reflected the existential menace of fascist dictatorships and were thus an "irreplaceable source of contemporary self-understanding." Fritz Stern echoed that historical judgment, writing that Jünger had lived through, described, re-interpreted and perhaps unwittingly prepared people for all the temptations of German life in the century while keeping his distance.

What will remain of Jünger's work? Will he find a permanent place in the pantheon of German classics? Will he be considered a "national poet?" Will Wilflingen become an "Upper Swabian Weimar?" The answers to these questions were mixed and pointed to the problem that no single work by Jünger had the unambiguous

---

52 "Das Jahrhundert in einem Leben," *Berliner Zeitung* 41, Feb. 18, 1998.

53 "Stimmen zum Tode von Ernst Jünger," *Süddeutsche Zeitung*, 40, Feb. 18, 1998.

54 The comments by Hans Georg Gadamer, Felipe González, Frank Schirrmacher and Fritz Stern are in the *FAZ*, Feb. 18, 1998, 41, and Hans Mommsen and Ernst Nolte are in the *Berliner Zeitung*, Feb. 18, 1998, 12. Wolf Lepenies' comments are in the *NZZ*, Feb. 18, 1998, 47; See also Lepenies, "Le siècle de Jünger, *Le Monde*, Feb. 20, 1998. Michel Tournier and Oscar Lafontaine in *Le Figaro*, Feb. 18, 1998, 13.

feel of a classic work. Stefan Breuer ventured the prophesy that not many of his novels or stories will be read, and the political writings only by historians of ideas, but the diaries will remain the best source for the history of everyday life in the Federal Republic.[55] Michael Krüger argued, in this vein, that the novels will probably not be read in the next century, but the diaries and essays will count as "central histories of our times," in particular in regard to the unsolved problem of the relationship between revolution and reaction.[56] Heinz Ludwig Arnold noted that Jünger's books and diaries seem to revolve around the same themes, an "eclectic and metaphysical philosophy without a system," a constant return to the self-engagement of the author with himself.[57] An editorial in the *Frankfurter Rundschau* captured this problem best: Jünger lived through so many different phases of German history, but always inside himself; he "hibernated."[58] Perhaps all these reactions explain why when the man who had survived so much adversity in the twentieth century finally died, there was much belated, sometimes grudging, sometimes enthusiastic respect expressed for the solitary warrior, but not much mourning. In the end, the man who could never shake the reputation of being an extreme nationalist, seemed to live for himself, not the nation.

---

55 Stefan Breuer, "Der Krieg ist unser Vater," *Berliner Zeitung*, Feb. 18, 1998, 3.

56 Michael Krüger, Diagnostiker der Leere, *Neue Zürcher Zeitung*, Feb. 18, 1998.

57 Heinz Ludwig Arnold, "Krieger und Künder," *Die Woche*, Feb. 20, 1998, 3.

58 Wolfgang Schütte, "Jahrhundert Gestalt," *Frankfurter Rundschau* (Feb. 18, 1998), 3.

II.
Intimité:
Ernst Jünger's French Connections

The forty-six-year-old German writer Ernst Jünger, highly decorated World War I hero, leader of the revolutionary nationalist youth in Weimar, chastened esthete and apparently a Christian convert in the 1930s, was a member of the occupation army in Paris from February, 1941 until July, 1944. He was peripherally involved in the Rommel conspiracy against Hitler, but not a member of the inner core of the activists.[1] He was opposed to assassinations and thought that the war would have to run its course until the bloody end, when a new order would emerge. He returned to Germany after the Stauffenberg plot against Hitler failed (July 20, 1944) and the army command in Paris had been flushed out, its highest officers forced to commit suicide or return to Berlin to face the hanging judge, Roland Freisler. Jünger was put on trial before the People's Court but his superiors refused to name him as a co-conspirator and the case was dismissed for lack of evidence. It was a very close call.

---

1 Field Marshal Erwin Rommel, the "desert fox," was one of Hitler's best generals. He just about defeated the British in Northern Africa in 1942-43. But he turned against Hitler as the war on the Eastern Front turned into a rout for the Germans. He was counting on Hitler to make an inspection of the Atlantic Wall sometime in May, when the landing of the Americans was expected in the Normandy. Inexplicably, Hitler continued to direct the war from Berchtesgaden. After the invasion of Normandy, Hitler made an unexpected visit to the Western Front and was planning to come to La Roche-Guyon on June 19. Rommel had a golden opportunity to strike. As so often in the history of assassination attempts against Hitler, uncanny fate intervened. The bombing of England with the V-1 had begun from French territory on June 15. On June 18, one of the rockets strayed off course and came down near Margival, just about hitting the bunker where Hitler was meeting with Field Marshall Rundstedt. Depressed and disappointed with the performance of his Wunderwaffe, he returned immediately to Berchtesgaden. After that, the conspiracy against Hitler shifted to the Stauffenberg plan to kill Hitler at his bunker in East Prussia.

Jünger was a highly accomplished diarist and chronicled the entire war period, first in a book, *Gardens and Paths*, published in France in 1942, and then in a set of secret notebooks, not published until 1949, entitled *Radiations*, or *Emanations* (*Strahlungen*). The German army command in Paris was led by aristocratic Prussian officers who disliked the interference of the party into their business and who gradually turned against Hitler in 1942 as the Russian campaign floundered. Jünger's diaries reflected their position and mentality. But he was perhaps even more sensitive than most to the to the suffering of the Parisians under occupation, and eloquently expressed his contempt for the ideological warriors of the SS, whom he called lemurs and sadistic monsters. On February 8, 1942, he received a report of the mass shootings and exterminations taking place on the Eastern Front and wrote, there "is no question that there are individuals who are responsible for the murder of millions.[2] On June 7, 1942, he encountered for the first time the yellow star and noted being "embarrassed to be in uniform."[3] On September 10, 1942 he fears that he will soon despise all of mankind, because the masses have abandoned free will.[4] These sentiments reflected elitist haughtiness, but were uncommon opinions for the majority of the German officer class, and were, needless to say, hardly the sentiments of the average German soldier, let alone of the hated "boche" whom the French regarded as a primitive barbarian in uniform.

The diaries endeared Jünger to the French reading public in the postwar years, and until his death in 1998, he was considered *le plus grand écrivain allemand*, despite the fact that Jünger's own countrymen hardly shared that enthusiasm. Why Jünger had such a different reception in his home country, why there was indeed a gulf of understanding, a mutual puzzlement over the treatment of this enigmatic writer, is a subject of continuing speculation among observers of the French-German cultural exchange during the war and its aftermath. My contribution here attempts to clarify the historical background of Jünger's activities in Paris and to offer some

2 *Jünger, Sämmtliche Werke*, 1979, hereafter *SW*, 2, 303.
3 *SW*, 2, 336.
4 *SW*, 2, 375.

insights into the often contradictory and harshly polemical stands taken by critics on the subject of Ernst Jünger's work and person. In doing so, I wish to address the larger issues of the memory of the holocaust in France and Germany and the persistent fascination in France with ideas that derive from the epoch of European fascism.

Let us begin by examining Jünger's role as an occupier comfortably lodged in Paris at the Hotel Majestic on Avenue de Kleber during the war years. He enjoyed the protection and patronage of two high-ranking cultural connoisseurs, Karl Heinrich von Stülpnagel, the commander of the occupying forces in France, and his chief of staff, Hans Speidel, (later to become chief general of the Bundeswehr). Jünger's had a plum job because it didn't take up much of his time, was ethically unoffensive and it had to do with literature, or at least with writing: he had to sift through the daily correspondence of German soldiers and their mail from home. He even saved some soldiers from the grip of the SS by discreetly destroying letters that would have been viewed as seditious.

In Jünger's spare time, which was apparently considerable, he was a flaneur, casing the sidewalks of Paris, browsing through the museums, studying the urban architecture, and strolling through the galleries, antique shops, and bookstores. Every new book or art purchase was meticulously registered. The aura attached to objects that weathered the ravages of time fascinated him. Besides collecting art and books, Jünger also nurtured contacts with famous writers and artists. In the salon of Marie-Louise Bousquet, a writer for Harper's Bazaar, he came into contact with "l'Hitlerisme Francais", with Drieu la Rochelle, Marcel Jouhandeau, Paul Léautaud, and Henri de Montherlant.[5] Right from the beginning Jünger straddled both sides of the occupation, threading ties to resistors and collaborators. He knew Alfred Fabre-Luce, a supporter of the Pax Germanica, and contributed several pieces, mostly from his World War I diaries, to Fabre-Luce's well-known collaborationist anthology.[6]

5 See Philippe Simonnot, *Hitlerisme Français* (Paris: Perrin, 2015). See also Phillipe Burin, *France Under the Germans; Collaboration & Compromise*, trans. Janet Lloyd (New York: New Press, 1996).

6 See the collaborationist journal of Alfred Fabre Luce, *Journal de la France* (March 1939-July 1940), 175 ff.

But he was also a favored guest of the "Thursday salon" where the avant-garde met, particularly one run by socialite and patron of the arts Florence Gould (alias Lady Orpington), the wife of Frank Jay Gould, a wealthy American businessman.[7] Jünger rubbed shoulders with Jean Cocteau, Georges Braque, Pablo Picasso, Sacha Guitry, Julien Gracq, Paul Léautaud, and other luminaries, including Jean Paulhan, one of the founders of the resistance newspaper _Lettres Françaises_.[8] Jünger was also happy to be seen at the salon of Lucienne Didier, a Belgian sculptor. Her husband, Edouard Didier, in contact with the German ambassador Otto Abetz since 1933, had founded an association called "Jeune Europe" as a forum for Franco-German intellectual exchange. He introduced Jünger to Hendrik de Man, the famous Belgian Neo-Socialist and collaborator.[9] The gathering at the Didier salon of progressive Catholics, socialists, as well as fascist sympathizers, organized by Otto Abetz and Max Liebe, contributed to what Thomas Fries calls the "unholy alliance of the first period of the occupation."[10]

The warm reception of Jünger in leading French literary and artistic circles contrasted sharply with the experience of most German intellectuals in France, in particular when one considers the enormous difficulties faced by the German exile community in prewar France. The French academy closed its doors to German professors and most exiles experienced a social cordon sanitaire. As Arthur Koestler wrote, "the great mass of refugees in France lived cut off from French contacts and led a kind of ghetto existence."[11]

A particularly unsettling aspect of Jünger's name-dropping and romps through the art and book world of Paris's cultural elite is the dissonance between his cultural exploits and the terrorization

---

7 See Jünger, SW, 14, 383 ff. Jünger used the pseudonym "Lady Orphington" to hide an affair with her from his suspicious wife.

8 Jünger, SW, 14, 127.

9 Henri Plard, "Ex ordine shandytorum," in Armin Mohler, ed., _Freundschaftliche Begegnungen_ (Frankfurt: Klostermann, 1955).

10 Thomas Fries, "Paul de Man's 1940-1942 Articles in Context," In Werner Hamacher et al., *Responses: On Paul de Man's Wartime Journalism* (Lincoln: University of Nebraska Press, 1987). 198.

11 Frederic V. Grunfeld, *Prophets Without_Honor* (New York: Kodansha, 1955). 21.

and starvation of Parisians under Nazi occupation. Beginning in the summer of 1942, the city was being plundered and Jews deported. Although Jünger expressed his displeasure at the treatment of the Parisians by the SS, he seemed to be unaware that the German Army was also an object of hatred for most of the occupied population. On August 18, 1942, he entered a stationary store and was greeted by the cold, spiteful stare of a young salesgirl behind the counter. He notes with surprise that the hatred in the girl's face might spread like a virus or a spark "that would take a lot of strength to put out inside oneself."[12]

It is true that Jünger allotted considerable space to ruminations about his distaste for Hitler and the Nazis. But he was ambivalent about his position vis-a-vis the other *frondeurs*. The manner in which he characterized the members of the George V circle, "spiritual knights who meet in the belly of the Leviathan,"[13] points to an act of distancing, of displacement, into an almost medieval fantasy, even though his precarious situation called for utmost discretion and cunning. He kept his journal notes hidden in a locked safe in his room, but with Gestapo agents and informers crawling all over the Hotel Majestic, the project was not without considerable risks. Hitler was always characterized in the diaries as "Kniébolo," (a word-play on "diabolo,"), for whom he had nothing but sneering contempt. And the Führer appeared menacingly in his dreams.[14]

On the Eastern Front, Jünger talked to officers who related stories of the brutal activities of the notorious Special Action Units,

---

12 Jünger, SW, 2, 367.

13 Jünger, *SW*, 272. Hotel George V was a hub of intellectual and cultural life in occupied Paris, where dinners and salons were attended by German officers and French collaborators. After the city's liberation in 1944, the hotel served as the headquarters for Allied forces, including Eisenhower. From 1940 to 1944, the hotel hosted a "round-table" of German officers and French intellectuals, including Jünger, Carl Schmitt and French collaborators Jean Cocteau, Paul Morand and Henry Millon de Montherlant, among many others. George V was not used as a command center like the Hotel Meurice, where the German military governor of Paris surrendered.

14 Jünger, SW, 3. 41-42.

the *Einsatztruppen*. Like many others, he heard of atrocities committed in the concentration camps.[15] Though shaken by these events, his detachment is evident as well. Historical events had for him the force of nature; they sweep human beings along as if by the irresistible power of a hurricane or the destructive fury of an earthquake. As much as the barbarism of the Nazis was repellent, he could not help but interpret the persecution of the Jews and others as part of a fated, cosmological scheme. Particularly in the last books of the war diaries, where Jünger contemplated the issue of German guilt, what he called his "stereoscopic" vision searched for a metaphysical explanation behind the perplexing evidence of the senses. In the following example, Jünger invokes a Biblical image, rendering literal the meaning of "sacrificial" in the term Holocaust: "Was our persecution the last birth pang before the appearance of the Second Messiah, the Paraclete, with whom the epoch of the spirit shall begin? It is impossible that such a sacrifice won't bear fruit."[16]

Jünger's question is troublesome because it provided a metaphysical justification for the suffering of the Holocaust, a kind of theodicy that survivors would vigorously disavow.[17] Jünger's interpretation of death as the sole authentic experience of life, indeed as having a higher reality than life, is another recurring topic in the war diaries. The Nazi mass murders interested him not so much from the point of view of the victims, but rather the abstract historical significance of the method applied in committing the crime.[18] In

---

15 The main source for his knowledge of the concentration camps and the atrocities in the east are his World War Two diaries, see Elliot Neaman, Introduction to *A German Officer in Paris; The War Journals 1941-1945* (New York: Columbia University Press, 2019), ix-xxvi. See also Walter Bargatsky, *Hotel Majestic; Ein Deutscher im besetzten Frankreich* (Basel & a Vienna: Herder, 1987). 101.

16 Jünger, SW, 2, 415.

17 Levi, Primo, *The Drowned and the Saved* (New York: Simon & Schuster, 1988). 167-197.

18 There are no hints of anti-Semitism in any of Jünger's published writings after the World War II. But after a thirty-year friendship, Jünger's Belgian translator Henri Plard broke off their relationship because Jünger allegedly defended Pierre Laval's anti-Semitism (Henri Plard, interview by author, March 7, 1990).

a commentary on the concentration camps, he noted that death had become standardized, mechanized and sanitized, like everything in the technical world.[19] He thereby linked the administration of death to the general impoverishment of the "modern world." In the final pages of the war diaries, Jünger varied this theme with a not-too-subtle attack on the thesis of collective guilt. The engineers of the atom bomb make Tamerlane and his atrocities look absolutely royal, since death becomes cheaper and responsibility untraceable, when millions are killed. The advancement of technology brings with it a concomitant impoverishment of the world, because rational calculation takes precedence over the higher faculties of the imagination. Finally, the collective guilt assertion is just a mantle the allies use to hide their real interests:

> The thesis of collective guilt has two strands which run together. For the defeated it means, I have to stand for my brother and his guilt. It gives the victor an excuse for undifferentiated plundering. If the bow is pulled too tightly, the dangerous question arises whether the brother was really so unjust.[20]

After Germany's defeat, Jünger was prohibited from publishing his books (except in the French occupation zone) and remained on the blacklist in the American and British sectors until 1949 because he refused to fill out the infamous Questionnaire distributed by the allied occupation forces, used to classify the guilt of ordinary German citizens in the much maligned process of "denazification" (the "big fish get away, the smaller ones get caught.") In the postwar years, Jünger retreated from the political battles of his youth and was content to write books about obscure topics for rather esoteric audiences. He published science fiction, a book about his entomological pursuits, and another about his drug experiences with LSD, mescaline and other hallucinogenic substances. His grand project remained his diaries, chronicling world travels and daily reflections on books, insects, nature and the cosmos. He also became a kind of good will ambassador for the Federal Republic to the France, a

19 Jünger, *SW*, 2, 448.
20 Jünger, *SW*, 2, 510.

surprising activity considering his distrust of the state and his suspicion of democracy. Jünger played the role with increasing satisfaction as his fame in France grew. French president François Mitterand invited him to the Elysée on practically every visit to Paris. As a war hero and last surviving bearer of the pour le mérite (Germany's highest medal of valor), he was constantly invited to openings of museum exhibitions, and military commemorations of World War I. Already in 1975, German President Carstens invited Jünger to Bonn as a cultural ambassador of French culture to help him prepare for a state visit.

In June, 1979 the "old German fighter of the First world war" was invited by the mayor of Verdun to address the annual commemoration of the famous battle of 1916. Five years later, Jünger returned to Verdun to lay wreaths with the French president and German Chancellor at the memorial cemeteries at German stronghold Fort Douaumont and the Meuse heights area of Consenvoye. Although French newspapers reported that hardly a spectator ventured out to observe Kohl and Mitterand clasping hands while the Marseillaise played, camera teams were omnipresent as an "eye witness."[21]

Although Le Figaro called the ceremony "clumsy" and some German commentators thought the event was a consolation for the absence of an invitation to the fortieth commemoration of the landing at Normandy in June, it was without doubt an important gesture of reconciliation, contributing to a strengthening of Franco-German relations. This little-noticed event can be seen in hindsight as a prelude to the much more problematical reconciliation over the graves, in the blaze of publicity, when Reagan and Kohl met at Bitburg in May, 1985.[22]

In May 1985, François Mitterrand and Helmut Kohl met in Konstanz to iron out tensions that had emerged in the course of a recent economic summit in Bonn, due to divergent reactions to the S.D.I. (Strategic Defense Initiative) of the United States. Before the

---

21 Joachim Fritz-Vannhame, "Langer Händedruck zur Marsellaise: Die historische Geste von Verdun," Mannheimer Morgen, Sept. 24, 1984.

22 Deborah E. Lipstadt, "The Bitburg Controversy," *American Jewish Yearbook* (87, 1987), 21-37.

meeting started, Mitterand insisted on flying by helicopter to Wilflingen to visit Jünger. Kohl knew his visit would irritate the left in Germany, but with socialist Mitterand in attendance, how much of a fuss could critics raise? The story is told that Kohl and Jünger had a hard time starting a conversation. Finally the Kanzler asked "how did you start your beetle collection?" and Jünger had an opening. Kohl tried to talk about literature, but the conversation was halting. Finally, he asked about the Argentinean writer Jorge Luis Borges, whose photograph from a recent visit was within view. In the end, they chatted about the World War I. As a departing gift Jünger gave Kohl a copy of his just-published novel, *A Dangerous Encounter*. In sharp, calligraphic letters, Jünger entered a wry inscription in the book: "In memory of an un-dangerous encounter."[23]

The meeting between Mitterand and Kohl failed to erase the fears of the French that the German support for SDI, and relative neglect of the European defense program (Eureka) represented "the first step towards a Germanized Europe," (as the headlines of the Jean-Paul Sartre-founded newspaper *Liberation* claimed). (*Liberation*, May 31, 1985) Many Parisian newspapers commented unfavorably on Mitterrand's meeting with Jünger, whose 1932 anti-bourgeois book *The Worker* had not yet been translated into French. The French reading public knew little of the role Jünger had played as part of the Conservative Revolution and the rightwing intellectual mobilization against the Weimar Republic. Would Jünger's popularity be diminished, it was asked, if *The Worker* were to be published in French?[24]

---

23 Jürgen Busche, *Helmut Kohl: Anatomie eines Erfolgs* (Berlin: Berlin Verlag, 1998.

24 *The Worker* (Der Arbeiter) is a still very controversial book, which sets out, in programmatic fashion, the contours of a new fascist order in Europe and beyond, brought about by the revolutionary transformations of industrial society. Jünger's answer to the political stalemate of Weimar democracy as seen from the vantage point of the fateful year 1932 was a broad alliance between Catholic and independent trade unions and the Nazi labor organizations with the backing of the army, in other words, the kind of social revolution that Gregor Strasser and other radicals in the SA hoped to achieve. Parliamentary democracy would be replaced by a corporatist state and a benevolent military dictatorship. This was very close to the plan that General Kurt von Schleicher tried

Jünger's popularity, often bordering on adulation in France, was an intriguing phenomenon. His relationship to French culture and history was complex, but one can point to a number of historical reasons why Jünger's past was seen in an entirely different light west of the Rhine. First, Jünger's attachment to French literature distinguished him from most right-wing intellectuals of the Weimar period, who generally disdained French civilization as inferior to Germanic Kultur.[25] Jünger had been an avid and admiring reader of French literature ever since he imbibed the works of the fierce nationalist politician and writer Maurice Barrès (1862-1923) shortly after the end of the World War I.[26] French writers, especially Stendhal, Baudelaire, J.K. Huysmans, the Goncourts, and the anti-modern Catholic intellectuals Leon Bloy and Bernanos had a profound influence on him. Jünger cultivated relationships to French writers in the interwar period and was in turn, regarded by them as an avant-garde artist of some stature.[27] When the German writer Joseph Breitbach introduced Jünger to later Nobel Laureate André Gide (1869-1951) in 1938, Jünger obtained a crucial introduction to the world of French letters.

Second, The French have generally judged Jünger's role positively, as a sympathetic captain of the Wehrmacht at the eye of the storm in occupied France. In hindsight, Jünger was looked back upon as "the perfect type of occupier," charming, cultivated, and cosmopolitan. He gained recognition as a curator and protector of

---

to enact in his capacity as the last Weimar chancellor before Hitler took power in January 1933. The plan failed because Hitler sabotoged it and crushed Strasser's power base in the party, but the program remained as an option until Hitler finally eliminated the power of the SA in the so-called Röhm Putsch of June, 1934.

25 Walter Laqueur, *Weimar: A Cultural History, 1918-1933* (New York: Putnam, 1974). 79 ff.

26 Following the Franco-Prussian War and the Dreyfus Affair, the focus of Barrès shifted from a symbolist cult of the individual to traditional nationalism based on a theory of "the earth and the dead" (*La Terre et Les Morts*). He now emphasized ancestral values, rootedness in one's native soil, and embraced xenophobia, as exemplified in his trilogy *The Novel of National Energy* (*Le Roman de L'Energie Nationale*), which included the novel *Les Déracinés* (*The Uprooted*).

27 Albrecht Weber, *Ernst Jünger und der französische Geist*, Ph.D. diss., Universität Erlangen, 1949.

French culture. He was on a first name basis with luminaries like Jean Cocteau and Sacha Guitry. Even Sartre's leftist monthly journal of political debate, *Le Temps Modernes*, called him a "dreamer of peace during the war" and a "critic of Kniébolo-Hitler."[28] He was considered a mole in the system; someone who worked to save what could be saved. In particular, the protection from plunder of valuable manuscripts in the Bibliothèque Nationale, and the refusal to carry out orders to dynamite a medieval church in Laon, endeared the German to many a French patriot. Even among former members of the French resistance, Jünger's reputation was generally untarnished—in fact he was often revered.[29] Joseph Breitbach testified that the occupation officer passed on important information—the dates and times of deportations of Jews from Paris—to the maquis (Mühleisen, 1986). Henri Plard observed that Jünger represented for the French a kind of stereotype that can be traced as far back as Madame de Stael's search for the "good German" in contrast to the Boche.[30] Whereas Nazi propaganda denigrated French culture as decadent, weak, feminine, or "Judaized," Jünger's books, from this perspective, displayed a deep indebtedness to French traditions.

Third, Jünger's circle of wartime admirers in France, including non-conformist and anti-modern writers Julien Gracq, Antoine Blondin, Robert Poulet, Marcel Jouhandeau, and Denis de Rougemont, began immediately after 1945 to propagate the image of a "great" European writer of classical stature. Gide had famously called Jünger's war diaries the "most honest book ever written about the war."[31] When the *oeuvres complètes* of French Minister of Cultural Affairs Georges André Malraux (1901-1976) were published in France in 1989, Le Figaro sought and won an exclusive interview with Jünger, "le plus grand écrivain allemand," to solicit

---

28 Jean-Henry Roy, "Journal," Le temps Modernes 74 (December, 1951).

29 Maurice Nadeau, "Le combat d'Ernst Jünger," *Combat*, (Sept. 20, 1951).

30 Henri Plard, "Ernst Jünger in Frankreich," Text & Zeichen 105/106 (January, 1990), 142-43.

31 Michael Klett, "Aristocrat, il rêvait d'autre chose," *Le Monde* (Feb. 19, 1998. Michael Klett is from the third generation of the Klett family, the esteemed conservative publishing house in Stuttgart, to which Jünger was closely connected.

his opinion on matters concerning Malraux's life and works.[32] One of the questions posed to Jünger would very unlikely have been phrased in the same way by a German intellectual: "Isn't the type of man that you represent, Malraux and yourself, a product of very exceptional epochs, and could such types still exist today?"

Fourth, one cannot overestimate the contribution made by Henri Plard to Jünger's success in France. His translations are almost universally regarded as brilliant productions, and Jünger responded to his increasing popularity in France by devoting more attention to his French publishers. In fact, his late novel, _Eumeswil_, appeared in Plard's French translation chronologically before the original German version.

Finally, the case of Jünger in France deserves the kind of treatment that Jeffrey Mehlman labelled a "politics of literary adulation.[33] Without addressing the thorny argument Mehlman made about certain forms of literary criticism, when a figure is celebrated to the point that followers ignore or misrepresent inconvenient aspects of their work, relevant here is his interpretation of the writings of Jean Paulhan, an acquaintance of Jünger, who had been an early recruit to Jacques Doriot's extreme right Parti Populaire Français (PPF), worked with the Nazi occupying forces and collaborators, and at the same time grounded the first resistance journal *Les lettres françaises*.[34] Mehlman established a connection between Paulhan's linguistic research into homonymic antonyms and his criticism of the postwar purge of collaborationist writers by the National Committee of Writers. The meaning of the words "resistance" and "collaboration" tends to slide from one pole to another, a reversal of direction, like the translated pun *Sauerkraut*, which becomes *choucroute* in French. Paulhan's objective was that France might one day forget the bitter divisions caused by this unfortunate period

32 André Brincourt, "Malraux: La legende du siécle," *Le Figaro Littéraire* (May 2, 1989).

33 Jeffrey Mehlman, "Writing and Deference: The Politics of Literary Adulation," *Representations* 15 (Summer, 1986), 1-14.

34 Paulhan was managing editor at Gallimard after 1945. See Michael Syrotinski, "Some Wheat and Some Chaff: Jean Paulhan and the Post-War Literary Purge in France," *Studies in Twentieth Century Literature* (16, 2, Summer, 1992), 249.

in French history. Mehlman controversially suggested that the "radical forgetting" of the linguistic origins of Derrida's originally Heideggerian concept of deconstruction was proof of the success of Paulhan's call for amnesty (from: amnesia) of collaborationist writers.[35]

In this context, Mehlman introduced the figure of Gerhard Heller, an "anti-Nazi Nazi occupant" like Jünger, who worked with the German Propaganda Service in Paris as a censor, allowing many good books, including *Gardens and Paths*, to be published.[36] After the war, Heller emerged as a strong proponent of Franco-German reconciliation and was awarded the Grand Prix by the French Academy. It is intriguing to ask whether the accolades imparted to Jünger were in fact part of the same complex process of repression of memory of collaboration, that Paulhan worked out linguistically, and Heller's superficial papering over of differences in his double-agent role as occupier and French culture enthusiast exemplified. After all, beyond the factual basis for the French people's admiration for Jünger, there also existed psychological projection. Jünger's interpretation of the events of the war and the roots of fascism may have helped ease the shame of defeat and collaboration. They provided a basis for the illusion of shared suffering and the toleration of crimes by an imposed and unwanted regime. François Mitterand's own checkered past as an early supporter of Vichy may explain his attraction to Jünger and his government's eagerness to enlist the old warrior in symbolic acts of reconciliation.[37]

---

35 In the wake of the De Man Affair in 1987, Mehlman's linking of deconstruction in toto to French collaboration in World War II, and amnesty attempts afterward, has, of course, been met with indignation by many literary critics. See for example Ian Balfour, "Difficult Reading: De Man's Interaries;" See also Mehlman's contribution (324-33) and many other selections in Werner Hamacher, et. al., *Responses, On Paul de Man's Wartime Journalism* (Lincoln: University of Nebraska Press).

36 Gerhard Heller, *Un allemand à Paris, 1940-44* (Paris: Editions du Seuill, 1981).

37 After escaping a German prisoner-of-war camp in late 1941, Mitterrand returned to France and secured a position in Vichy's government. Through connections, he began working in a department responsible for the welfare of French POWs. His official work for Vichy overlapped with his involvement in the Resistance, leading some historians to describe

One of the most fascinating aspects of the French reception of Jünger was the role Jünger's writings played in what Richard Wolin in the 1990s called the "French Heidegger Wars," referring to the hotly contested debates between the French Heideggerian Left and its critics over Heidegger's purported attempts to shift the blame for his support of National Socialism from personal engagement to the de-personalized "fate" of Western metaphysics and the "forgetting of being."[38] Derrida and some of his followers attempted to interpret Heidegger's attraction to Nazism as a philosophical, rather than a political error; he conceived of the movement, so the argument goes, as a spiritual and cultural return to a pre-Socratic, polis-based renewal of German and occidental culture, that would shift theory and praxis away from the subject/object legacy of Western thinking and consequently, away from the planetary domination of technology, modern science and the "flight of the gods."[39] Derrida argued in *On Spirit*, that the use of the term "spirit" in Heidegger's infamous rector's address of 1934, indicated a step backwards from his own critique of the German humanist and idealist tradition, explicated so adamantly in *Being and Time* (1927). In this debate, Jünger's intellectual trajectory might have helped support such a vindication of Heidegger, because Jünger had an important influence in the 1920s and 1930s, particularly on Heidegger's thinking about technology, but by contrast, Jünger put much greater distance between himself and the National Socialist regime. Jünger also "spiritualized" his revolutionary battle against the Weimar Republic in a way

him as a "*vichysto-résistant.*" By 1942, he was already associating with other escaped POWs and taking part in early Resistance activities. Pierre Péan revealed in 1994 that Mitterrand expressed admiration for Pétain. A photograph of Mitterrand shaking hands with the Marshall in 1942 became public, providing undeniable proof of this contact. See Pierre *Péan, Une Jeunesse Française: François Mitterand, 1934-37* (Paris: Fayard, 1994).

38 Richard Wolin, *Labyrinths: Explorations in the Critical History of Ideas* Amherst: University of Massachusetts Press, 1995), 42-61.

39 Jacques Derrida, *Of Spirit; Heidegger and the Question*, trans. Geoffrey Bennington and Rachel Bowlby (Chicago: University of Chicago Press, 1989).

that was generally free of völkish, Nordic, or racial contamination.[40] Following thus route, some French Heideggerians (along with the general French reception) overemphasized Jünger's distance from National Socialism, or turned him into an oppositional, rather than resistance figure.

A good example of this spiritualization of politics can be found in *Heidegger, Art and Politics*, in which Phillipe Lacoue-Labarthe attempted to "think" Auschwitz in a Heideggerian manner against Heidegger, locating in the *Ereignis* (Event) of the Holocaust, a caesura which revealed the "truth of the West" as *techné*.[41] Explaining the essence of Nazism is, of course, different from approving it, but Lacoue-Labarthe left himself open to misunderstanding when he called fascism "no more aberrant or inadequate" than any other of the "age's possible political forms."[42] In another context, Michael Zimmerman stressed the indebtedness of Heidegger's understanding of the rueful effects of "planetary technology" to Ernst Jünger's influential essays of the 1920s, including "The Total Mobilization," in which Jünger postulated that modern technology was a revolutionary force about to sweep away all the stable structures of bourgeois society.[43]

Pierre Bourdieu, seemingly in the minority of contemporary French intellectuals not bewitched by the legacy of Nietzsche, had shown how important Jünger's work was to Heidegger, and how the ambiguous ideological structure of Jünger's Weimar writings could function as a surrogate revolutionary philosophy, both for the conservative revolutionaries of the 1920s and radical Heideggerians.[44] Whereas Bourdieu remained wary of the continuing appeal of the

---

40 Phillipe Lacoue-Labarthe, *Heidegger, Art and Politics: The Fiction of the Political*, trans. Chris Turner (Oxford: Basil Blackwell, 1990, 45.

41 Ibid., 107.

42 The distinction between "spirit" and "race" erases the large gray zone, in which plenty of room remained to support alternative, equally problematic "solutions" to Germany's Weimar dilemma. See Anson Rabinbach, *In the Shadow of Catastrophe* (Berkeley: University of California Press, 1997) esp. 97-128.

43 Michael Zimmerman, *Heidegger's Confrontation with Modernity: Technology, Politics, Art* (Bloomington: Indiana University Press, 1990), 28ff.

44 Pierre Bourdieu, *The Political Ontology of Martin Heidegger*, trans. Peter Collier (Stanford: Stanford University Press, 1991).

anti-technological metaphysics of the conservative revolutionaries, Jean-Michel Palmier argued against rejecting *The Worker* simply because of its intellectual affinities with the revolutionary right, while applauding the "immense intelligence" of its analysis of modern life.[45] Philippe Lacoue-Labarthe likewise stressed Jünger's social, rather than racial, understanding of politics. Jünger's intellectual association with National Bolshevism led Lacoue-Labarthe to claim, misleadingly, that Jünger "refused from the outset to have any truck whatever" with National Socialism.[46]

The shock in France that greeted the publication of Victor Farías's book *Heidegger et le Nazisme* in 1986—an exposé of Heidegger's involvement in Nazi politics revealing some, but not much already known in Germany—showed how extensive the radical forgetting of the Nazi era had become in France. How else can one explain the fact that the collaborationist past of writers like Ferdinand Celine, André Therive, Pierre Benoit, Jean Giono, and Abel Hermant had not been exposed to nearly the kind of scrutiny that comparable German authors had been treated?

The above five points summarize some important reasons for the success of Jünger's career in France. Beyond these verifiable contentions, many people have speculated more loosely about Jünger's popularity. These theories might better be taken as a kind of barometer that registers attitudes and inclinations, rather than factual arguments. It is important to remember that the French heroization of Jünger, his lionization as a "great" writer, had been supported and propagated, on the whole, by the conservative press, Jünger's personal friends and national-conservative circles in France.[47] As in Germany, the Jünger reception in France was

---

45 Jean-Michel Palmier, *Ernst Jünger: Rêveries sur un chasseur de cicindèles* (Paris; Hachette, 1995).

46 Phillipe Lacoue-Labarthe, *Heidegger, Art and Politics: The Fiction of the Political*, 24.

47 This is particularly true of readers who grew up in the 1930s and 1940s. See Georges Schlocker, "Fernweh nach den Göttern: Was die Franzosen an Ernst Jünger fasziniert," Süddeutsche Zeitung, (July 4, 1978). But in both France and Germany a new generation of the counter-culture, interested in esoteric subjects, (and unbothered by the disputes over Jünger's past), discovered Jünger's mysticism and celebration of drug experiences. See Jacques Le Rider, "Les nouveaux lecteurs d'Ernst

marked by deep divisions between critics and apologists.[48] Still, in comparison to Germany, where his books were purchased by a relatively small number of devoted readers, Jünger remained a household name among the substantial French reading public. An article on Jünger in the French press rarely appears without the epithet "le plus grand écrivain allemand contemporain," or similar designations. It seemed self-evident to the French that Jünger was "anti-Nazi" and "defiantly opposed to Hitler."

German observers of French intellectual life have advanced, over the years, several explanations for the "fascination" that draws readers to Jünger. Opinions differ as to whether the French had been seduced by a kind of evil genius, or, on the contrary, if the German resisted recognition of a real genius in their backyard. Rolf Hochhuth argued for many years that the confused discourse about the past made Germans blind to a "great living author."[49] For the author of the famous 1962 play *The Deputy*, (condemning the Catholic Church's involvement in fascism), Jünger was an example of a world celebrity who had been recognized everywhere except in his own country, condemned as a "Nazi or even an anti-Semite" by peo-

---

Jünger," *Le Monde*, (July 19, 1981). Currently forty-eight titles of Jünger's books are available in French translation, twelve of them in paperback. Albrecht Betz contends that Jünger's popularity in France has been exaggerated and points to the small influence he has had on other French writers. But does the testimony of writers constitute the decisive criterion? How does one explain the many official kudos, the lavish praise of politicians, and a wide range of intellectuals? See A. Betz, "Qui lit Jünger?" *Le Monde Dimanche*, Sept. 19, 1982.

48 See Elliot Y. Neaman, *A Dubious Past; Ernst Jünger and the Politics of literature after Nazism* (Berkeley: University of California Press, 1999). Also Lianne Dornheim, *Vergleichende Rezeptionsgeschichte; Das literarische Frühwerk Ernst Jüngers in Deutschland, England und Frankreich* (Frankfurt: Lang, 1987).

49 See "L'autre Goethe: Jünger, le viellard inspire," L'Express, May 19, 1989. Other examples could almost be quoted at random. Variations include "un très grand écrivan," Jean Louis de Rambures, "L'enigma Ernst Jünger," L'Express, Feb. 11-17, 1974; "le plus Francais des écrivains allemands," "Ernst Jünger un veilleur solitaire," Telerama, May 22, 1978; "En France, c'est le plus populaire des auteurs d'outre-Rhin." Lèopold Sanchez, "Jünger 87 ans: tous ses cheveux et la dent dure," S, Sept. 4, 1989.

ple who have never read his books or knew anything about his personal history. For Hochhuth, Jünger was "by far Germany's most interesting author, and it was no coincidence that the French esteemed him above all others."[50]

Jünger's onetime personal secretary Armin Mohler attributed Jünger's popularity in France to the fact that, in contrast to other German writers, Jünger was viewed as a home-grown author (*einheimischer Autor)*, one who even the normally anti-German right could embrace.[51]

Georges Schlocker pointed to Jünger's advocacy of anarchism as another plausible explanation for the French embrace. The French harbor special reverence for the outsider and iconoclast, one might argue, and Jünger's notorious elitism and refusal to conform can easily became enshrined in the pantheon of French radical individualism: In the mind of the Parisian intellectual, Jünger's Icelandic mysticism suddenly became transformed into enlightened individualism,

> Someone who says no to the majority, like Montaigne and so many writers after him .... They see in Jünger the man who can grasp the big themes and locate the place where the individual stands. It is a contradictory attitude which says "The writer should not become a hostage to political parties," and "It makes no sense to revolt against the state."... Jünger's works seem to the French to represent a battle against logic and functionalism, an emancipatory goal that in the meantime has attracted even the left.[52]

Schlocker clearly viewed the lionization of Jünger by some French intellectuals as a symptom of the yearning for a new radicalism, even if its origins were on the right. This question of the French attraction to German philosophy considered "tainted" in Germany (From Nietzsche to Heidegger) traveled well beyond the Jünger reception. After Solzhenitsyn's disclosures on the Soviet gulags were

---

50 Rolf Hochhuth, "Der Dichter in Uniform," *Abendzeitung* (Hamburg), (March 29, 1975).

51 Anton Madler, "Ernst Jünger ein Kennwort in Frankreich," *Die Welt* (Feb. 2, 1976).

52 Georges Schlocker, Fernweh nach den Göttern," Süddeutsche Zeitung, (July 4, 1978).

published in the 1970s, not a few disillusioned French Marxists turned to German philosophy in search of a different language with which to speak about alienation and bourgeois politics.[53] Jünger even encouraged the conversions. He reported to Henri Plard in 1977 his satisfaction of being informed that a group of French philosophers, "meta-Marxists" as he calls them, were giving seminars in Paris on *The Worker*. Clearly the alleged postmodern abandonment of the "grand narrative" did not stop some intellectuals from searching for a re-enchanting cosmology that would integrate mythology and Nietzschean post-metaphysics into a new anti-logocentric synthesis.

The French reception of Jünger points to the enormous difficulties involved in coming to any final judgments about Ernst Jünger's literary and political legacy. Almost everything he said or wrote becomes interpreted in the context of a complicated web of contested memory and historical associations. It seems that a core difficulty with Jünger's world-view lies in the suspicion that he attempts, in multifarious ways, to exonerate the majority of perpetrators and bystanders alike from any responsibility for the rise of Nazism. Primo Levi has written of the concentration camps that

> Many knew little and few knew everything about what happened, but that whatever the case, since one cannot suppose that the majority of Germans lightheartedly accepted the slaughter, it is certain that the failure to divulge the truth about the Lagers represents one of the major collective crimes of the German people and the most obvious demonstration of the cowardice to which the Hitlerian terror had reduced them .... Without this cowardice the greatest excess would not have been carried out, and Europe and the world be different today.[54]

---

53 Jünger mentions a certain "Lévy," presumably the philosopher Bernard Henri Lévy, who coined the phrase "New Philosophy" and, like André Glucksmann, was at this stage reevaluating student radicalism after reading Solzhenitsyn's memoirs. Jünger to Plard, Aug. 15, 1977 (PAP, Private Archive Plard). On Lévy see Paul Berman, *A Tale of Two Utopias: The Political Journey of the Generation of 1968*. (New York: Norton, 1996), 278-79.

54 Levi, Primo, *The Drowned and the Saved* (New York: Simon & Schuster, 1988), 15.

Jünger's message was just about the opposite. Since the original root of Hitlerism was to be found in an exaggerated Enlightenment faith in reason and domination of nature, culminating in a series of catastrophes and civil wars in the twentieth century, the German people were victims of history, at least as much as anyone had a right to the claim: "all suffered and therefore all must share the fruits of peace."[55] Many Germans did in fact suffer under Hitler's tyranny, while just as many were intoxicated by Hitler's victories and the ideology of the Super Race. Jünger conflated these two attitudes by lumping together the everyday German experience under Nazism with heroic, Spenglerian stoicism: "*das Ausharren auf verlorenem Posten*" or waiting out a hopeless situation.[56] Like many of the protagonists in Jünger's novels (the two brothers in *The Marble Cliffs*, Lucien de Geer in *Heliopolis*, and Michäl Venator in *Eumeswil*), Jünger could only imagine a "spiritual" resistance to tyranny. His response to the rise of Nazism was to watch from a distance. As Jean Cocteau said, some had dirty hands, others had clean hands, but Jünger had "no hands."[57] Henri Plard aptly described the World War II diaries as a log of a sinking ship, the daily observations of the catastrophe by a sober mind.[58] Jünger's philosophy of male, aristocratic virtue valorized the tragic heroism of facing up to destruction and defeat with silence. For Jünger to be a victim became a kind of test of strength and honor.[59]

One way of interpreting the very different reaction of the French to Jünger is to consider their own difficulties with coming to terms with the occupation and their initial acceptance of, even at

55 Jünger, *SW*, 7, 207.

56 Jünger borrowed the phrase from Oswald Spengler, see *Der Mensch und die Technik* (Hamburg: Beck, 1931/1961), 82.

57 Nevin, Thomas, *Ernst Jünger and Germany: Into the Abyss, 1914-1945* (Durham: Duke University Press, 1996), 169.

58 Henri Plard, "Ex ordine shandytorum," in Armin Mohler, ed., *Freundschaftliche Begegnungen* (Frankfurt: Klostermann, 1955), 110.

59 The philosopher Alfred von Martin called Jünger's heroism "*das schweigende Heldentum*" (Silenced Heroism) and pointed out that Jünger was particularly fascinated by cities like Catharge and Jerusalem that had experienced fateful destruction in battle. See *Der heroische Nihilismus und seine Überwindung* (Krefeld: Scherpe, 1948), 169-70.

times enthusiasm for Petain. I have emphasized how Jünger's impeccable posture and his adoration of French culture set him apart from the caricature of the ugly, boorish Nazi *boche*. Even more than that, collaboration with an enemy like Jünger could be made to appear reasonable, even civilized. Jünger never abandoned the notion that collaboration was in fact in the service of a noble cultural goal. As he wrote to Plard in 1975,

> Both the resistance and the collaboration have shades of light and darkness. The history of the resistance included a large number of murders, also of innocent people. I think of my friend Medan, whose friendship with me cost him his life. The youth movements in Germany and France found themselves in a circle called "Jeune Europe" standing for ideas that even today have not yet been realized ... Goethe says there is hardly a crime that he couldn't have committed; that is true, more or less, I think for everybody.[60]

Jünger's understanding of the history of the occupation was read by many in France as a story of shared suffering in a situation that offered few good choices. When all are victims, there remains no moral basis for differentiating good from evil, the murderers from the murdered. These are soothing nostrums, but the more historians examine the epoch of fascism, the clearer it becomes that there were far more choices than courageous people willing to make them. Moreover, the Vichy government could depend on the attitude of a large number of the French people who thought that the Third Republic and the Popular Front had justifiably failed in its attempt to create a French version of secular republicanism. The deep resentment of the French Revolution and its aftermath, modern mass democracy, remained very much alive in the tradition of French Catholic anti-modernism and Jünger's writings spoke directly to that constituency.

The reception of Jünger tells us much about the very different ways the memory of fascism is confronted in France and Germany. In France the memory of Vichy has always been fraught with controversy, as became clear when Vichy officials like René Bousquet,

60 Jünger to Plard, PAP, (Sept. 19, 1975).

Paul Touvier, and Maurice Papon would be prosecuted and convicted for crimes against humanity in the 1990s. Marcel Déat, Louis Darquier de Pellepoix were charged but escaped justice by fleeing France. Many French still consider the Vichy regime to have been an honorable arrangement in a period of national humiliation, and the trials of Vichy official were considered examples of illegitimate "Victor's Justice."[61] In a broader context, the French reception of Jünger threw into relief the continuing appeal of critiques of Western liberal civilization, held responsible for the planetary domination of technology, historical triumphalism, the destruction of the environment and the homogenization of culture, among many other sins. After the decline of Marxism as an attractive option for intellectuals, self-regarding radical intellectuals on the left and right joined forces by distilling a broad critique of western civilization from unorthodox conservative ideas of the Weimar period.

For too long historians have denigrated fascist intellectuals as mediocre, misguided or naive and have conceived of the intellectual grounding of fascism as opportunistic, irrational, muddled and anachronistic. The reception of Jünger (and Heidegger) in France shows that intellectual fascism can and is read as a potent critique of liberal humanism and modernity. I have argued that French intellectuals have the dubious distinction of being less burdened by the taboo of taking fascist ideas seriously than in Germany, a difference which explains, along with other peculiarities of French culture and the French memory of fascism, why Jünger was so much more popular east of the Rhine and why his ideas have consistently enjoyed a broader forum in the home of both the Enlightenment and Catholic Romanticism than in his native land.

61 The term Victor's justice was popularized by historian Richard H. Minear in his 1971 book about the International Military Tribunal for the Far East, see Richard H. Minear, *Victor's Justice; The Tokyo War Crimes Trial* (Princeton: Princeton University Press, 2015).

III.
Hiding in Plain Sight:
Ernst Jünger's Own Inner Emigration

Ernst Jünger's novel, *Auf den Marmorklippen*, was published in 1939, the year Adolf Hitler led a somewhat reluctant German nation into the catastrophe of the World War II[1]. Since the story's anti-hero is a dangerous, violent, eccentric warrior, who plunges a peaceful maritime civilization into an apocalyptic war. The novel has gone down in literary history both as an astounding prophesy and as an influential message of opposition to the tyranny of the Third Reich. These bold claims demand a critical, historically informed appraisal.

The first question about this unusual novel is, why it was allowed to be published at all, after Joseph Goebbels' propaganda ministry brought under its umbrella every aspect of literature after 1934, establishing pliant cultural organizations, excluding Jews, communists, and other so-called undesirables, deemed insufficiently loyal to the *Volksgemeinschaft*? The answer must be sought first, by taking into account Jünger's status as a larger-than-life hero of the Great War, second, his political trajectory, including a break with political activism after 1934 and third the evolution of his political orientation during the course of the 1930s.

Jünger became a public figure at the tender age of twenty-three in 1918, when personally bestowed by the Kaiser, the Pour le Mérite, the highest medal of the German army for acts of outstanding bravery. Jünger suffered multiple wounds as a daring storm trooper in northwest France, carrying out daring raids across enemy lines by a newly devised tactic to try and break the four-year-long stalemate, due to the unsuccessful and unimaginative strategy of attrition. Urged by his father, Jünger published the notes jotted down throughout the war in a memoir, In Stahlgewittern (In Storms of Steel), published first in 1922 and then in six different, heavily

1 Ernst Jünger, *Auf den Marmorklippen* (Hamburg, Hanseatische Verlagsanstalt, 1939, 1941).

re-edited versions in the course of the 1920s and 1930s. Hitler was an admiring fan of the book, which he regarded as the most eloquent expression of the front generation's experience in battle. In 1925, he sent Jünger a copy of Mein Kampf and Jünger responded with an enthusiastically dedicated copy of his essay "Fire and Blood" in 1926. A planned in-person meeting never materialized, and Jünger had no further personal communication with the national leader. (Jünger's inscription to "the nationalist leader" could mean, and probably meant, "a" leader, rather than the "sole" leader, based on the fact that the nationalist movement had many leaders at that point in time)[2].

Jünger did come into contact with Goebbels in the early 1930s when Jünger was residing in the capital, living from a veteran's pension and supplementing his income as a writer, art critic and journalist. Goebbels tried to enlist Jünger to run for a seat in the Reichstag as a National Socialist, but was rebuffed. Although Jünger continued to write political pieces until the fall of 1933, he was an independent analyst, advocating an alliance between workers and soldiers along the anti-capitalist, corporatist lines envisioned by Kurt von Streicher, the Catholic trade unions, Nazi labor groups and the aristocratic officer class. Jünger's famous treaty, *Der Arbeiter* (*The Worker*, 1932) can be seen as the most cogent expression of his version of a "Revolution from the Right," as advocated by various young conservatives at the time.[3]

After 1933, Jünger retreated from politics, into what has been called the "inner emigration." The term refers to a strategy developed by intellectuals in the Third Reich who later claimed they opposed the system but chose to hide their disgruntlement by turning to non-political pursuits or launching subtle critiques that could be read between the lines of seemingly innocuous texts. After the war and even today, the extent to which the inner emigrants were really opposing the regime is a matter of great controversy. The term was

2 See Elliot Y. Neaman, *A Dubious Past: Ernst Jünger and the Politics of Literature after Nazism* (Berkeley: University of California Press, 1999). The copy of *Mein Kampf*, with the inscription, is currently in the Library of Congress in Washington, D.C. 31, see footnote 45.

3 See Thomas R. Nevin, *Ernst Jünger and Germany: into the abyss, 1914-1945* (Durham, NC: Duke University Press, 1996), 27-28.

coined by the jazz age novelist Frank Thiess, who responded to a BBC broadcast by Thomas Mann, who had declared that all Germans bore collective guilt for the crimes of the Nazi state. Thiess responded that Mann had spent the war in comfortable security in Switzerland and the United States, so could know nothing of how citizens had to survive in a police state[4].

A good example of the inner emigrant controversy was the debate over Martin Heidegger's Nietzsche lectures of the 1930s, which supposedly contained a sharp critique of biological racism and signal Heidegger's turn away from National Socialism. Directly after the war, Thomas Mann had also accused the inner emigrants of being treasonous fellow travelers, whose various cultural activities accomplished nothing but grant some respectability to the regime. The reception of *On The Marble Cliffs* revolved around a similar question: how should we interpret the fact that Jünger kept publishing, even non-political texts, such as his travelogues, under the Nazi regime? *On the Marble Cliffs* was given official imprimatur in 1939, becoming a bestseller within weeks, and was banned in 1942 by the censor, ostensibly because of a paper shortage.

For Thomas Mann, Jünger's position directly revealed the central problem with the "inner emigration." Though we now know that Mann hesitated to leave Germany and had to be persuaded by his daughter Erika, he early on recognized the ineffectiveness of working to change the system from within. In 1943 Mann specifically pointed to the contradiction in Jünger's actions: having contributed to the rise of Nazism through his "saber rattling," Jünger retreated into hiding when he found the results displeasing. Mann wrote to the writer Harry Stochower, "Jünger now expresses his contempt for the torturers and their thugs, but he himself flayed a few skins and wallowed with pleasure in inhumanity."[5] Jünger's response to Mann's criticism was indicative of the bitterness of those intellectuals who felt they had no choice but to stay in Germany and do what

4 On the"Great Controversy" ignited by Mann and writers at home in Germany after the war see Tobias Boes, *Thomas Mann's War: Literature, Politics, and the World Republic of Letters* (Cornell: Cornell University Press, 2019), Ch. 6.

5 Thomas Mann, *Briefwechsel* (Frankfurt am Main: S. Fischer Verlag, 1963), 289-90.

was possible to maintain some cultural standards even as German culture went down with the shipwreck of National Socialism. By contrast, when asked about Mann, Jünger told a French journalist: "Thomas Mann just packed up and left. An emigrant cannot understand. He didn't share the tragedy of his people. How could he hope to find an echo among the people after that?[6]

On the surface, Jünger's *On The Marble Cliffs* is a story about two brothers living on a subtropical marina who become involved in a violent struggle against a powerful war lord in the mountainous interior, the Chief Ranger, an evil genius who suddenly disrupts the quiet life of the coastal community. Interspersed in a mosaic of philosophical and botanical observations is a narrative of almost orgiastic violence. The novel could be read as a statement of opposition to the Nazi regime based primarily on the similarity between Jünger's description of the power struggle between the aristocracy and the church on one side and the Chief Ranger and his armed thugs on the other. The Chief Ranger commands a paramilitary group known as the *Mauretanier* (Mauritanians, or Moors), an army of ruffians whose warrior camaraderie and vigilante mentality resemble the veterans' leagues of the Weimar period. The brothers come into contact with the forces of opposition, including a priest, Father Lampros and two warriors, Prince Sunmyras and a fanatical subaltern named Braquemart, who attempt to assassinate the Chief Ranger, but are caught and tortured to death. Sunmyras may be read as the aristocratic resistance to Hitler, and his plans to kill the Chief Ranger presciently end in failure. The climax of the story is an apocalyptic battle described in the language of deadly fascistic kitsch: giant knife-collared dogs and great poisonous snakes join in the fray. Some figures might almost have stepped out of an action comic book, like the old Belovar, whose ears are hung with golden rings and his head swept by a red bandana. He fights with medieval weapons, and joins in battle with the two brothers. The Chief Ranger finally succeeds in engulfing the entire island in flames, his men murdering and plundering in an orgy of destruction. The two brothers escape at the last moment in a ship filled with fleeing refugees and return home to their father's house in a mythical place

6 Ibid.

called Alta Plana somewhere to the north of the island, ringed by marble cliffs.

The entire story could be read as a dark fairy tale, or a gothic horror story. The very first lines of the book immerse the reader in a macabre and ghostly remembrance of things irretrievably past.

> How irrevocably beyond recall (are moments of happiness). We are more mercilessly separated from them than from any other distance. In the afterglow the images stand out even more enticingly. We think of them as we do of the body of a dead lover who lies deep in the earth and who appears to us like a desert mirage, in an enhanced and more spiritual splendor.[7]

Nostalgia is cast here as the memory of a *dead body*. The contrast could not be sharper between the first image of remembrance of happy things past and the second image of a ghostly corpse. In Jünger's surrealistic pastiche, death, love, and memory can be intertwined without seeming incongruous because the author camouflages the language of violence in natural metaphors—the desert mirage, the deep earth. The link between the morbid-surreal style, not unlike Salvador Dali's *The Face of War* (1940), and the gothic novel has been overlooked in the critical literature about *On The Marble Cliffs*, but the sense of impending horror brought on by the increasing violent incursions of the Chief Ranger and the ossuary extravagance of a site of torture called Köppelsbleek, fit perfectly into the tortured mood that is a hallmark of the gothic tale. The "happy past" elicits in the reader the *relative* security of the interwar period, now threatened by the face of war.

The characters in the novel only vaguely mirror actual Nazi leaders. The Chief Ranger is an earthy, sadistic man with insatiable carnal appetites, hardly consonant with the hypochondriacal, petit-bourgeois Adolf Hitler. And although Goebbels felt himself satirized by Braquemart, his unceasing devotion to Hitler contradicts the image of the fictional rebel. It took the Nazi censors a few years to recognize the fact that the book had subversive undertones; Goebbels became furious and eventually had the book taken out of print.

---

7 Ernst Jünger, *On the Marble Cliffs, A Novel*, trans. Stuart *Hood*, (London: New Directions, 1947), 3.

Though no longer available for purchase, the work continued to be publicly discussed. In occupied Belgium and France, reviews of the work even passed the military censor as late as the summer of 1942. After the war, a circle of personal friends of Jünger, many associated with rightwing journals such as *La Table Ronde, Rivarol, Figaro, La Patrie, Renaissance*, and *La nation française* propagated an image of the German writer as the most vigorous voice for a revival of occidental culture, against godless communism and secular materialism. In German treatments of the novel, it was often regarded as a rare example of nonconformity among the books published with the imprimatur of the Third Reich. It is not enough, however, to remain on the surface of the narrative of opposition.

Earlier works by Jünger, such as *The Adventurous Heart* (1928/1939) and the techno-utopian *The Worker* (1932), each in different ways, promised alternatives to modernity. The style was avant-garde, futuristic, disruptive, and subversive, in short, modernism of the extremes. The unlikely pairing of immediate and deferred time was hostile to certain aspects of modernity—for example the drive for increasing equality—but seeking to channel the energy of the modern into alternative utopias. By contrast, *On The Marble Cliffs* has none of this eruptive energy; it is elegiac and nostalgic, combining premodern and the liminal, between past and present. At most one could argue that the style reflected some aspects of literary expressionism. Goebbels in fact first championed a version of a so-called 'Nordic' expressionism in his struggle over the future of German art. He believed that modern art could be repurposed for propaganda purposes, even expressionism, which he viewed as a useful marketing style for captivating the masses. Goebbels perhaps initially supported the publication of Jünger's novel because of his distaste for antimodern, vulgar-realist art and literature championed by his opponent, chief party ideologue Alfred Rosenberg.

One cannot ignore the testimony of the novel's contemporary civilian readers. Many intuited the story as predicting a bad end for National Socialism, though soldiers on the battlefields read the novel in a more immediate fashion. One wrote, "When we could steal away a moment from the horror of the bombs flying overhead and read a few pages of *On The Marble Cliffs*, suddenly we knew what we were experiencing.[8]" Another wrote that it was taken up by the soldiers as gospel truth about their own struggles. If it was a gospel, what did it proclaim? Most soldiers recognized the allegorical significance of the tale as some kind of commentary on the regime that had sent them into battle, but how would the war end? Heinrich Böll, who disliked the mysticism and symbolism in what he considered Jünger's antiquated German, nevertheless felt constrained to acknowledge the personal courage of the author of *On the Marble Cliffs*, a book that he felt deserved a place in the resistance to tyranny. Jünger—cleverly—never revealed his own thoughts, but rather communicated his distaste for the regime by not conforming to its expectations. Readers in the Third Reich were starved of political literature not slavishly enforcing the party line. Jünger wrote for those who distrusted the Nazi *Bonzen* (the Bigwigs), those who had never voted for the Nazis or wanted them in power, as well as for those who initially may have welcomed the Third Reich, but felt trapped, in 1939, between their sense of loyalty to the nation and deep anxiety about the path of war taken by Hitler. *On The Marble Cliffs* might have appeared more oppositional than it really was simply because readers were desperate for a narrative that refused to conform to Goebbels's screeching triumphalism. It is unlikely that the book would have gone through so many printings in the first two years of the war had the censors detected an obviously oppositional stance. Once the state secret police and the SD, the Security Service, learned that the book was *perceived* as unorthodox, however, it had to be taken out of circulation because of, not despite the ambiguity of the messages contained in the literary bottle.

Jünger's own reading of *On The Marble Cliffs* was as an "unfinished" novel, having possibly influenced historical events, but also a product of history.[9] He perceived a kind of metaphysical interaction beyond time that resisted contemporary events. It would be simplistic to read the novel as an allegory of National Socialism.

---

8 Egon Mayr, "Zweideutig, ästhetisch und verkannt," (*Vorwärts*, March 27, 1975).

9 Neaman, *A Dubious Past*, 116.

Much more pertinent is its aestheticization of fascism, its transformation of fascist ideology into a conquest of the imaginary that ultimately failed to become reality. The moment of flight that ends *On The Marble Cliffs* can be followed recursively as an instinctive response in many of Jünger's literary works. At the historical juncture when German intellectuals had to decide for or against working within Nazi state ideology, the message of futility and escape at the close of the *On Marble Cliffs* is homologous to the strategy of the Inner Emigrants. Jünger and his brother Friedrich Georg return to the mythological north, that is, to the imaginative locus of their original fascination with, and then intellectual abandonment of, right-wing politics. in the same way, the conservative revolutionaries opposed the reality of the existing regime by deferring the into authoritarian utopia into the future or the subjunctive category. When they finally abandoned pursuing an alternative political order altogether, a new opponent, the liberal-democratic Federal Republic, was firmly in power in West Germany, a reality that called forth different tactics of opposition and sometimes new paths of inner emigration. Jünger self-deported to a small village in Upper Swabia, where he remained reclusive, mysterious, and, against the grain, a celebrity writer in old age, admired, detested, fought over, and ultimately accorded a post in the uncertain pantheon of German literature.

IV.
A Crononaut in Swabia:
Ernst Jünger and Postwar German Conservatism

Halley's Comet is the only known, short period naked-eye comet that humans can possibly observe twice in a lifetime. Ernst Jünger witnessed the comet in 1910 and then in 1986. He was born under the Wilhelmine Empire, marched off to war in 1914 and ended service as a highly-decorated hero. He worked as a writer in Berlin at the height of Weimar Germany's cultural rebirth, beginning in 1927, and stayed in the capital just long enough to see Hitler seize power. He fought as a captain in World War Two, spending much of his time in occupied Paris close to a resistance circle of aristocratic Prussian generals. He lived out much of the rest of his life in a small Swabian village through the period of the Cold War and after the downfall of communism. He lived long enough to see Germany reunified and died in 1998, a celebrated centenarian and Olympian figure.

Jünger was born 1895 in Heidelberg, the oldest of six children, two of whom did not survive infancy. Of his siblings, he was closest to his younger brother Friedrich Georg, born in 1898. From his father Ernst Georg, a chemist, he inherited the sharp analytical skills of a scientist, and from his mother Karoline Lampl, artistic capacities and an eye for natural beauty.[1] In an essay from 1930, *A Sicilian*

---

1 Of the many reliable biographies, see most recently Thomas Amos, *Ernst* Jünger_(Hamburg: Rowohlt, 2011), Allan Mitchell, *The Devil's Captain; Ernst Jünger in Paris, 1941-44* (New York: Berghahn, 2011), Heimo Schwilk, *Ernst Jünger; Ein Jarhundertleben* (Munich: Piper, 2007), Helmuth Kiesel, *Ernst Jünger; die Biographie* (Munich: Siedler, 2007), Steffen Martus *Ernst Jünger* (Stuttgart: Metzler, 2001). From the 1990s also important are Paul Noack, *Ernst Jünger; eine Biographie* (Berlin: Fest, 1998), Thomas R. Nevin, *Ernst Jünger and Germany; Into the Abyss* (Durham: Duke University Press, 1996), and Martin Meyer, *Ernst Jünger,* (Munich: Hanser, 1990). Of earlier biographies, see Gerhard Loose, *Ernst Jünger, Gestalt und Werk* (Frankfurt: Klostermann, 1957).

Letter to the Man in the Moon, he combines both these capacities by developing the notion of the stereoscopic gaze, whereby a third dimension is added to the normal vision of the left and right eye, a magical and synesthetic quality which he claims takes our understanding deeper into the observable phenomenon. The childlike fantasy that the moon is actually the face of a man points for Jünger to a deeper reality worth exploring. A red fragrant carnation, for example, is not stereoscopic, involving merely sight and smell separately, but a velvet carnation that emits the fragrance of cinnamon is stereoscopic, because the nose both smells and tastes the qualities of spice simultaneously.[2] One sense organ has to take over the function of another. Jünger may have physically experienced synesthesia, or at least he was able to simulate the ability of having one sense organ take over the function of another in his writing.

In his youth Jünger's family moved from place to place, partly in search of a good school for Ernst, who daydreamed too much and got poor grades. The father went in search of a stable income, abandoning ambitions to work as a scientist and opening an apothecary in a small town in the Erzgebirge, near the eastern border of today's Czech Republic. Jünger retained fond memories of the pristine landscape of forests and meadows in the surrounding area that he remembered as enigmatic and magical. The family did not remain in the idyll very long. Between 1905 and 1913 the boy was sent to various educational institutions, including boarding schools, which rendered him even more alienated from adults and their rules. He and his brother joined the *Wandervogel* in 1911, one of the many prewar youth groups that sprung up all over Germany, offering adolescents an escape from the benevolent tyranny of regimented life in late imperial Germany.[3]

In 1913, Jünger broke out for his first genuine adventure. He diverted money given to him to pay for half a year's food at school, boarded a train to Verdun, then to Marseilles, where he lied about his age and joined the Foreign Legion. He was shipped off to Algeria,

2 See Eliah Bures and Elliot Neaman, Introduction to Ernst Jünger, *The Adventurous Heart* (Candor NY: Telos Press, 2012), xix.

3 See Walter Z. Laqueur, Young Germany; A History of the German Youth Movement (London: Routledge & Kegan Paul, 1962), 66-73.

but had no desire to become a legionnaire. Escaping from his camp in Oran he darted off to discover Africa on his own. Quickly captured by foreign Legion soldiers, he was held until his father, through the German Foreign Office, arranged for his release. The furtively proud father instructed the boy to have a photograph taken before departing. The *adventure*, as a spiritual concept will play a central role in much of Jünger's life and writings.

Upon his return, the young man was promised a trip to Kilimanjaro if he finished school. This plan was interrupted the following year by the guns of August. Jünger rushed to Hanover and volunteered for the 73rd Regiment of General Field Marshal Prince Albrecht von Preussen. He quickly finished an emergency high school degree and arrived at the Western Front in Champagne by December. In November 1915, he was promoted to Lieutenant and quickly earned a reputation as a daring storm trooper. After suffering fourteen battle wounds, he received the Pour le Mérite on September 22 1918, the highest honor awarded by the Prussian military, rarely given to soldiers of his tender age.

The World War I was the single most defining experience of Jünger's life. He carried with him at all times in battle a slim notebook, sixteen of which he filled with impressions and observations. Upon the urging of his father, he assembled these notes into a war memoir, titled *In Storms of Steel*, which was first self-published in 1920, and then in heavily revised published editions over the next decade (he even made revisions as late as 1961). The book was influenced by school books of that era, above all Homer and Dante, but also by Nietzsche. Educated German soldiers more often carried *Thus Spake Zarathustra* than the Bible into battle during World War I.[4]

Storms of Steel, as well as other essays from the postwar period, such as the "Battle as Inner Experience" (1922) and "Fire and Blood" (1925) transformed the young soldier into a recognized leader of the "New Nationalists," veterans who were intent on bringing the war experience to bear on the heady politics of the fledgling Weimar Republic. These writers inflated the war memories into

4 See Stephen E. Aschheim, *The Nietzsche Legacy in Germany 1890-1990* (Berkeley: University of California Pres, 1994), 135.

mythic proportions to justify the enormous loss of life on the battlefields and to create a nationalist and collectively utopian narrative as an alternative to the unpopular republic, which was founded on liberal-democratic principles. Jünger described the experience of battle with astounding clarity, but not without expressionist pathos. In his view, war brings men back into a natural, unchanging order, subject to elementary forces that reveal the primordial violent rhythms of life below the thin veneer of civilization. Some modern critics, such as Klaus Theweleit, have accused Jünger of thus legitimizing the embrace of death and destruction by means of a fascist literary imagination.[5]

Jünger remained in the *Reichswehr* until 1923, but left disillusioned with the empty socializing and alcoholic excesses of the fraternizing officers. He enrolled in the natural sciences in Leipzig for the winter semester of 1923. There he joined the illegal paramilitary *Freikorps* and the legal Veterans' group *Stahlhelm* and began writing for various nationalist newspapers, including the Nazi *Völkischer Beobachter*. The years from 1923 to 1927 mark the high point of Jünger's engagement with the extreme right. He was one of three editors of the weekly *die Standarte* (later *Arminius*), which included the writers Friedrich Hielscher, Franz Schauwecker, Hans Friedrich Blunck and Friedrich Georg Jünger, all intellectuals who Armin Mohler will later identify as proponents of a "Conservative Revolution" in Germany.[6]

Mohler's book *The Conservative Revolution in Germany 1918-1932* (1950) attempted to forge a common identity between many different kinds of writers and thinkers, from fairly obscure and now forgotten journalists of the Weimar era to highly original thinkers who didn't necessarily act or think in concert with one another, such as Carl Schmitt, Martin Heidegger, Julius Evola, Oswald Spengler, Thomas Mann and Hans Freyer. To add to the somewhat

5 Klaus Theweleit, *Mannerphantasien*, 2 vols. (Frankfurt: Roter Stern, 1977). See in particular Vol. 1, 57 ff. and Vol. 2, chapter 3.

6 See the latest edition, Armin Mohler & Karlheinz Weissmann, *Die Konservative Revolution in Deutschland 1918-1923* (Graz: Ares Verlag, 2005), 115 ff. Jünger's journalistic writings of the period have been collected and annotated by Sven Olaf Berggötz, ed. *Ernst Jünger: Politische Publizistik 1919 bis 1933*. (Stuttgart: Klett-Cotta, 2001).

artificial nature of the "revolutionary" designation, Mohler included "father figures" from the nineteenth and early twentieth centuries as disparate as Nietzsche, Sorel, Pareto, Mosca, Veblen, Barrés and Houston Stewart Chamberlain.

A common theme that characterized the conservative revolution was to pit the "ideas of 1914" against the "ideas of 1789." For Jünger's circle, the "ideas" of the last war meant an emancipation from liberal civilization and a return to the organic *Volk* community. The war had signaled the death knell for the nineteenth century belief in progress. These young firebrands did not accept the old conservative desire to uphold the moral and judicial fundamentals of the state. They wanted instead to establish a charismatic base for politics outside democratic institutions and looked for a figure like Louis Napoleon, whose appeal went beyond warring factions, classes and parties. A social Darwinian influence made them view world politics as a fight for existence in which a national collective either triumphed or was destroyed.[7] Their critique of parliamentary political systems follows in many ways the path laid out by Carl Schmitt in his seminal 1923 essay, "The Crisis of Parliamentary Democracy."[8]

In these years Jünger worked to establish a Central Council that would unite workers and soldiers until a Führer could be found who could put the revolution into practice. This was a "National Bolshevik" strategy, and explains his close friendship with Ernst Niekisch, a politician and writer from Saxony who founded the journal *Widerstand*, with the aim of grafting Soviet bolshevism onto Prussian nationalism. But by 1927 Jünger became disillusioned with the various nationalist groups fighting one other as the Weimar government entered a relatively stable period, which lasted until the Great Depression doomed Germany's first experiment with democracy.

---

7 See Elliot Neaman, *A Dubious Past; Ernst Jünger and the Politics of Literature after Nazism* (Berkeley: University of California Press, 1999), 32-33.

8 Carl Schmitt, "The Crisis of Parliamentary Democracy," trans. Ellen Kennedy, (Cambridge MA: MIT Press, 1985).

Jünger had married Gretha von Jeinsen in 1925 and moved to Berlin with their infant son in 1927. He continued to engage in political journalism but moved increasingly away from the fixation on war and nationalism of his Leipzig years. In the revisions of his war memoir for example, he removed the opening epigraph, "Germany Lives and Germany shall not Perish."[9] His artistic eye shifted to the bustling metropolis whose vitality and energy were on display around the clock. In Berlin he wrote *The Adventurous Heart*, notes written down by "day and night." The first edition, published in 1928, and the second, very different version in 1938 has been called "surrealist," but the approach was only loosely connected with André Breton's famous movement of the same period. Karl-Heinz Bohrer has memorably labeled Jünger's style an "aesthetics of shock," since this book contained a phantasmagoria of scientific and poetic vignettes, a collage of wild associations and ghostly images that recalled the war inspired art of painters like Renée Magritte, Salvador Dali and Max Ernst; also the expressionists Otto Dix and George Grosz.[10] The method was stereoscopic, a journey into magical sub realms below quotidian existence. A key term Jünger borrowed from the French was *desinvolture*, the casual and innocent observation of actuality from a distance (as in Nietzsche's *Unschuld der Werdens*).[11] Jünger had a two-fold purpose, not only to capture the horrors of bodily deformation and disfiguration suffered by most soldiers in the recent war, but also to expand his aesthetic reach to reflect the deformities and disruptions caused by modern urban life.

Jünger's circle of friends and literary acquaintances expanded in Berlin as he moved beyond his ties to war veterans. On the left he interacted with Bertolt Brecht, Ernst Toller, Elke Lasker-Schüler, Erich Kästner and the anarchist Erich Mühsam, on the right with Gottfried Benn, Ernst von Salomon and Arnolt Bronnen. He also began to travel, especially to France, where he made contact with

9 See Helmuth Kiesel, ed. *Stahlgewittern; Historish-kritische Ausgabe* (Stuttgart: Klett-Cotta, 2014).

10 See Karl Heinz Bohrer, *Ästhetik des Schreckens; die pessimistische Romantik und Ernst Jüngers Frühwerk* (Hamburg: Ullstein, 1983).

11 "The Innocence of Becoming" was a title given by the Nazi philosopher Alfred Baumler to a collection of Nietzsche's unpublished works in 1931.

French literary circles, facilitated by the well-connected German-French author Joseph Breitbach. A lifelong association with French intellectuals and politicians began at this time. As the Nazis begin their final ascent to power after winning 107 seats in the Reichstag in the elections of September 1930, Jünger distanced himself from the party while at the same time advocating his own, in some ways more radical version of the nationalist revolution, authoritarian and ruthless, but not racist. He rejected the Nazi fixation with blood and soil. In 1927 he refused to accept an offer from Hitler of a seat in the Reichstag. When the Nazis published excerpts from *Storms of Steel* without permission, he forbade any further use of his writings.[12] The one anti-Semitic tirade that came from his pen during this period was phrased in cultural terms, the "Gestalt" of Germans and Jews were as separate as "oil and water."[13]

During his last two years in Berlin he published two "proto-fascist" works, *The Total Mobilization* and *The Worker*, both odd mixtures of social analysis, political polemic and cultural pessimism. These books are often taken as evidence of Jünger's role as a "pathbreaker" for National Socialism, but in fact the Nazis used the title of the former solely as a powerful slogan, disregarding its contents, and rejected the esoteric metaphysics of the latter. Jünger's vision of a brave New World, set forth in steel cold prose in *The Worker*, was uncompromising but also too global to be of use to the racially-obsessed Nazi ideologues. He heralded a collective new age of The Laborer in epochal terms, while the Nazis concentrated on the specific situation of Germany's supposed superior racial characteristics. National Socialism appeared to him a purely technical execution of the total mobilization. He later said that it "lacked metaphysics."[14] As a political platform *The Worker* was entirely useless to the new regime. Even worse, the Nazi ideologues took his ideas as heretical. Thilo von Trotha, a personal assistant to the Nazi chief ideologue Alfred Rosenberg, wrote in the party newspaper, just after

12 Letter to the *Völksicher Beobachter*, June 14, 1934, cited in Heimo Schwilk, *Ernst Jünger; Leben* und Werk, 142.

13 Ernst Jünger, "Über Nationalismus und Judenfrage," *Süddeutsche Monatshefte* 12 (September 1930), 843-845.

14 Interview in *L'Express*, Jan. 11-17, 1971, 105.

The Worker appeared in print, that Jünger was "entering the zone of the head shot" since his work lacked any sense of racial biology and sacrificed the nationalist for a planetary perspective.[15]

The threat from Trotha was not idle. Because of his ties to the National Bolshevist Ernst Niekisch, the Gestapo searched Jünger's apartment in early 1933. (Niekisch was arrested in 1937 and spent the war years in a Gestapo jail, where he was liberated by the Red Army in 1945, a broken, nearly blind man).[16] At this time Jünger began burning papers and letters from the last decade. At the beginning of December 1933 the family left Berlin for Goslar, in Lower Saxony on the slopes of the Harz Mountains.[17] During the so-called Röhm Purge at the end of June 1934, in which the SS eradicated the leadership of the unruly Brown Shirts, Jünger was vacationing on the island of Sylt, but felt the threat palpably. The mood was ominous, wrote Jünger's wife.[18]

He now entered a period of "inner emigration," a term possibly coined by Thomas Mann, but one Jünger never embraced.[19] He remained in Germany, and continued to publish, but studiously avoided employing the language and themes that characterized writers who ingratiated themselves with the new regime. In November 1933 he rejected membership in the Nazi synchronized Prussian Academy of the Arts, which in May 1933 had forced out many luminaries, including Thomas Mann and Alfred Döblin. The Nazis staffed the writing (*Dichtung*) section with party hacks, though it was headed by Gottfried Benn, a major poet who was on friendly terms with Jünger.[20] In 1934 Jünger published *Blätter und Steine* (Leaves and Stones), a collection of his essays on language, travel and philosophical topics which offered a stark contrast to the daily

---

15 *Thilo* von Throta, "Das endlose dialektische Gespräch," *Völkischer Beobachter* (October 22, 1932). https://www.dhm.de/lemo/biografie/ernst-niekisch

16 Thilo von Throta, "Das endlose dialektische Gespräch," *Völkischer Beobachter* (October 22, 1932).

17 https://www.dhm.de/lemo/biografie/ernst-niekisch

18 Neaman, *A Dubious Past*, 104.

19 Inge Jens, *Dichter zwischen rechts und links*, (Munich: Pieper, 1971), 33 ff.

20 Helmuth Kiesel, "Ernst Jüngers Marmorklipen," http://iasl.uni-muenchen.de/register/kieselauf.htm. See Section 2.

reality of the Third Reich, as Hitler's popularity soared to unprecedented heights. In 1936 he published the diversionary *Afrikanische Spiele* (African Games), a novel about his short adventure in the French Foreign Legion.

The Jünger family moved several times in the 1930s, once down to Überlingen, on the north shore of Lake Constance, to be near his brother Friedrich Georg. But Jünger didn't like the soft climate there and so they finally settled in Kirchhorst in 1939, near Hannover, where Gretha had found a large, somewhat run down old house with a large garden, which would be very useful since food would soon be rationed in Germany. Here Jünger would live until 1950, though he was away for much of the World War II.

In 1939 he published *Die Marmorklippen* (The Marble Cliffs), which he started writing on Lake Constance. The book has gone down in the history of the Third Reich as a subtle novel of opposition, but the fact that it received the official imprimatur of the regime shows how successfully the writer was able to camouflage the tale, wrapped in an allegory. On the surface the fable tells of a peaceful agricultural people living contentedly on the shores of a large bay, who are increasingly threatened by a primitive nomadic people from the hinterland, and by the followers of an unscrupulous tyrant named the Head Ranger, whose thugs torture their enemies in a spooky camp called Köppelsbleek. The site is surrounded by the skulls and flayed skins of the victims. At the end of the novel, the Head Ranger conquers and destroys the entire marina area, while the two protagonists, modeled after Ernst and Friedrich-Georg Jünger, are forced to flee. Jünger resisted the tendency to view the novel as an allegory about concentration camps and totalitarianism (the Head Ranger had similarities to Goering, who was in fact the "Imperial Forest Ranger" of Nazi Germany), since the fictional tyrant could have have represented Stalin, Franco, Hitler or any dictator of that era. Despite the framing of the story in the gothic horror style, many readers in the 1940s, both in and outside of Germany interpreted the novel as an aristocratic and conservative critique of National Socialism.[21]

21 Neaman, *A Dubious Past*, 122-26.

Soon after the war broke out in 1939 Jünger enlisted as a lieutenant then was promoted to captain. His troops were stationed first at the West Wall by the Maginot Line. Then a lucky break—in April 1941 his regiment was ordered to occupied Paris. The Germans allowed the French to administer the metropolis, under supervision, so Jünger found himself in the enviable position of enjoying the charms of the City of Light in a position of near casual authority. He would even be permitted to stroll through the streets and markets in civilian clothing. His official job was to censor the mail but also surreptitiously to write reports about internal conflicts between the army and the party, in particular the SS, the SD, the Embassy and the Gestapo, which all operated their own surveillance systems in Paris. He found an admirer in the aristocratic General Otto von Stüpnagel, and then a distant cousin, Carl Heinrich von Stülpnagel, who succeeded Otto in February 1942. Through the latter Jünger came into contact with officers involved in a conspiracy to overthrow Hitler, centered around the legendary General Erwin Rommel.[22] After the failed Stauffenberg plot of July 20, 1944, the SS made a sweep of the military command in Paris, but Jünger had kept enough distance from the plotters to avoid arrest. As Jean Cocteau (who socialized with Jünger in Paris) once wittily observed, under the occupation "some people had dirty hands, some people had clean hands, but Jünger had no hands."[23]

Jünger's eldest son, his namesake Ernstl was killed in November 1944, of all places in the marble cliffs of Cararra, Italy. He had expressed sentiments hostile to the regime, was denounced and arrested in January 1944. Jünger received permission to leave Paris in February and met with the authorities in Berlin, displaying his Pour le Mérite insignia ostentatiously across his chest. The son was allowed to return to military service, but given a dangerous assignment in the Italian mountains. Jünger was never sure if his son had been shot by the enemy or murdered by the SS. The war diaries are written with cold, emotionless precision, except for the entries about

22 Nevin, *Ernst Jünger and Germany*, 169.

23 SW, 3, 270 (May 27, 1944). 10

his son's death, which reflected the deep and enduring pain he felt all his life at the loss of his eldest son.[24]

In France Jünger worked at the Hôtel Majestic, on the Avenue Kléber across from the Arc de Triomphe, and lived next door, at the luxury hotel Raphael. He kept his notes about the rivalry between the party and the army, as well as a diary and other writings, safely locked away in a vault. The diary entries formed the basis for his later published war memoirs *Strahlungen* (Emanations).

These war diaries offer a unique perspective from "inside the Belly of the Leviathan" as Jünger put it. Some critics have accused the writer of posing as a *flâneur* and dandy while others suffered. In one infamous scene, Jünger climbed up to the roof of the Hotel Raphael and, holding a glass of burgundy, observed a night bombing of Paris, as "its red towers and spires lay in stupendous beauty, like petals blown over in an act of deadly fertilization."[25] Whatever moral judgement one wishes to make about this aesthetics of violence, the diaries are indispensable as first-hand accounts of Paris under the German occupation and provide sharply observed portraits of Jünger's contemporaries as they struggled with the apocalyptic destruction of Germany and during the first years of *its* occupation.

The Paris Diaries from 1941to early 1944 read like entries in the log of a sinking ship. The sections written after the summer of 1944 project the stark mood of a shipwreck. Under occupation Jünger haughtily refused to fill out the mandatory questionnaire that was part of the Allied Military Authority's denazification program. As a result he was blacklisted and cut off from the larger world. Messages in a bottle washed up on his shore, as he gradually received news about friends, acquaintances and relatives. Some alive, others barely alive after brutal treatment by the Russians in the Eastern zone, others dead by fate or their own hand. Throughout the years 1945-1948 waves of expellees and refugees from the

24 http://literaturkritik.de/id/1652

25 *Ernst* Jünger, *Sämmtliche Werke* (Collected Works) hereafter SW, 1, 3, 494.

East flowed through Germany. In the first months some were quartered in his own house, delivering horror stories from their eviction and forced travels.

On July 21, 1945 Jünger wrote in his diary, "The Conservative mind aims to conserve, even conserve his enemy, that is part of his natural inclination.[26] This observation, written with bitterness, sums up the attitude of a writer entering a kind of second inner emigration. The British, he notes, share a fundamental misunderstanding of the German situation since 1918, one long civil war, in his view.[27] In other words, the allies were determined to punish the Germans, as they had done in 1919, which was a radical, not a conservative undertaking. "Unconditional surrender is the flip side of total war," he notes, by inference comparing Churchill, Stalin and Roosevelt to Goebbels.[28] In another startling association, he wrote that "Anti-Germanism, like Anti-Semitism appears to belong to the basic temper of our world."[29]

True to a style that will characterize all the diaries he kept until very old age, Jünger travels through four different dream worlds in these pages: the first made up of his actual dreams, the second in reflections of the natural world, the third composed of images and ideas from books and the fourth from historical figures and anecdotes. Quite naturally the trauma of the immediate past pre-occupied him. The descent into the catastrophe of National Socialism and the World War II are occasions for repeated reflections on the time travelers who accompanied him from the days of defeat in 1918 to the final apocalypse in 1945. In a series of arresting reflections on Hitler, he observed that he, like many in Germany, underestimated the demonic power that lifted the little nationalist drummer to the heights of power and then self-destruction. Hitler was a "moon character," who could reflect back to the German people their fears and desires in a way that the other Weimar politicians were incapable. It is striking that he goes to great lengths to dissect the personalities of some leading Nazis, in particular Heinrich Himmler

---

26 SW, 1, 3, 484.
27 SW, 1, 3, 493.
28 SW, 1, 3, 582.
29 SW, 1, 3, 609.

and Josef Goebbels, but says relatively little about the persecution of German Jews. The concentration camps are mentioned sporadically and in odd comparisons, as when six Jews liberated from nearby Bergen-Belsen appear on his doorstep. He makes the odd observation that the "suffering of millions" can only be measured by viewing a single individual. In another passage he speaks of "our persecution" of the Jews as the a possible sign of the coming of the second Messiah, the spiritual *Paraclete*, a redemptive trope that would surely be rejected by Holocaust survivors.[30] He compares the treatment of the German Sudeten refugees to the tragic fate of the Jews in Germany.[31] On the other hand he develops, around a decade and half before Hannah Arendt made the idea famous, the notion that some leading Nazis were extraordinarily mundane. Himmler was characterized by "penetrating bourgeois characteristics, he observes, and "evil in the modern world shows up in the ordinary actions of a bureaucrat behind a desk."

Politics make up only a fraction of these postwar diaries. Jünger often describes long walks in the moorlands around Kirchorst, noting the changing seasons, discussing philosophy, quoting passages from esoteric books. He dwells on the daily hardships of the Germans under occupation, the cold winters, the scavenging for food and basic necessities. In the end these are the reflections of a solitary man living in a world from which he feels both alienated and simultaneously deeply attached. He calls himself a Solitaire, rather than elitist.

Jünger hoped to make a comeback in the postwar period, despite the blacklist and his physical remoteness from German cultural life. He had to face a number of obstacles. The reading public, especially the youth, hungered for authors who were banned under National Socialism. American authors such as Hemmingway, Faulkner and Thomas Wolfe were in vogue. Sartre and the French Existentialists were starting their conquest of intellectual life across Western Europe. Jünger had kept another work, a long essay, in his secret vault during the war, which he hoped would provide a

30 SW, 1, 3, 415.
31 SW, 1, 3, 563.

vision for a peaceful postwar Europe that would put him back on the cultural map. He titled it simply *The Peace*.

This slim volume was published in various European countries outside Germany in 1946, but not until 1949 did the Americans allow it to appear in their occupation zone. Jünger viewed his own nationalist writings from the 1920s as his "Old Testament," and works like *The Peace* as part of his new evangelical spirit. They fit together: The "Total Mobilization" was just the flip side of *The Peace*, he wrote to his future secretary Armin Mohler in 1947. He argued that in the wake of the two disastrous world wars, Europe's future lay in overcoming nationalism through organic unity and integration. These ideas were fairly common after 1945, but Jünger's conservative contribution was first, unremarkably, to appeal to a return to Christianity as a solution to Europe's problems but second, quite contentiously, to relativize the question of war guilt, a topic widely discussed in public in this period by eminent figures such as the philosopher Karl Jaspers, the theologian Martin Niemöller and the psychologist Carl Jung. Jünger objected to laying blame on any one side or nation. He wrote, "We have seen the victims of this war. To their somber ranks all added their contingent. All shared the suffering and therefore the peace must bear fruit for them all. That is, the war must be won by all." This was an outlier position in the debates about German guilt, and *The Peace* did not play a major role in the public discourse.

Jünger held high hopes for a major novel he had been working on in these years. *Heliopolis* is a dystopian work about a power struggle between plebeians and an old aristocracy. In many ways it was a roman à clef about the period of National Socialism as seen from occupied Paris. Jews make an appearance as "Parser" and a civil war breaks out between a provincial governor who resembles the Head Ranger and a proconsul, who mirrors the Prussian aristocracy. The novel contains many theological diversions, a result of Jünger's intense reading of the bible he had begun in occupied Paris. The reception of *Heliopolis* was disappointing. One criticism was fairly common: the veiled references to the recent past in the book were tiresome. "Wouldn't it have been better," one critic asked, "to have made a collection of essays out of this novel, which wasn't one?" Even Carl Schmitt, writing in his *Glossarium* in 1949, displayed irritation with Jünger's apparent religiosity and his proclivity to mask history in metaphors and exotic characters.[32]

In 1950 Jünger moved one last time. He was offered an eighteenth century baroque villa by Freiherr Schenk zu Stauffenberg, a distant relative of the coup plotter against Hitler. The new home was in the small village in Upper Swabia, a few kilometers from the nearest train station and post office. Jünger became the famous recluse of Wilflingen, where he would live out the many years left in his long life.

In hindsight Jünger's turn to theology in the late 1940s misled his readers. He could best be described in religious terms as a neo-pagan, who considered Christianity just one interesting variant of Neo-Platonism, (though at the end of his life he did convert from Protestantism, his religion at birth, to Catholicism). A barely read novel from 1953, *Visit to Godenholm*, signaled his interest in esoterica and mystery religions, which would remain a life-long passion. The novel was written under the influence of LSD, which Jünger had imbibed under medical supervision with the drug's inventor, Albert Hoffman, in a visit to Bottmingen, Switzerland in February 1951. A character in the novel, Eimar, occupies himself with what Jünger describes as an older, more organic practice of science, gently bringing to the surface the secrets of nature, rather than through technological manipulation, which defines modern industry. Jünger's project was to recover the truths embedded in both past religions and metaphysics, which amounted to a rebuke of the positivist and materialist spirit of the postwar rebuilding period.

The early 1950s saw a series of works from Jünger's pen that expanded on this anti-modernist tendency. In 1950 he published an essay called "Over the Line", dedicated to Martin Heidegger on his 60th birthday, in which he echoes Heidegger's concerns about technology. As the economic boom was taking off in Germany, Jünger viewed feverish production by de-spiritualized workers and the increasing specialization of the human and natural sciences, as signs of an ever-diminishing ability to grasp the totality of life, as

32 Gerd Giesler & Martin Tielke, ed. Carl Schmitt (*Glossarium. Aufzeichnungen der Jahre 1947-1951* (Berlin Duncker & Humblot), 217.

proof of the growing nihilism of the age. In 1951 he published "The Forest Passage," which amounts to instructions for passive resistance to the modern condition. The individual walks in a metaphorical forest, taking her own path, to escape domination by the forces of technology, the omnipresent Leviathan state and the banality of modern culture. Religion, Counter-Enlightenment thought and myth are all put in the service of subverting the corrosive effects of instrumental rationality, which, he claims, undergirds all modern totalitarian forms of government. In 1954 he published an essay on hourglasses, which reconstructed the mythological timekeeping by calendars based on cyclical rhythms and thus by implication, counterpoising the synchronic experience of time in modernity to cyclical repetition. In 1955 he published a travel diary, "At the Saracen Tower," in which the lives of people, flora and fauna on the island of Sicily take on a timeless, magical quality.

Although Jünger could stand forth as a conservative defender of occident, for example in "The Gordian Knot" from 1953, which pits the freedom of the West against the despotism of the East, and even unvarnished internationalism, with strong advocacy for a world government in an eponymous essay from 1960, his political writing always contained a consistent strain of anti-democratic suspicion. A good example is a little-known essay he wrote in 1956 about the eighteenth century French writer Rivarol, a defender of the monarchy as an institution (but not necessarily the nobility) and a fervent critic of the French Revolution. Jünger was intellectually rooted in the progressive-conservative tradition that men like Rivarol (and Edmund Burke) represented. He sought a synthesis of eternal truths and contemporary reality. Jünger identified with Rivarol's rebellion against French society and viewed himself in a similar position of revolt against the imposed laws of the occupying posers in postwar Germany.

For Jünger the postwar world was characterized by the decline of Europe as a world power and the rise to dominance of purely technocratic societies, like the Soviet Union and the United States. Nothing new culturally would appear. Eclecticism in the arts, philosophy, science and literature would be the norm. He regarded the public sphere as little more than an expression of the power of the mob that threatens to displace dwindling authority in modern states. Conservatism consisted of resistance to all these assaults by any means possible.

Gretha Jünger died in the fall of 1960. Her husband cared for as she declined in health for two years. This was a difficult period. Jünger had suffered from depression and melancholy at times throughout his life and the sadness of losing his wife was added to an already darkening mood. Depression ran in the family. His second son Alexander, who had a medical practice in Berlin, suffered from non-reactive depression and took his life in 1997.

After his wife's death Jünger lived an ascetic lifestyle for several years before marrying Liselotte Lehrer, an archivist and editor twenty-two years his junior in 1962. She helped him publish a ten volume *Collected Works* in 1964, in which he left out all of his journalistic writings from his nationalist period of the 1920s. He evidently viewed these works as excesses of youth, unworthy of his ambition as a neo-classic author, though some observers from the right, such as his ex-secretary Armin Mohler, viewed the omission as a betrayal of the values of the Conservative Revolution.

On March 29, 1965 Jünger turned seventy, He began a new set of diaries that he would maintain until the last days of his life. The diaries are replete with reminiscences, metaphysical speculation, notes about nature and history, but increasingly less about the contemporary world. Jünger observed the world not even from a bird's eye view, but rather from the perspective of a distant planet, or as a naturalist would view insects (he was a respected amateur entomologist). The day after the Berlin Wall fell he noted, "I never doubted that reunification would come, just that I would experience it. I didn't expect a national awakening as much as I expected a melting of borders in the general development towards a world state." The next entry is nine days later and nothing more is said about European politics for the rest of the autumn of 1989, a revolutionary period that held the world's breath as communism fell in state after state.

In his old age Jünger saw his time increasingly through a post-historical lens. For the European right after World War II, thinkers such as Martin Heidegger, Arnold Gehlen, Carl Schmitt, and others, in various versions of the same idea, postulated that the postwar world would be characterized by the decline of Europe as a world power and the rise to dominance of cookie-cutter technological systems that would expand to the entire globe. For Schmitt and Jünger, the new technical-industrial drive for hegemony was reaching into space, following the model of British global colonization of the sea. As a result, ancient cultures were now doomed. The "end of history" implied that after the demise of European culture, intellectuals could only take stock of what had been handed down.

Jünger captured this mood in his 1949 introduction to the war journals, in which he postulated that the Copernican quest for ordering the cosmos, and the diary as a modern literary form fall together chronologically. They have in common "the bifurcation of mind from object, the author from the world." The World War I marked the end of history, because it represented the demise of heroic action in a pre-technological sense. The end of history, he once said, can be equated with the end of the aristocratic order.

The technological conquest of Europe coincides with the end of mythological time. Jünger regarded the imperial colonization of space and its reflection in science fiction as signifying of the end of the historical novel. *Posthistoire*[33] thinkers could only contemplate the stranded objects of history washed up on the shore. Jünger seems to have believed that the rise of fascism and communism in the 20th century constituted another kind of effacement of history. As he told a sympathetic French interviewer, "We have had the huge school of herrings, the masses, and several sharks as well, Hitler, Stalin, Mao. That was the age of Leviathan, according to Hobbes.

In his own science fiction novel, *Eumeswil* from 1977, posthistorical themes are omnipresent. The book marked a change in literary topography from the guarded optimism characteristic of Jünger's early postwar political tracts like "Over the Line" and "The World State." There he expressed hope that the catastrophic experience of the two world wars would galvanize mankind into transcending national differences, overcome nihilism and create a rational system of world organization. This novel, by contrast, transports the reader into a post catastrophic twenty-second century, in

---

33 On the history of *posthistoire* in European thought, see Lutz Niethammer, *Posthistoire; ist die Geschichte zu Ende?* (Hamburg: Rowohlt, 1989).

which the world state had disintegrated and nuclear-armed warlords have imposed static tyrannies on their emasculated subjects. *Eumeswil* may be modeled on the *Eumenides*, the final play of Aeschylus's *Oresteia*, about the breakdown of social order as the gods punish Orestes for the murder of his mother. The book places us in a desolate future empire where culture is atrophied and history and the arts are left in the hands of dilettantes, lexicographers, and collectors.

Readers of *Heliopolis* recognized the symbolic montage of *Eumeswil*. The state is governed by the tyrannical Condor, who has recently put down a mass uprising led by a demagogic tribune of the people. The story takes place in the fortress residence of the Condor, outside the city on the Kasbah. Throughout the novel, the tribune is scheming to regain power; and the Condor responds by implementing increasingly repressive measures. The protagonist of the novel is a young historian, Michael Venator, whose double life as a bartender at the private nightclub of the Condors' generals gives him insider access to the power games of the elite. Venator is the prototype *Anarch*, Jünger's word for the conservative anarchist we encountered in *The Forest Passage*. The Anarch's subtle subversion consists of undermining the state by stealth rather than confrontation.

Venator operates computers with databanks full of sources on the history of past civilizations, and through a kind of virtual reality can transport himself back in time. The book appealed to three distinct audiences; to conservatives nostalgic about past worlds, to the war weary German middle-class eager to return to respectability, and to the young generation seeking an explanation for the catastrophic course of recent history. For the conservative temperament, Jünger described a period when the old values were in in decline and being replaced by machines of democracy. The protagonist projects medieval aristocratic values and Faustian personal perseverance in the face of defeat.

In October of 1982 the conservative Christian Democratic Party came to power under Chancellor Helmut Kohl. The end of the Social Democratic era was viewed as a turn (*Wende*) towards soft patriotism and an attempt to gradually come out from the shadows of the fascist past; to replace the politics of reparation and shame with a larger view of German history and Germany's place in the world that wasn't reducible to the twelve years of Nazi rule. Kohl famously said he had been born with the clemency of a late birth (he was born in 1930). The Chancellor turned to Jünger as an appropriate symbol of this fundamental shift in Germany's view of itself from a conservative perspective.

In same fall of 1982 Jünger was awarded the Goethe Prize, the most prestigious literary award in Germany, by the conservative city administration of Frankfurt am Main. The bestowal of the prize was greeted by howls of protest from hostile commentators across Germany and street demonstrations in the city of Frankfurt on the day of the ceremony. According to the critics, this award in the name of Germany's most hallowed humanist should not be bestowed on a writer who had "paved the way" for the rise of fascism in Germany.

A decade later, as Jünger approached his hundredth birthday, this unsympathetic sentiment had shifted towards a more favorable appreciation of an Olympian figure in whom many Germans could take pride. He was also honored with a visit in Wilflingen by Chancellor Kohl and French president Francois Mitterand on July 20th, 1993, the historical date of the failed Stauffenberg plot against Hitler. Jünger still had many critics, but the German public was prepared, some grudgingly, others enthusiastically, to accept the fact that Ernst Jünger's life work was pan-European, a century long and that his talents could be seen as on par, or at least approaching, the likes of the almost universally adored Goethe.

Jünger's place in the conservative European pantheon is hard to place. His younger self undoubtedly belonged to the generation of radicals who rejected the bourgeois state and welcomed the overthrow of the European order that had been tenuously re-established after 1918. He both foresaw and welcomed some combination of nationalism and socialism as a revolutionary solution in the 1920s and early 1930s but just as clearly rejected the actual party that carried out the coup in Germany after 1933. In the wake of two disastrous world wars, he predicted that modern technology and the growth of the power of the state would lead to planetary integration on a scale never seen before in human affairs (a phenomenon we today call globalization). In his late post-historical analysis, he predicted the decline and eventual eclipse of temporal and geographical particularity as European culture melted away to be replaced by a sterile planetary culture and a new cosmopolitan elite lacking specific cultural roots. The result, he feared, would be the rise of demagogues and tyrants who knew how to manipulate modern technology to play to the anxieties of the masses. The only answer for the individual would be to retreat to the security of an autonomous self, to become a forest wanderer, an Anarch. His life work offers a model for those who accept his cultural pessimism. But considering the decline in faith in politics in our own age, particularly among the young, the rise of petty tyrants and demagogues, and the current revolt against elites across the globe, his vision may also have been prophetic.

V.
L'Ernst Jünger in the Sky with Diamonds:
A Visit to Godenholm

One will search in vain for a single explicit reference to drugs or intoxication in *Visit to Godenholm.*[1] But since 1970, at the latest, when Jünger included the story in his encyclopedic exploration of narcotics and pharmaceutics, *Drogen und Rausch*, it is clear that an LSD or Mescalin trip was at the heart of the story. When the book was first published in 1952, many readers were somewhat at a loss as to what to make of this strange tale. The novel takes the psychologist Moltner, and historians of prehistory Einar and Ulma, on a boat trip to the Nordic island-estate of Godenholm to visit its owner Schwarzenberg, a philosopher, retired explorer and adventurer. The plot is austere, while the dazzling metaphors, symbols and visions are plentiful, erudite and esoteric. A reviewer in *Der Spiegel* in 1953 threw up his hands and concluded "All in all, the *Visit to Godenholm* is nothing more than typical Jünger, which means that it is written in crystal clear form, somewhat doctrinaire and doesn't connect with those who are not already followers of Jünger."[2]

The attention-shy author was perfectly prepared for such a reaction. "I knew from the beginning that that this slim volume wouldn't make an impression or have any success, and I felt almost sorry for the book, as if it were freezing when I saw it in the book store window."[3] On the other hand, his friends and acolytes sensed that the controversial and unpredictable writer was on to something new and quite un-frozen. Gottfried Benn read it three times enthusiastically and told Jünger while on a visit to Berlin, "This is the

---

1 *Besuch auf Godenholm* was originally published in 1952. Republished by Klett-Kotta in 1958 and 1978. The English version, *Visit to Godenholm*, was translated by Annabel Moynihan, with an introduction by Elliot Neaman (Stockholm: Edda, 2015).

2 Besuch auf Sklavenland," *Der Spiegel* (January 1, 1953), 33.

3 Ernst Jünger, *Sämmtliche Werke* (Stuttgart: Keltt-Cotta, 1978). Hereafter *SW*. vol. 11, 365.

cleverest thing you have yet written."[4] Benn offered a phallic interpretation to the mysteries of Godenholm, which Jünger honored as a creative misinterpretation, just as he himself had mis-read "ocean" [*Meer*] instead of "moor" [*Moor*] in one of Benn's most famous poems, *Gesänge*.[5]

Jünger notes that even his intelligent readers found the story hard to order into his other works ("*Schwer einordnen*").[6] In the 1950s few people knew about Jünger's friendship with Albert Hoffman, the Swiss chemist who synthesized LSD for the first time in 1938 as an experimental medication for animals. The drug made animals nervous, but did not appear to have any pharmaceutical applications. Nevertheless, Hoffman prepared it again in his laboratory in 1943, at which time he accidentally ingested a small amount. The first recorded LSD drug trip, which lasted several hours, was the result. In his memoir, *LSD: My Problem Child*, Hoffman recounts how he had sent Jünger a birthday greeting on March 29, 1947, presenting himself as an enthusiastic reader of *Das Abenteurliche Herz*, a book that was published in two very different versions in 1929 and 1938, and that contained references to psychotropic drugs. The two men corresponded regularly from then on, leading to a life-long friendship. Jünger was working on *Heliopolis* at the time, depicting one of the novel's characters, the binder of exotic books Antonio Peri, as an adventurer and seeker of knowledge who keeps a log for years of his drug experiments, voyages out into the "dream regions," to find the answers to "certain world puzzles."[7] Hoffman then recounts how, two years after the publication of *Heliopolis*, Jünger embarked on his own acid trip:

> Two years later, at the beginning of February 1951, came the great adventure, an LSD trip with Ernst Jünger. Since, up until that moment, there were only reports of LSD experiments in connection with psychiatric inquiries, this experiment especially interested me, because this was an opportunity to observe the effects of LSD on the artistic person, in a nonmedical milieu. That was still somewhat

---

4 *SW*, vol. 11, 371.
5 *SW*, vol. 11, 372.
6 *SW*, vol. 11, 365.
7 *SW*, vol. 16, 266-67.

before Aldous Huxley, from the same perspective, began to experiment with mescaline, about which he then reported in his two books *The Doors of Perception* and *Heaven and Hell.*

In order to have medical aid on hand, if necessary, I invited my friend, the physician and pharmacologist Professor Heribert Konzett, to participate. The trip took place at 10:00 in the morning, in the living room of our house in Bottmingen. Since the reaction of such a highly sensitive man as Ernst Jünger was not foreseeable, a low dose was chosen for this first experiment as a precaution, only 0.05 mg. The experiment, then, did not lead into great depths.

The beginning phase was characterized by the intensification of aesthetic experience. Red-violet roses were of unknown luminosity and radiated in portentous brightness. The concerto for flute and harp by Mozart was perceived in its celestial beauty as heavenly music. In mutual astonishment we contemplated the haze of smoke that ascended with the ease of thought from a Japanese incense stick. As the inebriation became deeper and the conversation ended, we came to fantastic reveries while we lay in our easy chairs with closed eyes. Ernst Jünger enjoyed the color display of oriental images; I was on a trip among Berber tribes in North Africa, saw colored caravans and lush oases. Heribert Konzett, whose features seemed to me to be transfigured, Buddha-like, experienced a breath of timelessness, liberation from the past and the future, blessedness through being completely here and now.[8]

In a key scene in *Visit to Godenholm*, Moltner has a vision: "The light began to crackle, a blue thread rose from the edge of the flame. Moltner watched it at first with surprise, then with delight, as if his eyes had been *given new powers* [my emphasis]." Looking back Jünger notes, "I credit the spectacle of the blue thread to a morning in Bottmingen" (that is, his visit to Hoffman's Swiss residence in February 1951), which he combined with a different inspiration, a visit to the South German town of Heuneburg, an important archeological Celtic site from the middle bronze period.[9] Here is to be found one of the keys to the book: that mind-altering substances

8 Albert Hoffmann, *LSD; My Problem Child*, trans. Jonathan Ott (Sarasota FL: MAPS, 2009), 159-60.

9 *SW*, vol. 11, 365.

extend conscious powers and open up vistas into the symbolic-geography of prehistory.

Hoffman is perceptive in linking the book *The Adventurous Heart* to the adventures in *Heliopolis* and to the *Visit to Godenholm.* The concept of *adventure* is in fact another hidden and sometimes not-so-hidden red thread sewn into the fabric of all of Jünger's writings. In one of the most insightful essays ever written on the topic, Georg Simmel defined the adventure as an out of order experience, without reference to all the neighboring parts of life: "it is like an island in life, which determines its beginning and its end according to its own visionary powers (*Bildungskräften*), and is not at the same time determined, as in the case of a part of a continent, by the one side or the other."[10] Moltner comes to Godenholm is in search of a spiritual adventure, something out of order, but he has his doubts that an island is the right place. "The surface was indeed solemn, Protestant, mercantile. It was boring, like reading a Scandinavian novel." But Schwarzenberg knows better: "The plan to assess the situation in small groups—and test their limits in experiments—was not so senseless. There was nothing new about this idea—there has always been such a plan during great transitions—in deserts, cloisters, in hermitages, in stoic and gnostic communities, in circles surrounding philosophers, prophets and initiates." The reference to a "great transition" clearly points to the geopolitical situation of Germany in the 1950s, a complete break with the past, as a defeated nation lay powerless against occupation and then control by the superpowers in both its Eastern and Western parts. We learn that Schwarzenberg had fled Germany for Finland just before the World War II broke out. He experienced the destruction of Germany from afar, and inverts the Fatherland metaphor, as the devastated country becomes now a woman, "a mother lying in the dust." But the story transcends the context in which it was born and offers a post-histoire commentary on the "apocalyptic fear" of modernity unmoored from all past anchors. One message in the bottle from Godenholm is a call for a return to an older version of science. We are told that Einar occupied himself with prehistory, "although he

10 Georg Simmel, Philosophische Kultur *Über das Abenteuer, die Geschlechter und die Krise der Moderne* (Berlin: Wagenbach, 1983), 14.

did not consider this term valid. He wanted people to talk about 'primordial history.'" Schwarzenberg is not an enemy of science, but rather practices it in the nineteenth-century fashion, when the endeavors were part of organic and coherent growth, unlocking revelations about nature, rather than what it has become today, an unconnected patchwork of branches. Later we learn that prehistory cannot be understood by the usual scientific designation, but is rather to be understood musically, as an overture of "magical incantations and prophetic dreams, beyond the measurable world." Drugs act as to facilitate this journey back to this primordial world, in which symbols act as signposts back into the womb, from which the cosmos emerged.

Following this motif, the re-discovery of primordial forms of knowledge and the possibility of rebirth are symbolized by engulfing waters and the repeated appearance of fishes. When the weather changes on the sea around Godenholm, a Golden Redfish rises up from the depths and Ulma stares at "large saucer-like eyes that lent it a primeval character." Jünger was a diligent student of symbolism and knew that the fish symbol was appropriated by the early Christians as an ancient sign of female fertility. The *Ichtus* is in fact shaped like a vulva turned sideways.[11] Moltner sinks into this water-world vision. Many fishes appear, a frightening blue shark with a slate skin, sea horses that rises from coral gardens, divine salmon, a pale sea eel. In Moltner's altered state of consciousness the "meaning of the fish and water" had been concealed to him until he grasps that his vision was "no longer water there were no fish anymore." Other animals appear as well: snakes, various birds, all versions of primordial gods and goddesses. The water is a form of amniotic fluid because in the final pages Moltner is reborn in a series of transformations, not unlike the hero of the *I Ching*, who traces through symbols the steps back to the origins of the universe.

Jünger does not allow the story to close with a resolution, nor does he attempt to tie all the pieces together. He wishes that every reader take the journey on his or her own. *Visit to Godenholm* might

---

11 Udo Becker, *The Continuum Encyclopedia of Animal Symbolism in Art* (London: Continuum, 1994). Originally published as Lexikon der Symbole, 1992.

best be compared to a *Vexierbild*, a picture or representation that, if one holds in the hand and turns one way or the other, transforms itself into different kinds of images. Gestalt pictures are the most familiar to us, though these kinds of brain tricks, distortions of the senses, reach back into the late Renaissance, as Giuseppe Arcimboldo's bizarre and proto-surrealist paintings manifest. Franz Kafka hit the nail on the head in his diary when he wrote that in *Vexierbilder*, the "hidden" appears as both distinct and invisible.[12] One might say the same thing about the island of Godenholm: its reality is occluded only for those who do not know how to redefine and see differently what is hidden in plain sight, with or without the help of consciousness-raising substances. This little gem of a book, here beautifully and expertly translated into English, is sure to delight anyone with a taste for exploration into those invisible but distinct mythological and cosmological realms that accompanied the birth of consciousness.

12 Ute Harbusch and Gregor Wittkop, *Kurzer Aufenthalt; Streifzüge durch literarische Orte* (Göttingen: Wallstein, 2007), "das Versteckte in einem Vexierbild sei deutlich unsichtbar. Deutlich für den, der gar nicht weiß, daß es etwas zu suchen gibt." 271.

VI.
Mutiny on Board Modernity:
Heidegger, Sorel and Soft Fascism

The work of Polish-born Israeli historian Zeev Sternhell and the German-born Berkeley philosopher Hans Sluga remain relevant because they demonstrate that fascism and Nazism were part of an early twentieth-century intellectual rebellion against universalism, liberalism, and Enlightenment rationalism. Western technology, values, and political institutions were seen as outmoded. Still, instead of wanting to return to the traditions of the past, as conservatives wished, these intellectuals thought that fascism could transcend modernity. Sorel, Heidegger, and other fascist modernists offered different radical solutions to what was conceived of as the decadence of liberal Western civilization. The question I pose below is whether or not the conservative-reactionary discontent with modernity of a century ago was a dead-end intellectual construction or a result of actual defects in modern life itself, which still haunt us today.

Hans Sluga's *Heidegger's Crisis: Philosophy and Politics in Nazi Germany* articulated how Germany's leading intellectuals of the interwar period, who were supposed to possess a broad understanding of German politics and societal reality, readily succumbed to the temptations of Nazi ideology.[1] Much ink has been spilled on Heidegger's relationship to fascism, but the originality of Sluga's work is that he showed how debates about Heidegger's complicity in Nazism fail to take into account the general development of German philosophy from Fichte to Nietzsche.[2]

In a series of brilliant intellectual portraits, Sluga established that German philosophers, starting around the turn of the 20th

1 Hans Sluga, *Heidegger's Crisis: Philosophy and Politics in Nazi Germany* (Cambridge MA: Harvard University Press, 1993.

2 Much of the recent scholarship revolved around the publication of Heidegger's Black Notebooks, see Richard Wolin, *Heidegger in Runs; Between Philosophy and Ideology* (New Haven: Yale University Press, 2023).

century, were shaken by the challenges to their profession posed by societal changes and the rise of the natural sciences. In response, these philosophers sought to construct a uniquely "German" basis for philosophy, distinct from the materialism and utilitarianism they attributed to French, British, and American thought. Sluga related these "crises" to a split in philosophy between radicals and conservatives; both camps, in different ways, helped set the stage for the rise of National Socialism.

Like Sluga's book, Zeev Sternhell's *The Birth of Fascist Ideology: From Cultural Rebellion to Political Revolution* (1995) placed fascism in the context of a broader reaction against the Enlightenment, rationalism, and the belief in progress. Where Sluga argued for the complicity of a wide range of German intellectuals in the fascist alternative to bourgeois society, Sternhell outlined a comparable development among important French and Italian sociologists, philosophers, and economists. As in his other books, he convincingly demonstrated that important strains of fascist ideology were present in the anti-materialistic reformulations of Marxism to be found in Georges Sorel, Edouard Berth, Arturo Labriola, Hubert Lagardelle, Enrico Leone, and other Italian and French theorists of radical syndicalism. In Sternhell's view, fascism could be seen as a movement that "corrected" Marx's economic critique of capitalism by leaving private property and "productive" capitalism in place, but shifting the active fight against exploitation and bourgeois society to a moral and "ethical" realm.

The Sternhell Argument

Zeev Sternhell's book on the ideological foundations of fascism was informed by a determination to expose the irresponsibility of intellectuals who denigrated ethics and academic integrity in favor of political crusades. In this way, as we will see, Sternhell's and Sluga's arguments were strikingly similar. Sternhell presupposed an explicitly liberal commitment to the universalism and humanism of the Enlightenment in order to build his case against the heterodox Marxists who, he claims, laid important theoretical foundations for Italian and French fascism. Those who would deny the validity of universalistic Enlightenment ethics faced the task of establishing some other criteria for the responsible interaction between ideas and politics. If Sternhell differed from Sluga, it was his willingness to explicitly embrace Enlightenment standards, rather than trying to draw a strict division between the two realms.

Sternhell established his reputation as an historian of the radical intellectual right in the Third Republic. His book on the preeminent nationalist, Maurice Barres, stressed the anti-Semitic and antiliberal tendencies in French ultra-patriotism.[3] In his second major work, he traced the emergence of Third Republic political movements that were both nationalist and socialist and whose aim was to overthrow the liberal order.[4] The book that followed, *Neither Left nor Right*, established Sternell's international reputation and was also the cause of a cause célébre among intellectuals in France, because he argued that French fascism was neither a foreign import, nor was France immune to fascism, but rather the ideology had long laid roots in prewar French culture.[5] Here Sternhell went beyond the rather uncontroversial, exhaustive chronicling of the various fringe groups on the right and presented two daring theses. First, he argued that the radical right was not composed of mere polemicists and cranks but also weighty thinkers who integrated the most advanced and sophisticated theories in contemporary social science and philosophy with elements of cultural modernism.

Sternhell argued further that out of this brew emerged a form of French fascism that was already well constructed by 1914 and did not need the events of the war to become consolidated or politically viable. French fascism, in other words, was homegrown, not a copy of Nazism or Italian corporatism. Second, Sternhell argued that a multitude of political thinkers on the right in the 1920s and 1930s, even when they never explicitly embraced the self-styled fascist parties in France, helped prepare the way for the collapse of the nation in 1940 through their antiliberal, xenophobic, and chauvin-

3 Zeev Sternhell, *Maurice Barrès et le nationalisme français* (Bruxelles : Editions Complexe, 1985); originally published by A. Colin, 1972.

4 Zeev Sternhell, *The Birth of Fascist Ideology*, trans David Meisel (Princeton University Press, 1989/1994).

5 Zeev Sternhell, *Neither Right nor Left; Fascist Ideology in France*, trans. David Meisel (Princeton: Princeton University Press, 1983/1995).

istic agitation. Collaboration, in other words, was a domestic product, not an expression of opportunism or partiality towards German culture. Sternhell's second thesis, in particular, raised the ire of many French intellectuals, not least among whom were right-wing figures personally discussed in the book, and, by implication, named as traitors to French democracy. One of them, Bertrand de Jouvenal, successfully sued Sternhell for defamation of character, though the court denied Jouvenal a total victory by imposing only a minor fine and allowing the book to remain on the market unchanged.

In *The Birth of Fascist Ideology,* Sternhell took on his critics, but he also learned from them. Gone was the exclusive preoccupation with the French genre of fascism and the related, but (he tacitly admitted) not entirely convincing attempt to blame a diverse group of intellectuals for a series of complex historical constellations (French military defeat, collaboration, anti-Semitism, etc.). Instead, Sternhell built on the strengths of his previous books. In particular, he developed the insight at the core of *Neither Right Nor Left*, that fascism was not just a hodgepodge of unrelated nationalist impulses, as had often been argued, or just another version of socialism (as Hayek argued in *The Road to Serfdom*), but rather constituted a coherent attempt to go beyond Marxism on the left, and beyond liberal capitalism on the right, to locate a third way, a unique alternative to the modern economic and social lifestyle.

Sternhell traced the genesis of this intellectual movement to both French and Italian sources, in particular the syndicalist critique of Marxism and the consequent replacement of the category of class with the more socially potent, integrative and revolutionary category of the nation state. One of the most fascinating elements of this third way was its dependence on a highly sophisticated critique of Marxist economics from the left, beginning in the 1880s, that was associated above all with the name of the French engineer and amateur philosopher Georges Sorel. Sorel was influenced by the French anarchist Pierre Joseph Proudhon, a contemporary of Marx, but also by advances in the science of economics that had put to rest many of the flawed predictions of Marx and demonstrated that much of Marxist theorizing about capitalism was seriously deficient. Two Italian economists, Enrico Leone and Arturo

Labriola, followers of Sorel, attempted to rescue the revolutionary potential of Marxism by reconstructing a new basis for socialism, this time grounded in more rigorous economic theory. In this endeavor, Leone and Labriola were influenced in part by their understanding of the marginal utility theory of the Austrian school of Carl Menger, Friedrich von Wieser, and Eugen von Böhm-Bawerk. They added a "hedonistic" component, which they drew from the sociologist Vilfredo Pareto: the concept that economics must take into account idiosyncratic egotistical drives when attempting to calculate general economic processes.

The Revolutionary Sorel

Sorel was neither an entirely original thinker nor one of the many heterodox Marxists who tried to recast and modernize the master's system. Somewhere between an innovator and an epigone, his thinking led him to abandon much of the content while retaining the revolutionary form of Marxism. His strength was his ability to digest a large amount of difficult contemporary theoretical work in economics and philosophy and, having read them in the original German, English, or Italian, recast them for French readers. His writings attracted a generation of young intellectuals seeking a belligerent confrontation with bourgeois society.

Sorel's work is characterized by an uneven and repetitious quality. Instead of logical, step-by-step arguments, he confronts the reader with a barrage of polemical, moral, and tendentious propositions. Like the "fascist style" of the Futurists, his writing is evocative, heroic, dynamic, and anti-bourgeois to the core. It does not invite counterargument or further discussion, but demands and implores affirmation or rejection without any shades of gray. Originally, Sorel was attracted to the moral content of Marxism, principally the youthful Marx's romantic rage against the injustice and exploitation perpetrated by capitalism against the working class. Inspired by Nietzsche in his reading of Marx, he saw in revolutionary socialist terminology a transvaluation of values, a hope for a fundamental departure from the European past. Like the German philosophers discussed by Sluga, Sorel saw his society as decadent and effete, and he hoped to help sweep it away and herald a new age.

He was repelled by the petty nature of parliamentary politics in the Third Republic and by what he considered to be the unbounded materialism and hedonism of the middle class. Early on, departing from the historical determinism of Marx, he envisaged the battle of the proletariat against the bourgeoisie as an heroic, spiritual, and ethical movement (ethical in the original Greek sense of "character-building"). Marxist doctrine left the transformation of human character to the inevitable tendencies of history, so Sorel took it upon himself to complete the system in this direction. He was searching for the metaphysical, spiritual foundation for a politics of self-determination below the scientistic veneer of Marxian economic analysis.

For Sorel capitalism was not the enemy but, as portrayed in the *Communist Manifesto*, an historically necessary dynamic and revolutionary process to be welcomed, indeed, propelled forward. Yet Sorel rejected the central tenets of *Das Kapital*, the theory of surplus value and the demand for the socialization of private property. Where Marx prophesied (rather than demanded) a future of reconciliation, peace, freedom, and prosperity in a classless society,[6] Sorel did not claim to know what the society emerging from the apocalyptic self-destruction of capitalism would look like, nor was this his concern. As with the anarchists, for Sorel constant revolutionary activity was an end in itself. He thus attacked reform socialists who wanted the state to intervene in the economy so as to ease

6 Mainly in the preparatory notes to *Kapital*, the *Grundrisse*, six unfinished notebooks were written in the winter of 1857-58 as a reaction to the economic panic of 1857, caused in part by the overexpansion of the U.S. economy. The California Gold Rush had led to an overexpansion of the money supply. The global economy was now interconnected in an unprecedented manner, and the crisis spread rapidly from the United States to Europe. The telegraph had been invented in 1844 and was partly to blame. In Great Britain, the Palmerston government took the nation off the gold standard, causing the panic to spread there. Marx believed that the crisis heralded the collapse of capitalism as he had predicted. Sorel would not have known about these notebooks, since they were not published until 1939 in German in Moscow, but Sorel would have been able to read the *Critique of the Gotha Programme* (1875), which outlined a golden age in which all needs would be satisfied, "from each according to his ability, to each according to his needs."

class conflict, and instead he defended a truly free market of independent producers. Social arrangements that promoted class struggle were positive, while those relations, whether socialist or liberal, that helped reconcile the classes were deleterious to the revolutionary cause.

In all of this, Sorel's aim was the self-determination and self-organization of the proletariat into a militant movement. Thus, his defense of the free market was coupled with a repudiation of the philosophical and legal framework of natural rights and private property. He advocated an unbridled Darwinian economics, which he viewed as the motor of progress and as the final arbiter of success and failure in the work of society. This linking of the free market to revolution, based not on future predictions, as with Marx, but programmatically driven forward by the ethical goals of Italian syndicalism, was, according to Sternhell, the "essential early element of Italian fascism" (47).

As Sorel moved away from Marxism, he transformed Marx's vision into the symbols and myths of an idealized workers' revolt, ending in an apocalypse of destruction. In contrast to Marx, Sorel saw nothing inevitable about the impoverishment of the workers or class warfare. In fact, the socialist reform movements of the late nineteenth century were, for him, evidence of the opposite: as bourgeois society rendered concession after concession to the workers, the latter became complacent and supportive of the established order. If their character were to be transformed, the workers would have to be moved by a grander vision of an orchestrated, intentional drive toward revolution. Without it, they would succumb to the same materialism that enveloped the middle class. Sorel's revision of Marxism amounted to an anti-materialist embrace of the market economy.

Having emancipated himself from a rationalist understanding of Marxism with the publication of *The Illusions of Progress* in 1899—a book that ends with the wish that "socialism be transformed into a philosophy of morals" (75)—Sorel was open to all those prewar social movements that rejected the ideas of the Enlightenment and political liberalism. Sorel's conversion to "integral nationalism[7]" (which Sternhell dates to the summer of 1909, when he published a series of articles praising Maurras and the Action Française) was thus a predictable intellectual transformation. Action Française was antimodern, chauvinistic, and mystically Catholic; its constituency comprised many of the anti-Dreyfusard forces of the Third Republic. It was also the strongest prewar French political movement.

Sorel's attraction to the nationalist right can be explained both by his contempt for the proletariat and by his shift toward intellectual circles that cultivated Nietzsche's philosophy of heroic values and loathed the decadence of bourgeois civilization. Proudhon was a hero for members of *Action Française*, who admired his anti-intellectualism, anti-republicanism, anti-Semitism, and opposition to universalistic Kantian philosophy, as well as his championship of the nation and the family. Nationalism and syndicalism converged on any number of fields, rejecting bourgeois materialism while elevating ties of blood, the nation, and power above capitalism, despised as a system of plutocracy and Jewish manipulation.

Sorel was not a crude chauvinist, but he did admire the capacity of the *Action Française* to energize and mobilize the masses in a way that socialism had gradually proved itself incapable[8]. In Sorel's eyes the nation now replaced the proletariat as the locus of

---

7 Integral nationalism refers to an inclusive and homogeneous, as opposed to an open and heterogeneous, nationalism. Citizenship laws are a good measure for distinguishing between the two: any human being born on United States soil automatically becomes a citizen, according to the Fourteenth Amendment, while the integral nationalism inherent in current German law grants citizenship only to children born of persons with German passports, automatically excluding the children of immigrants. The integral nationalism of the fascist epoch was, of course, more extreme, since being outside of the integral nation could mean physical annihilation.

8 Today's *Rassemblement National* (RN) mirrors *Action Française* in having the same dynamic of converting socialist and communist voters to nationalist anti-capitalism of the right, but they are fundamentally different in their political structures and historical context. The RN is a modern, populist political party seeking power through democratic elections, while the AF was a counter-revolutionary, monarchist movement that historically advocated for the violent overthrow of the republic, along the lines for which Sorel advocated.

a new mythology capable of overthrowing the existing order. With this intellectual move, Sorel had arrived at a syndicalist-nationalist synthesis, an essential ingredient of the coming age of fascist ideologies. "Syndicalism" originally referred to the tactics of the French trade union movement, strongest in the French General Confederation of Labor, which was founded in 1895. The syndicalist-nationalist synthesis, however, envisaged that the trade unions would replace the bourgeoisie as the dominant elite of society, and in the process, abolish property and the market economy and take the place of the government. In France, this anti-Marxist synthesis remained exclusively a theoretical option because the socialist movement, led by Jean Jaures, was prepared to work through the Chamber of Deputies for incremental improvement of the workers' living conditions. The political and social environment in Italy, by contrast, was much more conducive to an authentic nationalist-syndicalist revolution.

Italian Revolutionary Syndicalism

In Italy, the emergence of revolutionary syndicalism can also be traced to a rejection of the reformist, evolutionary approach of parties like the French Socialists and the German Social Democrats. In contrast to their French and German counterparts, Italian workers, who were not as industrialized and had little experience with reform socialism of a parliamentary nature, found Marxism less attractive. The anarchism of Mikhail Bakunin, with its stress on insurrectionism and direct action, had more appeal.[9] The Italian Socialist Party (ITP), under Filippo Turati, remained a moderate and impotent force during the prewar period. The Italian parliament was run by a series of unstable coalitions, put together by the shrewd tactician Giovanni Giolitti, who was able to manipulate both liberals and socialists into moving across party lines in return for political favors.[10]

9 Gaetano Salvamini, *The Origins of Fascism in Italy*. Trans. Roberto Vivarelli. (New York: 1973), 73 ff.

10 Benedetto Croce, *A History of Italy 1871-1915*. Trans. Cecilia Ady (New York: Russell and Russell 1963), 214-37.

Disgusted by the sheepishness of the party, Antonio Labriola created a radical faction in 1902 and then split with the party in 1907, appealing to the militant syndicates, which he hoped would begin a revolution in the factories.[11] A number of important theoreticians of syndicalism—Michele Bianci, Alceste De Ambris, Filippo Corradini—converted to this form of direct action and helped organize and execute a number of successful general strikes between 1904 and 1908 that brought the entire country to an economic standstill, but did not result in the general expropriation of the bourgeoisie or an end to parliamentary democracy.

In time, syndicalist Italian intellectuals began to despair of the General Strike and turned to war as a remedy for what they considered Italy's maladies. In 1911, when Italy invaded Libya to conquer colonial territory, many supported the campaign. The Union of Italian Syndicalists (USI) was divided in 1914 when confronted with the possibility that Italy would take the side of its allies, Germany and Austria-Hungary, in World War I. Some of the syndicalists wanted the government to remain neutral, and some, like Corradini, wanted Italy to defect from the "reactionary" allies and join the side of the probable victors, Britain and France, as a matter of Italy's national interest.[12] In October 1914, the anti-reactionaries left the USI and created the Fascio R*ivoluzionario d'Azione Internazionalista*, the first fascist organization (established a full five years before Mussolini's *Fascio di Combattimento*). Mussolini joined the movement immediately. Although Sternhell insists that the syndicalist-nationalist synthesis had "come to fruition" before 1914, he makes the important concession that the war was necessary to "greatly accelerate its evolution" (140). Since the argument that fascism emerged full-blown before 1914 is central to Sternhell's position, the admission that the war sped up the emergence of a nationalist-revolutionary synthesis raises the question: exactly how important was the war as a catalyst for fascism?

---

11 On Labriola see Serge Hughes, *The Fall and Rise of Modern Italy*. New York: Macmillan, 1967, 37-59.

12 A.J. De Grand, *The Italian Nationalist Association and the Rise of Fascism in Italy*. (Lincoln: University of Nebraska Press, 1978).

The Bolshevik Revolution of 1917 had the effect of deepening both the syndicalists' rejection of Marxism and their embrace of nationalism. Unlike the rank-and-file French syndicalists of the prewar period, the Italian theoreticians of syndicalism were firmly procapitalist. Not only did the elimination of capitalism seem fundamentally erroneous from an economic point of view, but they also agreed with the nationalists that Bolshevism was a threat to the nation. The immediate postwar years in Italy were darkened by a huge national debt, depression, and unemployment. Moreover, the army had been humiliated by its performance during the war, and the postwar settlement denied Italy its territorial and colonial spoils. In the midst of strikes and general unrest, Mussolini founded the fascist combat units, based on the nationalist-syndicalist synthesis that he had learned from reading Sorel and the syndicalist journals in which Leone and Labriola published.

Free-Market Fascism

Labriola was an accomplished economist as well as a practical politician who served as Labor Minister in Giolitti's postwar cabinet. He believed that the solution to Italy's economic problems lay in a corporatist blurring of the distinction between workers and owners. All who contributed to the economy would be recognized as "free producers" and organized according to socioeconomic communities of interest. The true opposition was not a conflict between workers and the owners of the means of production, but between free producers and "parasites" who do not contribute to national wealth.[13] Commercial capitalism was nonproductive because it was speculative and parasitical (and ostensibly run by Jews); industrial capitalism was productive and positive.

The competition between free producers would lead to the emergence of a new industrial elite embodying the "New Man," the heroic, creative, inventive Superman dreamed of by Nietzsche and other nineteenth-century opponents of bourgeois culture and Marxist rationalism. Labriola criticized Marxism for restricting its idea of economic exploitation to the proletariat. Labriola's ideal of a society

13 Ibid. 144.

of free producers, and that of Enrico Leone, was to be an economy freed of exploitation by reducing the intervention of the state to a minimum and allowing individuals to pursue their hedonistic goals without limitation. Like the economist Leon Walras, from whom they borrowed the idea of a "hedonistic" basis for the economy, Leone and Labriola argued that social harmony, the final goal of socialism, was possible if individuals followed the law of egoism. "Pure" economics was valid because it was based on human nature. Leone believed that a "liberist" economy would eradicate the forces that impeded equality among producers: the state, parliament, bureaucracy, the legal system, reform socialists, and above all, intellectuals.[14] In a situation of "natural equilibrium," which Leone based on the subjectivist marginal utility theory of the Austrian school, the worker would not be forced to produce more than would satisfy his own needs. The "economic moment" would be reached, in short, before the effort to achieve hedonistic goals became painful.

The goal of syndicalism was to bring the entire economy into this general state of equilibrium, in which workers produced and satisfied their needs and capitalists could not inflict pain—that is, accumulate surplus value. Exploitation would be replaced not by central planning, but rather by the operation of the natural laws of the marketplace and economic egoism. Marx was wrong to base his economics on history rather than hedonistic forces. Once the labor syndicates broke down the barriers to pure capitalism by means of the General Strike, both the bourgeoisie and the proletariat would have the same access to the means of satisfying hedonic urges.

Syndicalist theorizing about the "liberist" economy was, like Marxism, production-centered; that is, it favored forces that contributed to the creation of unlimited abundance.[15] Unlike Marxism, however, it opposed any kind of intervention that would disrupt the economy, whether Soviet-style planning or the incipient social-dem-

14 Ibid. 147.

15 The French philosopher and sociologist Raymond Aron once famously quipped that Marx wanted to turn the world into a giant workplace. The comment is a concise summary of Aron's broader critique of Marxism.

ocratic bourgeois state. And unlike Sorel, Labriola and Leone opposed violence; the General Strike was to have the sole purpose of creating an *esprit de corps* among the workers and imposing on them enough discipline so that they could one day take over the means of production from the parasitical bourgeoisie.

The myth of the General Strike became problematic because, despite its recurrent successful implementation, it did not lead to revolution. Disappointed with the proletariat's lack of will, syndicalist intellectuals became interested in the nationalists' advocacy of war as a means of overcoming complacency. In the journal *La Lupa*, articles by *Action Française* authors began appearing side by side with the syndicalists in 1910. Filippo Corradini forged the synthesis between national identity and syndicalist revolution. In contrast to the old reactionary nationalism of the regional Italian aristocracy, he spoke of cultural nationalism as a force that would inspire the new elite of producers. Racism, which animated the *Action Française*, could blend easily with the syndicalist ideal of a heroic proletariat.

In contrast to Hitler, Mussolini was a genuine intellectual and did possess a fairly sophisticated theoretical basis for his political program. Like other syndicalists, he had come to doubt the revolutionary potential of the proletariat. He organized the fighting units that later became the *Blackshirts*, the *squadristi* as the avant-garde of a mass revolt against bourgeois democracy. But because Mussolini distrusted the workers' ability to revolt spontaneously, he regarded the entire nation as in danger of sinking into bourgeois decadence. Therefore the entire nation, not just the working class, had to be the locus of a revolution.

The main components of revolutionary syndicalism were taken up in Mussolini's evolution from Marxism, toward revisionism, radical nationalism, and, finally, fascism. Mussolini added a theory of elites based on the sociology of Vilredo Pareto, whom he studied while in Lausanne from 1904 to 1905. Pareto taught that history saw a constant succession of elites, the vigorous ones replacing the exhausted. Mussolini believed the time had come for the revolutionary syndicalist elite to take over from the exhausted worker's movement.

Apart from this elitism, though, Mussolini's disillusionment with Marxism duplicated much of the intellectual journey already taken by Sorel, Labriola, Leone, and other syndicalist intellectuals. Although one may want to view fascism as a revolt against modernity, it is clear from Sternhell's account that by embracing an ideal of economic freedom and championing allegiance to the state, the fascists attempted to incorporate key modern institutions into their vision. While it is true that nationalist fervor is anti-universalistic and thus a departure from the spirit of the Enlightenment, the same can be said of contemporary postmodernism and communitarianism.

None of these movements repudiate the main features of modern society. In fact, the resemblances may indicate the deep roots of these characteristics that, for all their disgust with the European status quo, fascist thinkers ended up apotheosizing the free market and the nation-state. Sternhell's illumination of the intellectual origins of "Roman" fascism dovetails nicely with Sluga's research on the crisis of modern German philosophy, which, he argues, is the indispensable background to Heidegger's fateful engagement with National Socialism. The fact that syndicalism had a decisive influence on Mussolini's political career, while Heidegger was "merely" a philosopher, should not distract us from the relevance of comparing the two intellectual traditions. Like Italian fascism, National Socialism was an attempt to transcend modernity, even if Hitler did not absorb much of the sophisticated philosophical heritage available to him. Heidegger's attraction to the fundamental tenets of National Socialism, which lasted, as we now know, far beyond his rectorship period, tells us that he saw in it the potential for solving what he considered to be the crisis of Western civilization. The comparison throws light, therefore, not only on some of the deeper sources of the European mutiny against modernity, but also—since some would point to a continuing crisis—why the radical impulses of that revolt have not subsided in our "postmodern" age.

The "Affaire Heidegger"

Sluga, whose philosophical roots were in logical positivism, turned his attention to Heidegger as a result of a series of debates initiated by the publication of Victor Farias's book, *Heidegger and National*

Socialism, originally published in France in 1967.[16] Heidegger had enjoyed a positive reception in the French intellectual community in the 1980s, mainly as a result of Derrida, Foucault, and a host of lesser postmodernist philosophers who were indebted to Heidegger's linguistic orientation (which stressed etymology and diachronic shifts, gaps, and concealment of meaning). The Farias bombshell shocked French intellectuals, who seemed to have suffered from amnesia regarding the well-documented association of Heidegger with Nazi politics.[17] Not only was there very little that was new in Farias's allegations, but even if French intellectuals did not know the vast evidence that we have today about Heidegger's Nazi-aligned views, much of the debate about Heidegger's activities as rector of the University of Freiburg in 1933, at a minimum, had already been carried out in the pages of Sartre's review, *Les Temps Modernes*, in 1946 and 1947.[18] In Germany, the research of Hugo Ott and Guido Schneeberger had also uncovered most of the pertinent facts about Heidegger's Nazi period known at that time.[19] One positive result of the Farias book was to provoke a new and extended examination of the relationship between Heidegger's philosophy and his politics. But the increasingly rancorous debate focused almost exclusively on Heidegger's activities and writings, without considering the intellectual and political context in which his ideas developed.[20] Sluga ventured beyond moralizing and psychologizing, focusing instead on the substantial interaction between philosophy and politics before 1933.

---

16 Viktor Farias, Hei*degger and Nazism*. Trans. Paul Burrell and Gabriel Ricci. (Philadelphia: Temple University Press, 1988).

17 Richard Wolin, *The Heidegger Controversy: A Critical Reader*. New York: Columbia University Press, 1991).

18 Anson Rabinbach, "Heidegger's Letter on Humanism as Text and Event." *New German Critique*, 62, 1994: 3-38

19 Guido Schneeberger, *Nachlese zu Heidegger. Dokumente zu seinem Leben und Denken*. (Bern, 1962: no publisher listed). See also Neske, Günther, and Kettering, Emil., *Martin Heidegger and National Socialism*. (New York: Paragon House, 1990). And Hugo Ott, Martin Heidegger: *Unterwegs zu seiner Biographie* Frankfurt: Campus, 1988).

20 Jacques Derrida, Richard Wolin, Didier Eribon, and Thomas Sheehan, "L'Affaire Derrida." *New York Review of Books* 41, 1993 (5): 65-67.

Sluga's book emerged as a result of discussions carried out at Berkeley, beginning in 1987, in an informal reading group that included the intellectual historian Martin Jay and the Heidegger specialist Hubert Dreyfus. Sluga's research undertakes to correct what this group saw as a deficient historical perspective on Heidegger's works. In the process, Sluga's study exposed how neither the indictment nor the defense of Heidegger touches on the more substantial question of how German thinkers, from Fichte forward, problematically integrated political issues into philosophy, and how this entire tradition was inextricably bound up in the cultural revolt that led to fascism. In other words, the singular focus on the fascistic elements of Heidegger's philosophy can obscure deeper issues inherent in the German intellectual tradition of integrative politics disguised as philosophy.

It should already be clear that this style of philosophy as cultural revolt was not a phenomenon restricted to Germany. On the eve of the catastrophe of the World War I, the mood of the intellectuals across Europe was unmistakably gloomy and exhausted. Despite the marvels of science and technology, despite the unprecedented rise in the standard of living of the masses, many felt that bourgeois Europe, with its dull routines and deadening bureaucracy, was a dying, exhausted culture. T. S. Eliot's poem "The Waste Land," though published in 1922, reflected the feelings of senselessness, irrationality, loneliness, and terror of modern life that made the coming of war in 1914 seem like relief and a possibility of renewal. Likewise, when W. B. Yeats wrote that European society, "that rough beast, its hour come around at last . . . slouches toward Bethlehem to be born," he expressed the hope that from the death of bourgeois culture in war, a changed civilization might emerge. The virulent antisemite and later propagandist for Mussolini, Ezra Pound, was more pessimistic. He wrote bitterly that the young soldiers had died "for an old bitch gone in the teeth, for a botched civilization."[21]

Although after the war many would wax nostalgic about the seeming innocence and stability of *fin-de-siecle* Europe, in fact, it

21 Paul Fussell, ed., *The Norton Book of Modern War.* (New York: Norton, 1990), 200.

was a period riven by social tensions and nationalistic conflicts that added to the intellectuals' feeling of impending doom. Historians have pointed out that in the countries that eventually fought each other in 1914, intractable problems involving women's rights, nationality, and class were solved only by the coming of war, and in fact may have been part of the cause of it. In England, struggles over the suffragettes and the Irish question overwhelmed the inflexible English parliamentary system and called out for more radical solutions.[22] In Germany, the achievement of a Social Democratic majority in the Reichstag elections of 1912 moved the Kaiser to consider disbanding parliament. Had the Great War not come, a civil war in Germany was a very plausible scenario.[23] In Spain, from 1917 to 1921, peasants rose up in the south and seized land, officers mutinied and Basques in the north fought against the central government. In France insurrectionary strikes, worker's revolts, and a mobilization of the extreme nationalist right threatened to undermine parliamentary rule.

The Third Republic had never been stable, shaken as it was by changing coalitions, scandals, and deep social division.[24] In Germany, the humiliation of defeat made it difficult to adjust to the reality that the old world was never coming back. Germany was seen by many as a hostile force, as threatening and vengeful as the hated enemies who had saddled Germany with the entire responsibility for the war.[25] When Heidegger began his career as a philosopher in the 1920s, he positioned himself against the *status quo* as an alienated and angry thinker who yearned for a new political beginning.

The Conservative Revolution

Pierre Bourdieu's influential *The Political Ontology of Martin Heidegger* (1991) places Heidegger squarely in the tradition of what

22 See George Dangerfield, *The Strange Death of Liberal England* (New York: Putnam, 1961).

23 James Joll, *The Second International 1889-1914* (Boston: Routledge & Kegan Paul, 1974), 145 ff.

24 Wohl, op. cit. 138.

25 Dagmar Barnouw, *Weimar Intellectuals and the Threat of Modernity* (Bloomington: Indiana University Press, 1988).

has been called the "Conservative Revolution" in Germany. This label has been applied to a diverse lot of thinkers—Oswald Spengler, Moeller van den Bruck, Ernst Jünger, Carl Schmitt, and others—who supposedly were united in their attempt to establish a purely Germanic anti-liberalism that was at once more revolutionary and more modern than orthodox Marxism. For Bourdieu, Heidegger belongs in this category because he undermined the only German tradition of humanism derived from the Enlightenment: neo-Kan-tianism. In contrast to other forms of German Idealism, Kantian philosophy was explicitly universalist in scope and thus could not be pressed into the service of historicism or cultural chauvinism. Sluga demonstrates, however, that simply equating Heidegger's anti-Kantianism with anti-humanism fails to take into account the fact that by 1918 the neo-Kantians no longer dominated the philosophical landscape in Germany. More importantly, Bourdieu's scheme leaves out all the other German schools and philosophers who, it turns out, were far from the humanistic and Enlightenment tradition that the rise of Nazism supposedly interrupted. Philosophy during the Weimar years was as divided and polarized as the political spectrum, which ran the gamut from extreme left to extreme right, every gradation with its own party. The neo-Kantian school still attracted a large following, but so did such logical positivists as Gottlob Frege and Ernst Mach. There was the essentially apolitical phenomenological method of Edmund Husserl, on the basis of which not only Heidegger, but a number of other more conventional philosophers, developed their ideas. There were right-wing and left-wing Nietzscheans and an entire spectrum of Nietzsche-influenced philosophers in between. There was also a wide range of Marxist philosophy, from orthodox to reform, and there were schools of philosophical anthropology and neo-Thomism. In each of these tendencies, furthermore, there were more humanistically minded and more scientifically minded factions, and divisions between realists and idealists, pragmatists and dogmatists, and so on.

Philosophical Radicals and Conservatives

In order to make sense of these complexities, Sluga offers a basic distinction between philosophical conservatives and philosophical radicals. The essential difference, he tells us, was whether one wanted to revive the great classical period of German philosophy that began with Kant's Critique of Pure Reason (1781) and ended with Hegel, or whether one was attached to the more radical hermeneutical and phenomenological schools inspired by Nietzsche and Dilthey.[26] Although this distinction is still somewhat misleading in lending itself to the impression of homogeneity within each group that Sluga criticizes in Bourdieu, it does bring the historical context of Heidegger's involvement in Nazi politics into clearer focus. The split between philosophical radicals and the conservatives during the Weimar period was especially dangerous because it became entangled in the polarization between republicans and antidemocrats that the Nazis would exploit so skillfully. Philosophical opponents turned into political enemies. After World War II, Heidegger defended himself by pointing out that Oskar Becker, a conservative Idealist, had reported Heidegger to Alfred Rosenberg's ideological office as a dangerous, Jew-loving phenomenological radical. Heidegger failed to mention that he, too, managed to ruin the careers of young academics whom he disliked, and that he was responsible for cleansing the Freiburg philosophy department of Jews. The politicization of philosophy was widespread and served the Nazi strategy, which was to transform all intellectual life into an ideological struggle between so-called pro- and anti-Germans. Sluga suggests two possible interpretations of how the philosophers of the 1930s reacted to the new political circumstances. On the one hand, both camps can be seen as ingratiating themselves with the new Nazi order, but as interpreting what this demanded in different ways. Alternatively, the two camps can be seen as having entirely different philosophical and political agendas, but as sharing similar theoretical assumptions, such as anti-positivism and an aversion to empiricism. Sluga suggests that these alternatives are not mutually exclusive and that both contain elements of the truth. A mood of deep crisis pervaded intellectual life and virtually everyone felt that extraordinary decisions would have to be taken in a time of danger. The subjective belief in (rather than the objective certainty of) a crisis undermined many intellectuals' faith in the liberal-democratic

26 Sluga, Heidegger's Crisis, op.cit. 12.

order, leading them to see National Socialism as an opportunity for philosophy to make a practical contribution to shaping Germany's destiny. This belief, was one that Heidegger shared not only with many of his contemporaries, but with an entire tradition since Fichte.

One problem with Sluga's classification of radicals and conservatives is that it leaves out certain important figures who did not succumb to the siren call of the Nazis for the sake of advancing their own version of philosophical truth. Karl Jaspers, Ernst Cassirer, Karl Lowith, and the philosophers of the Frankfurt school such as Theodor Adorno and Walter Benjamin are never discussed by Sluga. Jaspers, for example, although he his came wife from an orthodox Jewish family, could have bent with the prevailing wind and saved his career, had he been a man of less moral rectitude.[27] Of course, these figures were marginalized, cast out from the beginning because of their religion or radical politics[28]. But there were other philosophers who chose not to go along with the politics of the day. One who comes to mind is Nicholas von Hartmann (a figure Sluga mentions only in passing), a recluse who turned inward and quietly wrote book after book, surviving the Third Reich without doing anyone any harm. In the end, Sluga has chosen to tell another story, the narrative of a pervasive crisis, and he thus narrows the parameters in order to bring the picture into clear focus. Like Fritz Ringers devastating portrait of German academics in *The Decline of the German Mandarins* (1969), Sluga's book undoubtedly captures main

27 Jaspers was forced into retirement from his teaching position at the University of Heidelberg in 1937 and received a publication ban in 1938. Despite immense pressure to divorce, including threats of deportation to a concentration camp, Jaspers refused to leave his wife. The couple remained under constant threat until Heidelberg was liberated by American troops in 1945.

28 I thank Eduardo Mendieta for pointing out that it was Jaspers who convinced the American military authorities not to bomb the beautiful medieval city of Heidelberg, even though the Nazis had set up command headquarters in its old castles. Jaspers succeeded in persuading the Americans that the city was a cultural treasure for the whole world. In a parallel fashion, Jaspers would not condemn all of German philosophy just because some German philosophers anticipated or adopted National Socialism.

trends in the German intellectual community over a much larger time span. The question remains, however, whether this sweeping damnation accurately reflects the variations and counterexamples which are also part of the tradition. One might also ask if, by concentrating on the villains rather than more exemplary figures, did Sluga perhaps inadvertently excuse Heidegger's deep entanglement in Nazism by making them seem part of an inescapable web?

Was Fichte a protofascist?

Sluga traced four major concepts that characterize Heidegger's' thought: crisis, nation or race, leadership, and order. He contended that these concepts played a decisive role in encouraging an "extreme form of Europeanism," which politicized philosophical ideas in the name of saving Europe from the threat of non-European states and races. Of all of the works of the great post-Kantian Idealist philosopher Johann Gottlieb Fichte (1762-1814), none is perhaps more closely associated with his name than a series of lectures given in 1807 in Berlin, a city occupied at the time by Napoleon. A year earlier, in Jena, the Prussians had suffered a humiliating defeat at the hands of Napoleon. Fichte stood at the lectern as an official representative of the King of Prussia and addressed his countrymen on the somber topic of the future of the German nation. For Fichte, the turmoil of the French Revolution and the conquests of the new French Revolutionary Army had left the German people in a deep existential crisis. The Holy Roman Empire, within which hundreds of states, some miniscule, some substantial, coexisted in a loose juridical and administrative structure, was hopelessly moribund compared to the vital and unified French nation. In his Addresses to the German Nation, Fichte undertook to point to a way out of the crisis and to speculate about the future of Germany. He interpreted the role of philosophy as explicitly political; his words were not to be construed as mere detached, scholarly observations, but rather interjections into the course of world history. He even compared his lectures to a new gospel for a new age.

To Fichte, the Germans possessed two things of extraordinary and unique value: their language and their culture. The German language made German thought primordial and untouched by foreign influences, its culture more profound and authentic. Only the ancient Greeks possessed something of comparable worth. Heretofore, however, education into this culture, *Bildung*, was directed solely toward the cultivation of the individual. Now, in its hour of crisis, education must serve the future of the German nation. Young people should not view education as self-development, but rather as spiritual and practical labor for the benefit of the collective. Indeed, Fichte outlined a new kind of education, in which students would participate collectively not only in learning, but in military and manual labor so as to be prepared to serve the German state. When the Nazis came to power, the universities were reformed along lines Fichte had envisaged.

The extent to which Fichte's philosophy can be seen as "protofascist" is still a subject of some debate. Fichte's defenders point out that the crucial elements of biological determinism and racism were entirely absent from his thought. They argue that like his mentor, the romantic and *Sturm und Drang* theologian and literary critic Johann Gottfried Herder (1744-1803), Fichte saw all cultures, rooted in particular historical and linguistic configurations, as unique and valuable. He wanted the Germans to become conscious of their own cultural roots, but not lord over other peoples.[29] Sluga took an unambiguous stand against Fichte on this matter. "Fichte can truly be called a forerunner of what happened under the Nazis," he writes.[30] Without going too deeply into the controversy over Fichte's legacy, Sluga might have made his case even stronger had he shown how Fichte not only glorified the German language as a "whole" and "organic" *Ursprache*, but also compared German to the "disintegrative, cold, soulless Latin tongue," which only articulates abstract concepts such as "humanity" and "liberalism," ideas "deeply foreign" to the German "essence." Using this kind of language, Fichte established a model of German particularism that consciously imitates a supposed Greek profundity against the emptiness of Roman (and

29 Isaiah Berlin, "The Magus of the North." *New York Review of Books* 40, 1993 (15): 64-71.

30 Sluga, op.cit. 41.

later American) superficiality. Fichte's high hopes for German Idealism continued to exert a seductive power over German intellectuals, but with the rise of industrial society and the natural sciences in the nineteenth century, German philosophy lost its position as the theoretical arbiter of knowledge. At the end of the eighteenth-century Kant's grand project had been to restore to philosophy the role of stipulating, a priori, epistemological rules governing the human capacity to arrive at certain judgments about the external world, not only in the realm of empirical science, but also in the intersubjective realms of morality, religion, and aesthetics. But by the end of the nineteenth century, philosophy seemed on the verge of becoming an antiquated and irrelevant subject. Its only chance for rejuvenation was to search for a radical new beginning beyond the methodology and successes of the natural sciences. The most important pioneer in this undertaking was undoubtedly Nietzsche.

Was Nietzsche a Protofascist?

Not surprisingly, to tackle the Heidegger Question, Sluga first took up the Nietzsche Question, equally as vexing to historians of ideas: In making the case for the prosecution, Sluga pointed to Nietzsche's insistent affirmation of what enhances, strengthens, deepens, extends, or prolongs the experience of living in the world, and his denigration of what denies, degrades, or weakens it. This life-affirming orientation, in Sluga's view, had nationalistic implications even though it supplanted the explicit nationalism of Nietzsche's youth, when he hailed Richard Wagner as a German Homer, an artist who could provide a coherent and unified cultural expression for the German people. After the establishment of the German Empire (which he supported and for which he enlisted in the army as a stretcher carrier), Nietzsche became disillusioned with what he considered the philistine and unheroic culture of Wilhelmine Germany. In some of his writings, such as *The Genealogy of Morals* (1887), he seems to condone and even encourage the political use of violence, as when he sings the praises of ancient German tribes whose vital instincts were enhanced by raping and pillaging.[31] It is true that he found the reigning anti-Semitism of his day stupid and vulgar; he didn't want his writings to be used to support anti-Semites, and he said so unambiguously.[32] But his tirades against the unsalutary influence of Christian morality in Western culture, which he in turn traced to origins in Judaism, left his writings open to exploitation by the new populist, aggressively nationalist, and xenophobic right of Wilhelmine Germany.[33]

Sluga also condemned Nietzsche's apotheosis of the *Übermensch*, although it is a notoriously vague concept. Literally translated as "Superman," the term describes the self-contained individual, an autonomous breaker of cultural idols that inhibit life, one who possesses every attribute missing in the philistine, the dry academic, the snob and the cultural connoisseur. Nietzsche's idol is the aristocratic warrior, with the self-consciousness of being lord and master, while the bourgeoisie is embodied in Nietzsche's "Last Man," the final example of an inferior, slave mentality. Much of Nietzsche's hatred for nineteenth-century liberalism, social Darwinism,

---

31 Friedrich Nietzsche, *On the Genealogy of Morals*, trans. Walter Kaufmann and R. J. Hollingdale (New York: Vintage, 1967), I.11. See also Nietzsche's critique of "German culture" in *Twilight of the Idols*, "What the Germans Lack," in *Twilight of the Idols / The Antichrist*, trans. R. J. Hollingdale (London: Penguin, 1990), 29–40. Trans. Francis Golffing. (New York: Doubleday, 1956). 174.

32 For Nietzsche's explicit rejection of contemporary antisemitism, see Friedrich Nietzsche to Franz Overbeck, 30 July 1881, in *The Nietzsche–Overbeck Correspondence*, ed. and trans. Bruce Dundas (Chicago: University of Chicago Press, 1992), 112–13; see also Nietzsche to his sister Elisabeth, 29 March 1887, in *Selected Letters of Friedrich Nietzsche*, ed. and trans. Christopher Middleton (Chicago: University of Chicago Press, 1969), 262–63. In these and related letters, Nietzsche denounces the antisemitic movement as vulgar and deplores attempts to appropriate his work for any such endeavor.

33 For the way his critique of Christian morality (and its Jewish roots) could be appropriated by völkisch and nationalist readers, see Friedrich Nietzsche, *On the Genealogy of Morals*, trans. Walter Kaufmann and R. J. Hollingdale (New York: Vintage, 1967), I.7–14; Friedrich Nietzsche, *The Antichrist, in Twilight of the Idols / The Antichrist*, trans. R. J. Hollingdale (London: Penguin, 1990), §§24–27. On the right-wing reception of Nietzsche, see Steven E. Aschheim, *The Nietzsche Legacy in Germany, 1890–1990* (Berkeley: University of California Press, 1992), 23–62.

socialism, and all varieties of mass politics can be attributed to his almost obsessive fear that these forces in modern Europe were creating the exact opposite of the superman, a monotonous product of conformist, mass society. In order to create supermen, Nietzsche even speaks of "forming the future man through breeding and, on the other hand, the annihilation of millions of failures."[34] This kind of language was, of course, not difficult for the Nazis to interpret literally and for Goebbels to exploit his works in the service of the new regime[35]. At other times, however, in passages where Nietzsche's tone is less shrill, the superman sounds like nothing more than a nonconformist, aristocratic intellectual with anarchistic and revolutionary impulses, someone not much different than Nietzsche himself.[36] Since Nietzsche's style was poetic and evocative, his unsettling and rebellious tone resonated with groups all across the political spectrum, including even those whom he opposed, such as feminists and socialists. Nietzsche's bitterness pours out across the page like a hailstorm, yet Sluga notes that the Nazis were uneasy about the legacy of Nietzsche's philosophy. It was the dubious accomplishment of Elisabeth Forster-Nietzsche, the philosopher's sister, to establish the Nietzsche archives at Weimar as a kind of shrine to the Nazi worldview. But Hitler admitted never having read Nietzsche's works, though he praised him and assimilated many Nietzschean ideas second-hand.

After the Nazis seized power, ideology became less important as practical strategies for holding power became crucial. By the time the war began in 1939, Alfred Rosenberg's position as chief ideologue of the Nazi movement had been considerably weakened in the struggle with Goebbels over cultural appropriation of German philosophy. Historians of the Third Reich are of one mind that Machiavellian technicians of power, like Goring, Speer, Bormann, and

34 Ibid., 643.

35 See David B. Dennis, "Culture War; How the Nazi Party Recast Nietzsche," https://ecommons.luc.edu/cgi/viewcontent.cgi?article=1031&context=history_facpubs

36 See Max Whyte, "The Uses and Abuses of Nietzsche in the Third Reich; Alfred Bäumler's 'Heroic Realism'," *Journal of Contemporary History* (43: 2, 2008), 171-194.

Himmler, had the highest positions in Hitler's regime, while the ideologues, such as Rosenberg and Streicher, were marginalized.[37] As minister of propaganda, Goebbels still held much power and was primarily responsible for keeping morale high during the war. At the battle of Stalingrad, he quoted Nietzsche's famous maxim "that which does not kill me makes me stronger." As the war dragged on, he resorted to trivial forms of entertainment to keep people's attention diverted from the mounting toll the war was taking on Germany. Nietzsche and his ideas played a minor role in Goebbels's increasingly shrill propaganda tirades, in which it was, of course, Hitler, not Nietzsche, Fichte, or Schiller, or Beethoven, who was touted as Germany's greatest genius.

If the question of Nietzsche's contribution to the rise of Nazism remains unanswered, his influence on Heidegger and other radicals of the Weimar period is easier to trace. As we have argued, both Fichte and Nietzsche could be accommodated in the pantheon of Germanic heroes who were crudely assimilated into National Socialist ideology. But among philosophers, who were well aware of the the theoretical and methodological differences between these two very distinct thinkers, a conflict erupted over the question of whether Fichte or Nietzsche best represented the contribution of philosophy to the new nationalist movement. In this dispute, Fichte was hoisted on the flag of the conservative philosophers who longed for a return of the days when classical Idealism was the reigning queen of the sciences. The radicals seized on Nietzsche, whom they hoped would lead to an entirely new beginning in German philosophy.

The Conservatives under the Swastika

Of the two groups, the conservatives were the better organized. Two associations in particular, the Fichte Society and the German Philosophical Society (DPG), constituted the conservative institutional anchors. The figures who set the tone in these societies are today

37 Karl Dietrich Bracher, *The German Dictatorship*. Trans. Jean Steinberg. London: Penguin, 1980). 117.

largely and justifiably forgotten. Sluga can be commended for wading through the dusty tomes of such philosophers as Hermann Schwarz, Max Wundt, Felix Krueger, Hugo Fischer, Arthur Hoffman, and racial theorists such as Hans Guenther, whose work was key to Nazi race "science." Of all the conservatives, only the writings of Nicolai Hartmann and Arnold Gehlen have survived the ravages of time beyond historical interest. Gehlen wielded considerable influence in the postwar intellectual milieu of the Federal Republic. Gottlob Frege and Heinrich Rickert lent some respectability at the beginning to the German Philosophical Society, but they were not at the center of events. The leader was Bruno Bauch, the founder and leader of the society. Today his books make painful reading. But his ideas serve Sluga well in his attempt to show how ingrained were the nationalistic prejudices of German philosophers long before Hitler came upon the political scene. We learn of Bauch's 1916 article, "On the Concept of the Nation," which argued that Jews could never love the fatherland since they were an alien people. (Sluga could have emphasized the irony of this statement, since at that very moment Jews were fighting and dying for Germany in the trenches of France.) Bauch was terrified that German culture was dying, especially after Germany's defeat in 1918. He regarded the existentialists who followed Kierkegaard and Nietzsche as symptomatic of decadence and pleaded incessantly for a return to a realm of objective values, invoking Plato, Augustine, and Kant as upholders of truth, God, and the Good. After 1933, Bauch and the like-minded in the DPG were only too willing to grasp at the straw the Nazis held out. Sluga emphasized repeatedly that given the sense of pervasive crisis, many were convinced that the normal restraints on power could be abandoned. In this situation, men who were normally cautious and suspicious of change allowed themselves to be collaborators in the catastrophic course of Nazism.

For the conservatives, the emergence of National Socialism seemed to offer a chance of returning to the educational system that existed before the rise of the natural sciences. In such a system, which was hierarchical and elitist, philosophers would dominate highly selective universities. The conservatives dreamed of a new cultural elite that would guide National Socialism according to a program of reconstituted German Idealism.

Philosophic Radicals

That the radicals were only loosely organized may be explained by their status as individualists and outsiders. Besides Heidegger, Sluga focuses on the writings of Alfred Bäumler and Ernst Krieck. These three formed an alliance in 1933, but soon afterwards fell out with one another. The short-lived coalition was based on two central interests: the reformation of the German university and the Nietzschean critique of Idealism. Unlike the conservatives, Heidegger, Bäumler, and Krieck sympathized with the unemployed and disillusioned young veterans who agitated for a modernized curriculum, more practical training, and access to higher education for workers and previously excluded groups. The Nazis were able to win much support from students by promising to reform the German university along these lines. Since their theoretical origins were in Nietzsche and hermeneutics, the radicals also rejected the Idealist program of the conservatives. A student of Husserl's anti-systematic phenomenological method who was also persuaded by Nietzsche's claim to have overcome Western metaphysics, Heidegger interpreted the vocation of philosophy as a search for radically new beginnings. In this endeavor the entire German people, not just the intellectuals, had to become involved. History had called upon German culture to initiate a break with the past as decisive as Greek science had been.

With the Nazi revolution at hand, Heidegger thought the opportunity to change world history had arrived. These beliefs established a conjunction of interests between Heidegger and the other radicals, who wanted to reformulate the relationship between German philosophy and the state. Bäuemler, originally a fairly conventional specialist in Kantian aesthetics, became attracted to the "heroic realism" represented by young conservatives and nationalist youth after World War I. Bemoaning Germany's defeat and the "feminine" culture of Weimar, he turned to Hegel, Kierkegaard, Nietzsche, and romantic anthropology in a search for the foundations of a soldierly and masculine form of politics (an early version of the alt-right and the "Manosphere" By concentrating on the militant and aggressive side of Nietzsche, Bäuemler was able to turn the reticent philosopher into a bloodthirsty fascist in a book published in 1931 with the revealing title of *Nietzsche as Philosopher and Politician.*[38] On May 10, 1933, Bäumler gave his inaugural address at the University of Berlin, in which he spoke of the new political revolution in Germany and the role that the university must play in "spiritually" guiding it. That evening, the famous burning of works considered decadent and Jewish took place in front of the Berlin Opera. Bäumler joined the students in tossing thousands of books into the fire.

Less than two weeks after the auto-da-fé of books, Ernst Krieck also discussed the issue of philosophy's role in the new regime in his inaugural address as rector of the Goethe University of Frankfurt. Krieck's style and philosophical interests were much different than Bäuemler's. He came from humble origins, had never taken an *Abitur* (secondary school diploma) and had written a book on The *Philosophy of Education* that catapulted him into an academic career with an honorary doctorate from Heidelberg University. Krieck was neither a subtle nor an original thinker. His attraction to National Socialism derived from his conviction that the university had to serve the people and not the other way around. In his inaugural address, he spoke of the Nazi revolution as the beginning of a new epoch in which the university would break through the barriers of specialized disciplines and elitist attitudes. The workers and the students were to join together in forging a new community based on a "unified völkish-political worldview."

As the example of Krieck demonstrates, Heidegger was without doubt a much more profound and interesting thinker than any of

---

38 The book is back in vogue on the far-right. It was recently translated and published by Arktos Media, founded in 2009 by Daniel Friberg in Hungary, is a rightwing publisher that has been called a leading publisher of the "alt-right canon." The Southern Poverty Law Center (SPLC) and other extremism researchers have documented its deep connections to white supremacist and far-right movements. See https://www.vice.com/en/article/how-a-small-budapest-publishing-house-is-quietly-fueling-far-right-extremism/#:~:text=Arktos%20exists%20within%20a%20wider,extensively%20in%20Europe%20and%20Asia.

his contemporaries who supported National Socialist education policies. Nevertheless, Heidegger's philosophy, his proposals for the reformation of the universities, and his advice to the National Socialist movement, were by no means extraordinary. Heidegger's most famous book, *Being and Time* (1927), is still the central point of contention between those who claim that his early philosophy is contaminated by Nazism and those who insist that his engagement with the new order can be separated from his philosophical studies. *Being and Time* applies a Husserlian phenomenological account of being-in-the-world: instead of describing the factual existence of a subject confronted with "objective" reality, "Dasein" (or being-in-the-world) experiences "throwness," growing up in a particular culture with unique practices defined by self-contained linguistic structures. The being that emerges from this cultural process, *Seindes*, or Being-There, stands out against the background of "world" in a particular way that, Heidegger asserts, only human beings possess. In the first part of the book, Heidegger describes Dasein's anxiety at being lost in the world, dictated to by the customs and conventions of ordinary surroundings. Heidegger describes everyday coping in this environment but also the possibility of Dasein forging its own authentic existence.

In the second part of the book, Heidegger describes Dasein's political and social interaction with others. The most problematic concept used here is "resoluteness." There are any number of ways for Dasein to be in the world, since Dasein has no fundamental essence or nature, but is, at bottom, only that which it makes of itself. Dasein grows up in certain traditions and customs, but in order to achieve authentic existence, it must resolutely reappropriate this heritage and then forge ahead in creating its own destiny. This openness to possibilities of action can only take place in concert with others (*Mit-Sein*), with the people who have experienced the same fate and who will forge their destiny in the future.

Sluga argued that Heidegger did not spell out a specific form of politics: "He is not telling us how to choose in order to be authentic—he makes no moral prescriptions."[39] On the other hand, it would be wrong, according to Sluga, to conclude that Heidegger's

39 Sluga, op.cit. 138.

early philosophy had nothing to do with his later explicit endorsement of the Nazi regime. In his infamous inaugural speech as rector of the University of Freiburg, delivered on May 27, 1933, he explicitly invoked his own philosophical concepts as a panacea for the problems faced by Germany and as a guide for the future. Addressing not only students and professors also the Archbishop of Freiburg and important Nazi leaders in a large hall decorated by academic and Nazi flags, Heidegger clearly offered his speech as a political act. Like Krieck and Bäumler, he insisted that the university had a major role to play in the national awakening of the German people; Heidegger explained this by recalling concepts used in *Being and Time*. He talked of the "resolute openness of the German students," of the origins of Greek science as "embracing the whole life" of a people. He spoke of modern man's "abandonment in the midst of Sein" (i.e., the plenitude of reality), and how philosophical questioning would lead man back to a "primordial" confrontation with das Volk, the "destiny of the state," in a spiritual mission:

> This primordial concept of science obligates us not only to "objectivity," but, above all, to make our questioning in the midst of the historical-spiritual world of the people essential and simple.[40]

Heidegger and most other philosophers who engaged themselves politically were hopelessly misguided and naive in thinking they could guide the Nazi revolution. Sluga follows Karl Popper and other observers of totalitarian philosophy in demonstrating how this naiveté came naturally to those who followed in Plato's footsteps as claimants to the spiritual leadership of the state. Even Germany's radical philosophers saw themselves as the natural guardians of the state, whose boundaries may expand indefinitely depending on the slant of the particular philosopher.[41] If German philosophers were initially attracted to Nazism only to be disappointed that they didn't

40 Martin Heidegger, "The Self-Assertion of the GermanUniversity," (May, 1933, https://la.utexas.edu/users/hcleaver/330T/350kPEEHeidegger Self-Assertion.pdf, 5.

41 K. R. Popper, *The Open Society and Its Enemies* (London: Routledge, 1945); J.L. Talmon, *The Origins of Totalitarian Democracy* (New York: Norton, 1952/1970).

become guardians of the state, it was because they failed to recognize the polymorphous nature of its ideology. The Nazi worldview was a potpourri of conflicting ideas, nationalist and populist, conservative and radical, traditionalist, devoted to German custom while promoting revolutionary change, elevating the simple peasant life while advancing technological and military superiority, in short, a reactionary form of modernism.[42] Immersed in the Platonic understanding of the relationship between philosophy and power, the fateful mistake of the German thinkers was to believe that it was their role to make sense of and legitimate the confused worldview of Nazism. In the process, they assimilated and thus distorted, entire philosophical traditions to the political needs of the day.

Sluga concluded his book by turning to contemporary attempts by philosophers to gain political relevance by offering theories of power that might effect change in the "real" world. In particular, he took Foucault and his followers to task for speaking about power as if it were a metaphysical substance, an elusive, invisible energy or drive that permeates all social relations. Sluga pointed out that power is a much more complicated ensemble of diverse relationships that can only be elaborated by historical investigation. The experience of German philosophers in 1933 teaches us that we cannot know a priori how the relationship between philosophical truth and political power should be constituted. Heidegger and others thought they knew, and were led by their convictions to support one of the most destructive regimes of terror known to history.

Sluga's weighing of the evidence was always judicious and balanced, but his cautiousness led to one kind of timidity. In particular, the moral of the story was not always satisfying. In concluding, he wrote that "we live at a time when philosophy and politics have, on the whole, little to say to each other."[43] He suggested that the lesson to be learned from German philosophy's entanglement in National Socialism would be for intellectuals today, not only to keep a safe distance from politics, but also to be wary of the politicization

---

42 See Jeffrey Herf, Reactionary Modernism: Technology, Culture, and Politics in Weimar and the Third Reich (Cambridge UK: Cambridge University Press, 1986).

43 Sluga, op.cit. 255.

of theory. Is this a realistic or wise suggestion? The philosophers' embrace of Nazism represents a very specific historical constellation; it verges on anti-intellectualism to hold up their example every time philosophers claim that politics and philosophy have something to say to each other. Philosophy and the other human sciences stand in danger of even more marginalization and social indifference if claims to political relevance are abandoned. It is true that in an age where everything has become political, to an extent, nothing is political. But without taking a stand on what history can teach citizens in a republic how to distinguish between facticity and subjectivity, between the true lessons of the past and a distortion of the past, educators give up a powerful tool. Since Sluga believes that philosophy still has an important role to play in providing us with an understanding of human beings, he can hardly be in favor of its complete depoliticization. History is not necessarily a good guide for knowing what, in the future, may be politically dangerous and what might be beneficial to all. The usual standards of academic integrity, and the ethical responsibility of the citizen, but not the heavy-handed use of the sins of the past, must constitute the measure by which intellectuals gauge the political value of their work.

Helpless Antifascism

The synchronic developments situated in the epoch of fascism traced above hopefully illuminate some essential roots of fascism based in European intellectual history. One is left with a deeper appreciation of the extent to which fascism grew out of a long and genuine search for an end to social conflict and for a more perfect arrangement of social life. The fact that fascism ended in a historical nightmare does not necessarily detract from the noble intentions of many of those intellectuals who Sternhell and Sluga paraded before us as accessories to the crimes. While many of the theorists of revolutionary syndicalism ended up making compromises with the Italian fascist regime, Labriola and Leone went into exile and refused to support Mussolini. Most of the theorists of the conservative revolution in Germany came to see the Third Reich as a perversion of their ideals. Thomas Mann, for one, may rightly be considered incipiently an exponent of the Conservativ Revolution. Heidegger was reticent about his period of fascist involvement, and certainly lied (to himself and others) about how long he remained emboldened to the basic principles of National Socialism, but the question of of whether all of his philosophical contributions are tainted by fascism is still an open question, even after reams of books have been published on the topic.

The point is neither to blame nor absolve these thinkers, but to understand fascism by exploring its origins. Sluga does not so much illuminate the general German crisis of philosophy that contributed to Nazism, as to helpfully point to universal themes of discontent that were expropriated by a ruthless political movement. Sternhell does not so much trace the origins of fascist ideology

as he rather provides a series of intellectual biographies of former heretical Marxists whose hatred of bourgeois society made fascism appealing to them, even when the goals of radical syndicalism had been abandoned by the fascist regime. It is clear that the fascists in power didn't need intellectuals; in fact, most independent thinkers were persecuted or intimidated into submission. It is equally evident, however, that fascism would have looked quite different had it not drawn on ideas from the nineteenth century that attempted to "sublate" modernity, challenging it so as to improve on it. Integral nationalism, anti-Semitism, irrationalism, mythical collective memories and glorification of the state were all part of this equation, but so too were legitimate challenges to the premises of modern life.

Fascism was the other twentieth-century God that failed in this attempt. Does that mean that there is today "no ideology with pretensions to universality that is in a position to challenge liberal democracy," as Francis Fukuyama famously argued at the end of the Cold War?[44] Will political ascesis, as Sluga argues, or a renewed commitment to the ideals of the Enlightenment and universal rationalism, as Sternhell argues, save us from the current radical challenge to our unfinished modernity? Hard-headed rationalism

44 Originally published as an essay, Francis Fukuyama, "The End of History?" *The National Interest*, no. 16 (Summer 1989): 3-18.

easily degenerates into a blunt weapon when challenged by the seductive attractions of myths and grand gestures. Formalistic liberalism often proves impotent to the demand that politics be endowed with soul and meaning. But these issues take us beyond the subjects discussed here. An open question must suffice as a conclusion: was the failure of fascism inevitable because the contradictions of modern life are insoluble, or because intellectual dissatisfaction with modernity was misguided and fundamentally flawed? Might a higher synthesis combine legitimate criticisms of the deficiencies of the liberal democratic tradition, while rigorously defending its hard foundations, without which open societies cannot function? In an age when a softer version of fascism threatens to return in the guise of illiberal democracies, much harder to oppose because its operators tolerate a certain amount of dissent, such a project is no longer academic. The Other God, fascism, failed, but not as completely as did the original God of Lenin. Future studies of fascism will have to address this question, both in its historical form and in terms of contemporary political relevance.

Part Three: Leftwing Radicalism in Postwar Germany

My interest in the German student movement came about when I looked from the right side of the political spectrum to the left, and realized that, if 1945 was a caesura for radical conservatives in the Federal Republic, 1968 was a crucial turning point for German democracy because of the rise of the student movement and the challenges posed to the young West German democracy. The textbook reading of that era, often written by the sixty-eighters themselves, divided postwar German history into a before and after 1968, in which the students played a heroic role in overcoming the reactionary, still proto-fascist tendencies of the Adenauer era, and by challenging the status quo, guided the nation into a liberal-democratic future. I am exaggerating a bit here, but that was the tenor of much of the literature on that era when I began to do my research. I came to several very different conclusions about how we should think about the generation of 1968. As with Part One, I will let these two texts speak for themselves, but in summary, my central thesis is as follows: First, the generation of 1968 was not primarily responsible for the democratization of West Germany and its anchoring in the Atlantic alliance; quote the opposite, the two generations of genuine, classical liberals before them were responsible, since they had experienced the horrors of National Socialism first hand. Second, the student movement was the first major challenge to building a stable democracy in West Germany, since the ideology was based on a set of utopian ideas, some harmless, some quite threatening, that had to be vanquished in order for democratic norms and practices to take root. Finally, the 1960s experienced a wave of lifestyle changes that were genuinely emancipatory: civil rights, women's rights, sexual liberation, fashion, music, and popular culture in general. But the claim by the German generation that came of age in the 1960s, that they were responsible for these cultural shifts, gets the causation backwards. Whether for or against the rapid social change that occurred in the 1960s, the cause was global, not local, and had a lot to do with larger cultural forces, especially emanating from the United States, than what the often-provincial German students were doing at the universities and on the streets. The second piece in this section was written on the occasion of a Festschrift put out on the occasion of Martin Jay's 65th birthday in 2009. I collaborated with A. Dirk Moses, with whom I often have had political disagreements over the years, but with whom, I am grateful to say, I have a deep, and lasting friendship. I am in debt to Dirk for consenting to have this piece included here. Dirk employs his original concept in this article, the "Weimar Syndrome," to help analyze the issue of violence in relation to the German student movement. The "syndrome" describes the anxiety felt by post-World War II West German politicians and intellectuals about the stability of their democracy, rooted in the memory of the Weimar Republic's failure and the Nazi dictatorship. This condition led to a political dynamic by which opponents routinely accused each other of undermining the new democratic order. This dynamic mirrored the political atmosphere of the Weimar era, which was plagued by internal divisions and political turmoil that eventually led to its collapse in 1933.

I.
Ideas of and About 1968

A pastoral ballad on a revolutionary theme.
—European historian Conor Cruise O'Brien's reply
when asked about student protests in 1970.

According to many written accounts by the "68ers," The history of the Federal Republic can be divided into a *before* and an *after* of 1968; in other words a sharp line must be drawn between a period of conservative authoritarian restoration after 1945, with a lingering fascist mentality among a large segment of the German population, and by contrast an explosion of participatory democracy in 1968 and the creation of an increasingly liberal republic.[1] The fundamental historiographical question of whether "1968" led to a liberalization of Germany or, by contrast, constituted a destructive detour on that road, is still fiercely debated in German intellectual circles, even after all these years. The choice is most likely too binary, as are most options in life. Not in dispute however, is that the battles of '68 continue, this time not on the streets, but rather over who has the power to interpret the past *correctly*.[2]

Locating the generation of 1968 as agents of social change is at best only half *correct*, and much evidence points to the conclusion that the causal connection is backwards. In the 1960s the civil rights movement, the anti-war movement, and all the other isms of the decade that followed, environmentalism, feminism, gay rights etc. didn't come about because leaders finally emerged who were ready and able to fight for new causes. Instead, German society had changed organically, and many social, economic and political factors, all having to do with modernization across all of Europe, and especially the influence of American youth culture, that collectively

1 See for example, the collection edited by Lothar Baier, *Früchte der Revolte*, 85-88.

2 See Albrecht von Lucke, *68 oder neues Biedermeier; Der Kampf um die Deutungsmacht* (Berlin: Wagenbach, 2008)

created the possibilities, indeed the necessity of a fresh generation of leaders to guide innovative social movements.

This book situates the student movement within an enormous shift of attitudes that occurred in German society between the 1950s and the 1970s, what many historians now describe as the "long 1960s."[3] Rather than treating 1968 as an abrupt rupture, recent work has emphasized continuities from the student and youth politics of the 1950s: early campaigns against rearmament and nuclear weapons, protests against the reintegration of former Nazis, and the tentative emergence of a more critical public sphere in the Federal Republic (for example, in the V*erband Deutscher Studentenschaften* and the nascent peace movement).[4] The use of atomic weapons, the decline of the European colonial powers, and, above all, the economic and baby boom of the 1950s and the rise of an increasingly international youth culture were critical.[5] Social scientists have continued to debate how these structural shifts translate into waves of student activism, refining older "strain" and "modernization" theories with concepts such as political opportunity structures, transnational diffusion, and generational identity.[4] Yet in similar turbulent periods, in Germany and elsewhere, sustained student protest has not always been the result.[6] By the mid-1960s, a dense web of transnational connections—circulating through

3 Martin Klimke and Joachim Scharloth, eds., 1968 in *Europe: A History of Protest and Activism, 1956–1977* (New York: Palgrave Macmillan, 2008); Philipp Gassert and Martin Klimke, 1968: *The World Transformed* (Cambridge: Cambridge University Press, 2010).

4 Christina von Hodenberg, *Das andere Achtundsechzig? Gesellschaft, Generationskonflikte und die Protestbewegungen der 1960er Jahre in der Bundesrepublik* (Munich: C. H. Beck, 2018), 37–78; Lawrence S. Wittner, *Resisting the Bomb: A History of the World Nuclear Disarmament Movement, 1954–1970* (Stanford, CA: Stanford University Press, 1997), 177–216.

5 Ulrich Herbert, *Wiederaufbau und Neubeginn: Die Bundesrepublik Deutschland 1945–1965* (Munich: Deutsche Verlags-Anstalt, 1998); Konrad H. Jarausch, *After Hitler: Recivilizing Germans*, 1945–1995 (New York: Oxford University Press, 2006).

6 See for example David A. Snow and Robert D. Benford, "Master Frames and Cycles of Protest," in Aldon D. Morris and Carol McClurg-Müller, *Frontiers in Social Movement Theory* (New Haven: Yale UP, 1992), 133-155.

travel, media, and activist networks—was clearly propelling the German student movement, even as activists continued to narrate themselves as autonomous agents and prime movers within this global transformation.[7] More recently, cultural and literary scholars such as Susanne Rinner have traced how these events were subsequently remembered, forgotten, and reimagined in fiction and cultural memory debates after 1989, adding yet another layer to the historiography of the movement.[8]

The emphasis here on the larger geopolitical currents of change remains instructive, but newer research has filled out and complicated the picture. From its origins, the West German student movement located itself in an emerging anti-colonial and anti-imperial "world revolution," aligning rhetorically with struggles in Algeria, Cuba, Vietnam, and later Portugal's African colonies, as well as with Black civil rights and anti-racist movements in the United States.[9] Students targeted what they saw as the moral bankruptcy of European states that, after 1945, behaved as though the catastrophes of fascism and war had not discredited their claims to global authority. In 1956, Great Britain and France tried to use the Suez Crisis to reassert colonial prerogatives—soon followed by France's brutal war in Algeria—at precisely the moment when decolonization elsewhere was making such projects appear anachronistic.[10] The United States, still able to represent itself as historically anti-colonial, helped block the Suez adventure but then became enmeshed

---

7 Sidney Tarrow, *Power in Movement: Social Movements and Contentious Politics*, 3rd ed. (Cambridge: Cambridge University Press, 2011); Doug McAdam, Sidney Tarrow, and Charles Tilly, *Dynamics of Contention* (Cambridge: Cambridge University Press, 2001).

8 Susanne Rinner, *The German Student Movement and the Literary Imagination: Transnational Memories of Protest and Dissent* (New York: Berghahn Books, 2013).

9 Quinn Slobodian, *Foreign Front: Third World Politics in Sixties West Germany* (Durham, NC: Duke University Press, 2012); Kristin Ross, May '68 and Its Afterlives (Chicago: University of Chicago Press, 2002), 63–104

10 Tony Judt, Post*war: A History of Europe Since 1945* (New York: Penguin, 2005), 322–34; Matthew Connelly, *A Diplomatic Revolution: Algeria's Fight for Independence and the Origins of the Post–Cold War Era* (New York: Oxford University Press, 2002).

in its own post-colonial war in Vietnam, turning in German students' eyes from an ally of democracy into the principal imperial power.[11] In their readings of these developments, the US had simply taken up the imperial torch that Britain and France were losing, while the Federal Republic's tight Atlantic alignment made it complicit in that project.[12] By the mid-1950s, colonialism's legitimacy was indeed deeply eroded, but European powers waged a series of rearguard campaigns—from Indochina and Algeria to southern Africa—before a broadly post-colonial international order emerged in the 1970s.[11] Historians of "1968" have shown how West German activists appropriated this shift in world-view as both cause and justification of their own revolt, even though it was driven far more by the structural decline of European power and the assertiveness of actors in the global South than by any actions of student radicals in Frankfurt or Berlin. Yet in the contested political and cultural memory of these years, German students often continued to claim a disproportionate share of the credit—a tendency that more recent transnational studies of protest and of the "Third World" in the global 1960s have begun to scrutinize and revise.[13]

A look at the United States in the 1960s provides a parallel picture of how underlying fluctuating dynamics provide the impetus for change when old social practices have lost historical legitimacy. When Lyndon Johnson enacted the Civil Rights legislation in 1965,

---

11 Marilyn B. Young, *The Vietnam Wars, 1945–1990* (New York: HarperCollins, 1991); Fredrik Logevall, *Embers of War: The Fall of an Empire and the Making of America's Vietnam* (New York: Random House, 2012). Wilfried Mausbach, "'Auschwitz and Vietnam': West German Protest against America's War during the 1960s," in *1968: The World Transformed*, ed. Carole Fink, Philipp Gassert, and Detlef Junker (Cambridge: Cambridge University Press, 1998), 381–408.

12 John Springhall, *Decolonization since 1945: The Collapse of European Overseas Empires* (New York: Palgrave Macmillan, 2001); Frederick Cooper, *Africa Since 1940: The Past of the Present* (Cambridge: Cambridge University Press, 2002), 65–132

13 Norbert Frei, 1968: *Jugendrevolte und globaler Protest* (Munich: Deutscher Taschenbuch Verlag, 2008); Gerd-Rainer Horn, *The Spirit of '68: Rebellion in Western Europe and North America, 1956–1976* (Oxford: Oxford University Press, 2007); Klimke and Scharloth, *1968 in Europe*. op.cit.

(a southern Senator with no hitherto deep convictions in this direction), the spirit of the times announced itself as a repudiation of hundreds of years of established practices, both legal and by custom, between blacks and whites (for lack of more accurate designations) in the United States. The legislation of the Great Society was not possible without an emerging sense of guilt inside the dominant culture, which led to endeavors to enact rapid changes by the force of law (but not without bitter political battles). The guilt of the liberal elites was rooted in bad conscience, or the suspicion of bad faith, which created the possibilities of protest and then violence on the streets of the U.S. When four Black students in 1960 staged an actual sit-in, (in contrast to the German bland imitation) by sitting in the seats reserved for whites at a restaurant in Greensboro, their example set off a chain reaction within weeks all over the south. The tactic had been tried and failed as early as the 1940s in Chicago, but now the moment was ripe for change, because the laws separating whites and blacks were recognized as anachronistic and anti-constitutional. The constitution had not changed, but a new interpretation of its intent emerged. Laws that had stood the test of time only needed to be challenged on a broad basis to begin to fall like dominoes. As Illinois Senator Everett McKinley Dirksen said in in 1964, quoting Victor Hugo, "stronger than all the armies is an idea whose time has come."[14] The race riots of the mid to late 1960s happened after, not before the sweeping civil rights and Great Society legislation had been passed. That sequence of events proves the thesis, already charted by Tocqueville, that rapid social change occurs in the wake of loosening of authority along with the "J- Curve" of rising expectations, not in the cases of harsh oppression of social groups.[15] The student rebels came from the more affluent classes in

14 See Todd S. Purdum, *An Idea Whose Time Has Come; Two Presidents, Two Parties and the Battle of the Civil Rights Act of 1964* (New York: Henry Holt, 2014). The Dirksen quote adorns the first page of the book, and is attributed solely to the Senator.

15 J.C. Davies, "The J-Curve of Rising and Declining Satisfactions as a Cause of Some Great Revolutions and a Contained Rebellion," In Hugh Davis Graham & Ted Robert Gurr, eds., *The History of Violence in America; Historical and Comparative Perspectives*, (New York: Praeger, 1969),

Germany, not the downtrodden. The observation by Deirdre McLosky about the French students of the same period, that the radicals who threw cobblestones at the police on the Left bank in May 1968 came from comfortable bourgeois background, and were protesting against an economic system that had greatly benefited them, applies equally to the situation in Germany in the 1960s. The "clerisy" of artists and intellectuals who turn against the system that makes their lives economically feasible in the first place has a long history, dating back to the mid-nineteenth century, called romantic anti-capitalism and a "paradox of privilege."[16]

In Germany, historical guilt in the context of bourgeois privilege, contained specific contours. The Nazi past was the unspoken yet always present background, the "communicative silence" (Lübbe), against which the protest movements launched an assault on bourgeois complacency. Historians emphasize the importance of the fact that the 68ers were children born in the shadow of World War II, whose childhood memories were filled by the sounds and sights of allied bombs falling on German cities. They were only "Hitler's children" (Jillian Becker) however, to the extent that they accused their parents, whether justly or unjustly, of silence about the past. That was only half the story. The fact that around mid-1967 the APO moved in an anti-Zionist direction, chose the Palestinians out of all the possible liberation movements of the age to hoist on its flag, surely had something to do with the persistence of certain mental configurations from the Third Reich.[17] Was the progeny recapitulating ontology?

690–730. In *The Anatomy of Revolution* Crane Brinton wrote, "...the revolutionary movements seem to originate in the discontents of not unprosperous people, who feel restraint, cramp, annoyance rather than downright crushing oppression." *The Anatomy of Revolution* (New York: Vintage, revised and expanded edition 1965), 250.

16 See Deirdre. N. McCloskey, *The Bourgeois Virtues: Ethics for an Age of Commerce*, (Chicago: & London: University of Chicago Press, 2006). 18 ff. and 51-53.

17 Seymour Martin Lipset made a similar argument about the parallels between the American generation of 1968 and their liberal parents in *Rebellion in the University* (Boston: Little, Brown and Company, 1971), 80-123.

Anti-Americanism was also part of the mental baggage of the older generation. The claim by the generation of 1968 that without their prodding the Nazi past would have gone unexamined, certainly does not withstand historical scrutiny. We have had occasion to note the decisive impact of the Auschwitz Trials of the mid-1960s. The concentration camp survivor Fritz Bauer, born in 1903, whose class action lawsuits led to the Frankfurt Trials, and whose tips to the Mossad led to the capture of Adolf Eichmann, did far more to bring the crimes of the Nazis to public attention than anyone from the generation of 1968.[18]

Another shift in the Zeitgeist of the sixties may now be recognized as changes in the socio-political meaning of *youth culture*. As Philippe Ariès and other have noted, human childhood, in sharp contrast to animals, is not based solely on biological determinants, but rather equally on cultural norms, beliefs and attitudes. Childhood is a historical category.[19] One can argue that in very general terms, and allowing for many counter-examples, by the 1960s the longstanding reverence reserved for elders in traditional societies had been replaced in modern states by a fascination with and idolization of youth. The phenomenon was exemplified best by the vehemence with which the students began criticizing their elders (in Germany parents and professors in particular).

The German professor traditionally had enormous power and prestige. He or she (they were mostly male) could command and control associate and assistant professors, graduate students and an entire army of researchers and adjunct professors. According to polls taken in 1968, Professors commanded the most respect among the "honorary" professions, ahead of bishops, ministers, company directors and generals.[20] But suddenly the students lashed out, calling them "specialist idiots" (*Fachidioten*) and challenging their authority in numerous ways (including physical attacks). Early in this book we came across one of the most famous slogans of the 1960s, which lives on to this day, on the banner from November 9th,

18 See Irmtrud Wojak: *Fritz Bauer: Eine Biographie, 1903-1963* (Munich: C.H. Beck, 2009).

19 Philippe Ariès, *Centuries of Childhood* (New York: York: Vintage, 1965).

20 "Professoren; dies Herren," *Der Spiegel*, Nr. 8 (Feb. 19, 1968), 34.

1967 in Hamburg at the inauguration of a new Rector: "Under their gowns, a thousand years of mustiness."[21]

The respected German professors, used to adulation and privileges enjoyed only by royalty in other societies, were shocked by the impudence of the students. To make matters worse, on that November day in Hamburg, one of the robed gods, Berthold Spuler, a professor of Asian Studies, erupted at the students in a voice loud enough so everyone could hear, "you all belong in a concentration camp."[22] Despite what his outburst says about the German professoriate, there were more than a few liberal faculty members who recognized that the time was ripe to reform the feudal structure of the university. Reform of the medieval university was another powerful idea whose time had come, not a new cause the students initiated.

Power shifted incessantly towards youth in this age. From the margins of weakness, the students were pushed towards the center of influence, which had many consequences, some foreseen, some unintended. As much as the generation of 1968 opposed many of the fundamental social and political institutions of the Federal Republic, it is a delicious irony that by rebelling they also joined the family drama of German history and coveted, then protected their stake with unreserved possessiveness. One of the rebel students who carried that banner in Hamburg became a respected jurist and the other a university teacher himself. Their stories of transformation from anti-authoritarians to the new authority were typical.[23]

---

21 The two students were Detlev Albers, former student President and Gerd Hinnerk Behlmer, who wrote on the banner "Unter den Talaren—Muff von 1000 Jahren." *Muff* in German most commonly refers to stale air. The thousand years were meant to refer to the stuffiness and rigidity of the medieval university as well as to professors with a National Socialist background. The students wanted a say in the governance of the university. See "Unter den Talaren Muff von Tausend Jahren," *Die Welt* (November 12, 2007), 14.

22 Ibid. The outburst cost Spuler a disciplinary hearing.

23 Although it is a commonplace to suggest that the 68ers have moved into authoritative positions in law, politics, media, education and just about every aspect of professional life in contemporary Germany, one should-

As I have argued throughout this book (*Free Radicals*, 2016), the student theoreticians of the movement were steeped in the history of European revolutions and revolutionary thought, but erroneously applied that history and set of ideas to the political and social conditions of the Federal Republic. They interpreted the Grand Coalition in the context of the fall of the Weimar Republic and buffed themselves up into anti-fascist heroes who would not repeat the mistakes of the Weimar Left, which didn't recognize the Hitler threat until it was too late. Two texts were very important in situating the years 1966-1969 within the Weimar milieu of 1930-1933, delivering a concept, *authoritarianism*, against which to agitate: Max Horkheimer's *Authoritarian State* and Theodor W. Adorno's collection, *The Authoritarian Personality*. The Grand Coalition appeared against the foil of these books as a reincarnation of the last years of the Weimar democracy, as broad coalitions operated on the basis of emergency decrees that eventually gave Hitler the opening he needed to transform the crumbling structure into an explicit dictatorship. It also appeared to confirm Carl Schmitt's analysis of parliamentary democracy as the triumph of interest groups masquerading as representatives of the peoples' interests. The fact that Karl Schiller, a finance minister from the SPD, also succeeded in forging bodies of co-determination between the employers' associations and the unions, was greeted by the students not as progressive,[24] but rather misconstrued as yet another sign of the ultimate integrative power of the capitalist state to siphon off oppositional energy and exclude possibilities of other social and economic models. The students saw confirmation of the authoritarian personality thesis in the hostile attitude of the West German population to their own political goals. In particular they viewed the

---

n't forget that there are many forgotten or unknown fates from the sixties, brought down by drug and alcohol abuse, marital breakdown, mental health problems and suicides.

24 *Mitbestimmung*, or Co-determination, eventually spread to most other European Union countries and is considered today one of the most important achievements of the European Labor Movement. See Evan McGauhey, "The Co-determination Bargains; The History of German Corporate and Labor Law, *LSE Law, Society and Economy Working Papers* (10/2015), 1-43.

Springer media conglomerate through the lens of Marx and Freud as an incubator for the *fascist personality*: a product of a resentful middle class with ego-weak characteristics, the love of hierarchical order and the tendency to defer to authority. The rising popularity of the far-rightwing NPD in the late 1960s as well as the looming passage of the Emergency Laws only confirmed in the students' minds that the fascist state was just around the corner.

When one considers the concrete political goals of the student movement, it is clear, at least in long hindsight, that few of them were ever realized. Some university reforms were enacted, but historians of the German university have argued that the reforms would have occurred anyway, and perhaps have been even better without the deep animosity that was created by the disruptions of the student protests.[25] In regard to the fears that an authoritarian state was about to materialize, the Emergency Laws did not suppress democratic dissent; neo-fascist parties like the NPD were not prevented from entering parliament, but they quickly faded into marginality; the concentration of media power was not reversed but freedom of opinion in Germany thrived; and the US did finally end the war in Vietnam in 1973, not as a result of student protests, but rather from mainstream public opposition and because of Nixon and Kissinger's Machiavellian mistakes.

Despite German liberals' serious reservations concerning both the goals and tactics of the students, it is true that many leftwing intellectuals in the 1960s did sympathize with calls for reform of the university and for many social changes. They understood the weaknesses of the Federal Republic very well and were as worried as the student activists about the reactionary potential of the German population, only two decades after the fall of Nazism. But they also understood that many leaders of the movement, the theoretical heads like Rudi Dutschke, Bernd Rabehl, Christian Semmler, Hans Jürgen Krall, Wolfgang Lefèvre and others, emphatically did *not* embrace a democratic-capitalist, pluralist Federal Republic, but instead pined for another collectivist fantasy, in a long and bloody history of collectivist utopias, and rejected the post-1945 liberal world order. Older liberals could not help but associate the student

25 See Hartmut Boockmann, *Wissen und Widerstand; Geschichte der deutschen Universität* (Berlin: Siedler Verlag, 1999). 253-267.

radicals of 1968 with the same type they knew all too well from 1933. The crux of the matter was that the academics of the previous generation had experienced actual censorship, suppression and often exile, so they embraced tolerance as by natural reflex. They cringed often enough, but in the end supported the right of the students to have their say. German democracy had failed twice, in 1848 and 1918, and damned if the elders were going to throw sand into the gears of the first effective and functioning open society in German history. But, but—the last thing the young academic hotheads wanted was to be *tolerated*, since in their minds the result would be a more sinister, hidden "one-dimensional" form of repression. The students viewed the "free press" and other anchors of civil society suspiciously, as echo chambers designed to funnel off their excess energy. The anarchism of subversive Situationism, which Dutschke repackaged, mixing in hegelized Marxism and then passing it along to the SDS, was not derived from Enlightenment versions of anarchism like the unrealistic but very moral William Godwin, but instead from the violent and conspiratorial varieties of Mikhail Bakunin and the Russian *Narodniks* of the 1860s and 1870s. Students and marginal social groups were now supposed to step in as the historical agents delegated to ignite the final revolution. This revolutionary ideology, in other words, was about destroying systems of government, not reforming them, and certainly not holding them up to higher ideals, as the American students had done. The RAF may have been an extreme expression of this tendency, but it was not a deviation from the core logic built into the ideas of 1968.

In regard to reform, Dutschke's phrase about the "long march through the institutions" was misunderstood from the start among the activists of 1968, and then among some scholars, to mean that the students' long-term plan was to make incremental changes, in stages, to bourgeois society.[26] This reading was, and is still, based on false assumptions. Although the general phrase "Long March" was inspired by Mao's actual Long March of 1934-35, the specific SDS plan can be traced to the near obsession in the 1960s among student radicals with the high hopes attached to de-colonization af-

26 "Der Marsch durch die Instutionen hat auch die CDU erreicht," Jürgen Habermas im Gespräch mit Rainer Erd, *Frankfurter Rundschau*, 11 March, 1998.

ter 1945. As we have emphasized, it was not a coincidence that dozens of previously colonized peoples won their autonomy, often after bloody struggles, and were establishing new states in Africa and Asia, at the same time that youth revolts broke out in Western Europe in the 1960s. The promise of new forms of government and innovative social arrangements was mesmerizing. The appeal of Régis Debray, (an advisor later to French President François Mitterand, and today, in advanced age a "Radical Conservative"[27]), and his demand that the Cuban Revolution be exported to other Third World "focus" countries and then back to Europe, must be seen in this context. For theorists in the SDS, the "developments in the Third World" could not be separated from social relations in America or in Europe."[28] The Long March was meant to be *infiltration* of the commanding heights of the economic order (as Lenin would have put it), and then subversion of Germany's governing institutions.

Recent academic studies have developed the notion that 1968 represented a coherent "social movement" with a common identity and a coherent set of goals to challenge the established institutions of society.[29] In general the "cohesion" argument is correct, but one problem with this approach is the idea that a direct causal connection exists between the intentions of social actors and social change. The process of modernization mixes in a wild card that complicates the theory. In Germany, as in most industrial nations in the twentieth century, modernization was linked, among many other things, to the development (and sustainment) of democratic institutions and the rule of law.[30] German liberals were very aware of the idiosyncratic reading of the word "democracy" among student radicals,

---

27 Christopher Caldwell, "Règis Debray, Radical Conservative," *First Things* (June-July, 2021). https://firstthings.com/rgis-debray-radical-conservative/#:~:text=At%20the%20%C3%89cole%20Normale%2C%20he,a%20Catholic%20in%20the%20Church?

28 Interview mit Rudi Dutschke, *Konkret* (June, 1967), 25.

29 Among many studies, see Ingrid Gilcher-Holtey, *1968; Vom Ereignis zum Gegenstand der Geschichtswissenschaft*; also by Gilcher-Holtey, *Die 68er Bewegung: Deutschland, Westeuropa, USA* (Munich: Beck, 2008); See also Norbert Frei, *1968; Jugendrevolte und globaler Protest* (Munich: Deutscher Taschenbuchverlag, 2008).

30 See David Landes, *The Wealth and Poverty of Nations; Why Some are so Rich and some are so Poor* (New York: Norton, 1999), esp. chapter 3 on "European Exceptionalism."

as well as the structural factors that gave the Federal Republic a robustness, absent in Weimar, that allowed for gradual, nonviolent change. The students perceived this robustness as a challenge, not a *value* to be embraced. The students tended to interpret the strength of democratic institutions in Germany as a sign of *stagnation*. This view was, as the Germans say, alienated from reality (*Wirklichkeitsfremd*). The influential sociologist Wilhelm Hennis pointed out even at the time that only young people with a very constricted time horizon could come up with the "curious idea that (German) society was marked by immobility or stagnation."[31]

In our investigation, the events of 1968 were played out in public, in the glare of media exposure. As Tony Judt observed, the spectacle aspect of the sixties, the silly fashions and frivolous pop culture had a serious side as well, to make an ostentatious break with the gerontocracy that still ruled the world, embodied in figures such as LBJ, Macmillan, De Gaulle and Khrushchev.[32] But there was an important private aspect to 1968 as well, a generational experience that transformed the inner lives of many participants and observers. The events of the "hot years" from 1966-1969 had barely cooled when social historians tried to piece together the narrative of what had just happened. Already in 1972 they proposed that alienation in the 1960s was not perceived as personal, romantic agony, but rather as derived from psychic alienation, transformed into a political movement.[33] We have noted that this sense of cultural alienation can be traced back to the generally quietist but undeniably stifling period of the 1950s. At that time the rebels were not despairing intellectuals but rather authentic working-class youth, disaffected by the rigid rules and stuffy atmosphere of the father-figure Adenauer's no-nonsense attempt to return to normalcy after the wild ride of Nazism. These rebels, the "*Halbstarken*," were a 1950s social type, the German equivalent of James Dean and many rebels without a cause; anti-social young men and women who hung out

31 Wilhelm Henning, "Die deutsche Unruhe," *Merkur* Jg. 23 (February, 1969), 103-120.

32 Tony Judt, *Postwar*, 398.

33 See Walter R. Heinz & Peter Schröber, *Theorien kollektiven Verhaltens* (Darmstadt/Neuwied, 1972).

on the street, in jeans or black sweaters, with limitless cigarette dangling from their mouths. Especially in the sad, monotonous working-class districts of large German cities, a kind of expressive nihilism was acted out as bohemianism or vague existentialism. The alienated youths of 1958 were models for some parts of the 1968 youth revolt, particularly the Hash Rebels and others in the "turn on, tune in, drop out scene" that copied the American beatnik culture and served up cultural despair à la Bohémienne.[34]

The majority of the student rebels, like the hippies of San Francisco circa 1967, aimed their angst and anger at their middle-class parents and the consumer culture of the boom years. The identification with the poor and dispossessed of the world was entirely a projection or romantic idealization, not unlike later white youth in the 1990s who were the largest consumers of African American ghetto rap. But as the sociologist Niklas Luhmann has noted, the 1960s was also a period of rapid modernization when changes in the family structure and a loosening of social mores allowed marginal groups to break down social barriers to create authentic subcultures.[35] By the 1950s capitalist society, driven by internal dynamics, was itself posed to break down social barriers by dis-attaching the original, mainly Protestant values that accompanied the rise of capitalism from its parallel force of creative destruction. These "contradictions of capitalism, analyzed by Daniel Bell and others in the 1970s, were viewed in Germany as a disturbing new trend, the construction of a "risk society" in which the only antidote to materialistic culture could be a non-materialist ethos. A new kind of Critical Theory was necessary to understand this "post-traditional form of communitarianism.[36]

The idea of a revolutionary, "post-materialistic" subject, personified by marginal actors, was popularized by Jean Paul Sartre,

---

34 See Marina Fischer Kowalski, "Halbstarke 1958, Studenten 1968; Eine Generation und zwei Rebelionen," in Ulf Preuss-Lausitz, ed., *Kriegskinder, Konsumkinder, Krisenkinder*, 4th ed., (Landsberg: Beltz, 2010), 53-70.

35 Niklas Luhmann, *Soziale Systeme; Grundriss einer allgemeinen Theorie* (Frankfurt: Suhrkamp 1987).

36 See Ulrich Beck, *Risk Society: Towards a New Modernity*, trans. Mark Ritter (London: Sage, 1992). Quote is from the editors on p. 6.

who viewed outcasts and criminals, like the writer and petty felon Jean Genet, as enlightened critics of bourgeois society. In Germany Frankfurt School theorists like Claus Offe proposed that in "late capitalism" ever more social groups would be pushed to the margins, the unemployed, the mentally ill, the lawbreakers, who could eventually pose a real threat to the social order.[37]

The liberal defenders of the republic were also vaguely aware that the radical student program carried an aggressive *nationalist* subtext. Not enough attention has been paid to the fact that Habermas's famous remark about "left-wing fascism" implicitly contained this recognition. He was not only condemning "voluntarism" that is, the blanquist, gratuitous and violent tactics of the students, which Weimar revolutionaries did not hesitate to employ, but also the larger assault on West Germany's political accomplishments, which for Habermas meant an embrace of pro-western democracy, with warts and all.

With much passion Bernd Rabehl has argued that, at bottom, Dutschke was a "national-revolutionary" thinker in the context of a divided Germany and the Cold War.[38] Writing after the fall of the Berlin Wall, Rabehl was reacting to an "end of history" moment in the early 1990s when the collapse of communism seemed to signal the final triumph of liberal capitalism. Dutschke's project needed to be "recovered" in an age when anything not in tow to the "North American ideology" smacked of extremism.[39] For Dutschke, according to Rabehl, there was no contradiction between class and nation, since the latter tied together culture, the state, the workers' movement, liberalism and conservatism in a tradition that could be followed back to the heterodox revolutionary movements of the Reformation.[40] A genuine emancipation, in this reading, would have been

---

37 Claus Offe, *Strukturprobleme des kapitalistischen Staates* (Frankfurt: Suhrkamp, 1973). See also Theodor Adorno, ed., *Spätkapitalismus oder Industriegesellschaft* (Frankfurt, 1969).

38 Bernd Rabehl, *Rudi Dutschke; Revolutionär im geteilten Deutschland* (Dresden: Antaiois, 2002).

39 Ibid. 8. The nationalist theme is also developed by Rabehl in *Feindblick: der SDS im Fadenkreuz des Kalten Krieges* (Kiel: Philosophischer Salon, 2000).

40 Ibid. 26.

liberation from the totalitarian constraints of both free-market capitalism and state-directed communism. Just three days before he was shot in 1968, Dutschke told Wolfgang Venohr that Bismarck had solved the "German Question" from the top, and this time it would have to be revisited from the grass roots level.[41] In Dutschke's writings, particularly in the mid to late 1970s[42], there is much evidence for his continued preoccupation with the German Question and the Cold War geopolitical struggle, anticipating the oft-noted strains of anti-modernism wrapped in an ideology of anti-capitalism inside the broad spectrum of the early Green movement. Dutschke's nationalism was not an odd quirk of a contrarian.[43]

It is true that many other enraged 68ers rightly point out that opposing the American "way of life" did not mean the students embraced some romantic German alternative.[44] The students may have been naïve in their embrace of Third World emancipation movements but most were "cosmopolitan" to the extent that for them the future of Germany lay in a revolutionary transformation of global capitalism, rather than a specifically German revolution. Dutschke and others who grew up in East Germany may have had strong emotional reasons to concentrate on the issue of reunification, but that characterization cannot be said about the movement as a whole.[45] It should also be noted that up until the Paris Accords of June 1955 (integrating Germany into the Atlantic Alliance), the SPD had also held a firm position against rearmament, arguing that a militarized West Germany would render reunification of West and East Germany much more difficult to achieve. Seen in this light, the

---

41 Wolfgang Venohr, "Letztes Interview vor dem Attentat," *Neue Politik*, 17, April 27, 1968, 13

42 See Rudi Dutschke, "Pro Patria Sozi?" *Konkret* 20, Nr. 2, (Nov. 1974). "Die Deutschen und der Sozialismus, *das da/avanti* 4, Nr. 7, (July 1977). "Wer hat Angst vor der Wiedervereinigung?" *Das da/avanti*, 5, Nr. 10, (Oct. 78).

43 See Gayil Talshir, *The Political Ideology of the Green Parties* (London: Palgrave Macmillan, 2002) 162-3.

44 See Heidrun Kämper, "Der Faschismus Diskurs 1967/69," in Heidrun Kämper, Joachim Scharloth et.al.,*1968; eine Sprachwissentschaftliche Bilanz* (Berlin: de Gruyter, 2012), 259-286.

45 "Wir waren nie Nationalisten," Interview with Gisela Richter, Hanna Kröger and Bonni Baumann, *Junge Welt*, (Feb. 15, 1999).

"nationalism" of the SDS, which opposed the mother party's reluctant but politically expedient cooperation with the CDU in building a new German army after 1955, was as much a status-quo-ante position as it was "revolutionary."

Despite the above caveats, it is clearly the case that 1968 and 1989 are intimately connected as historic *nationalist* turning points. In 1968 social and national liberation was a theoretical program; in 1989 liberation became a historical reality, at least initially for East Germans. Rudi Dutschke would certainly have agreed with many East Germans in 1989 that the transition from "We are the People" to "We are One People" contained an inescapable historical logic. He would have been also severely disappointed that the dream of a "Third Way" (between capitalism and communism) was not fulfilled, even when the reform socialists seemed to have finally had their chance to implement what the East German state did so long to suppress. The fact that "the dream still lives," to quote the title of an early twenty-first century collection of socialist and communist writings, points to the manner in which the legacy of 1968 must be viewed in the context of Germany's special path to modernization, or a certain idea of German freedom that lives on as a romantic refusal to accept capitalism and globalization. [46]

In the aftermath of 1968, the organized extra-parliamentary opposition fractured into series of counter-cultural trends; deep ecology, feminism, esotericism, the peace movement, communalism and many other attempts to negotiate a new form of politics beyond bourgeois democracy. The legacy of the sixties in Germany was a gradual acceptance of the *status quo*, combined with a persistent extra-parliamentary *disposition*.

There were actually two countercultures in 1968. The street mutineers dreamed of a political revolution, which was acted out as theater, using old scripts. In their daily lives, politics became personal; emancipation came in the form of consumer choices. The first

46 Robert Kurz, ed., *Und der Traum Lebt Noch* (Berlin: Wagenbach, 2003), as well as Kurz, *Schwarzbuch Kapitalismus* (Berlin: Ullstein, 2002). See also Elmar Altvater, *Das Ende des Kapitalismus wie wir ihn kennen* (Münster: Dampfboot, 2011). Heinze Dieterich, *Der Sozialismus des 21. Jahrhunderts* (Berlin-Werder: Homilius, 2006).

was collective and failed, the second was libertarian, individualistic, futuristic, and carried the day. In the United States Stewart Brand, the visionary who founded *The Whole Earth Catalog* in 1968, pithily described the difference as between "Berkeley and Stanford":

Around Berkeley, it was Free Speech Movement, "power to the people." Around Stanford, it was "Whole Earth Catalog," Steve Wozniak, Steve Jobs, people like that, and they were just power to the people. They just wanted to power anybody who was interested, not "the people." Well, it turns out there is no, probably, "the people." So, the political blind alley that Berkeley went down was interesting, we were all taking the same drugs, the same length of hair, but the stuff came out of the Stanford area, I think because it took a Buckminster Fuller access-to-tools angle on things.[47]

In Germany this kind of technophile mindset was much more difficult to launch, given the entrenched romantic aversion to technology in the counter-culture. Heidegger's preference for *techné* (craftsmanship) over technology and the general aversion to industrial capitalism persisted well after 1968. The German street revolutionaries were right that the proletariat was about to be freed of its factory chains, but few anticipated the replacement of oily machines by computers, robots, cybernetics and virtual reality. The contrast between Berkeley and Stanford found its pale equivalent in Germany with the intellectual competition between Berlin and Frankfurt. The Frankfurters considered the Berliners not theoretical enough, and the Berliners thought the Frankfurters were not radical enough.[48] But they were both limited by the horizon of Marxism, beyond which they could not proceed.

Observers seem puzzled sometimes by the fact that not a few of the 68ers ended up on the political right, sometimes the extreme right of the German political spectrum, for example Horst Mahler, Günther Mashke, and Bernd Rabehl.[49] In France, Règis Debray, Alain Finkelkraut, Michel Onfray and Bernhard Henri-Lévy offer

---

47 Evgeny Morozov, "Making It," *The New Yorker* (Jan. 13, 2014), 70.

48 Hans Kundani discusses this in his generally perceptive *Utopia or Auschwitz: Germany's 1968 Generation and Auschwitz* (London: Hurst, 2009) 30 ff.

49 See "Vom Sponti zum Nazi," http://www.deutschlandradiokultur.de/vom-sponti-zum-nazi.950.de.html?dram:article_id=252681

other, more complicated examples of at least a shift in a conservative, nuanced nationalist direction. We have seen that figures such as Dieter Kunzelmann, from the beginning, combined socialist utopianism with anti-Semitism and German nationalism. An interesting parallel is the politics of cyber-anarchists like Julian Assange. The young Assange became a gifted hacker when he was in his teens, and worked with other hackers under the telling name *International Subversives*, a development which duplicated the Situationist International in a digital variety.[50] Just as Kunzelmann was attracted to Al-Fatah and called the German reparations to Israel a display of German neurosis, Assange has his ties to Holocaust deniers like the Israeli journalist Israel Shamir, and the Hezbollah leader Hassan Nasrallah.[51] Left and Right are not the key political categories to understand this phenomenon, but rather *power* and *subjection*. The German 68ers and today's anarchists share a hermeneutics of suspicion against any kind of authority.

Rainer Langhans (1940—) is another interesting case that confirms the idiosyncratic, spiritual drift of the old 68ers. After 1969 he "progressed" in an esoteric-therapeutic direction. He moved to Munich to inhabit a multi-apartment harem. Langhans regards fascism today as a "spiritual" movement and respects Hitler as a "great teacher." He also attended right wing fraternity associations, and contributed to the German Pirate Party and Julian Assange.[52]

What did the RAF represent if not a toxic mix of nationalism and socialism? The terror groups of the 1970s were not an aberrant development, some kind of accident or breakdown (*Betriebsunfall*), as when a factory has a bad accident). The student movement led inexorably to the RAF, even though the vast majority of participants halted before jumping off the cliff. The writer Peter Schneider was one of them. He himself flirted with the idea of joining the armed struggle in 1969 before tiptoeing back to ordinary life. In the early 1980s, Schneider wrote to Second Generation RAF member Peter Jürgen Boock,

---

50 Morozov, 22.

51 Morozov, 23.

52 Jörg Diehl, Langhans bei Burschenschaft: Rechts wie links, *Spiegel-online* (May 19, 2011).

> The idea of the urban guerilla hardly grew in the brains of just a few individual combatants. The idea swam, right from the beginning, in the river of thoughts and sentiments of the generation of 1968 and was discussed with unimaginable openness, from today's perspective, at Teach-Ins attended by thousands.

Schneider goes on to say that the idea of the armed struggle was nebulous, and discussed with a certain naiveté. One might hasten to add that in 1967, the SDS was and remained a small student group by membership count, reaching not more than 1500.[53] The organization attained fame and commanded attention far beyond its size in the wake of the killing of Benno Ohnesorg. A large segment of the left-liberal public in West Germany was intrigued and fascinated by this small clique of student radicals, because they announced they were ready to take direct action, rather than just talking about reform and change. Like Dutschke, many also had family responsibilities, so there remained definite boundaries to their sporadic Blanquist fantasies.

In lieu of actual militants, an entire sympathy wave emerged, the *Sypmpathisanten*, which represented a kind of radical-chic cheerleading squad supporting the goals of the revolution, including what the RAF later claimed were its goals, while always qualifying that "of course" they didn't support bank thefts and murder or anything else illegal. Almost forgotten today (or perhaps repressed) is the fact that when Hanns Martin Schleyer was kidnapped by the RAF and executed in 1977, many Germans on the left were celebrating the murderers. The Nobel Prize laureate Heinrich Böll felt a certain weakness for the anarchism of the RAF, which comes through in his strange depiction of the "war of the six against sixty million."[54] He wanted reconciliation. The ambivalence about the

---

53 Fichter/Lönnendonker, *Kleine Geschichte des SDS*, 9.

54 Böll sympathized with the RAF's challenge to power, even when he decried the methods. Was he alive today, might he have supported anti-globalism? He wrote, "Violence doesn't just exist in the form of bombs and pistols, but there is also violence and powers stashed in banks and traded on the stock exchange." See Torsten Krauel, "Die Armee der Sympathisanten muss sich auflösen," *Die Welt-online*, (March 14, 2014).

RAF persists to the present day and finds expression even in academic studies.[55] From the perspective of the RAF and its sympathizers, the battle did not set the RAF against the rest of Germans, but rather against the state, which was easier to justify. Irmgard Möller, a RAF member who spent twenty-three years in jail in Lübeck for triple murder said of the Böll statement,

> We were furious, since we didn't fight against 60 million, but against the government and the state. Böll constructed a kind of People's Front against us, which didn't exist—it certainly didn't exist then.[56]

The 68ers are well aware of their own limitations, contradictions and paradoxes. In late 1967 sixteen members of the generation of 1968 met with the intent to address their critics. *Der Spiegel* magazine cover captures the sense of self-irony well: "It Was Not all Bad—Mercy for the 68ers."[57] The critique they had to address was harsh. Even though "1968" was a worldwide phenomenon, the magazine noted that the legacy of that period has been more bitterly debated in Germany than in any other land. As an example, Eva Herman, (born in 1958), a controversial German television journalist and self-described post-feminist had been arguing for years that the 68ers had helped destroy the modern family, and she doesn't shy away from playing the Nazi card,

> The Nazis were bad, but they were at least good for mothers, children and families. The 68ers were so bad, that everything that had any

55 See for example Sarah Colvin, *Language, Violence and Identity; Ulrike Meinhof and West German Terrorism* (Suffolk: Camden, 2009). This book is an example of current leftwing justification for the RAF, of course trying to "contextualize" the violent tendencies of the RAF and also offers other examples of the *Sympathisanten* scene.

56 Oliver Tolmein, *Ein Gespräch mit Irmgard Möller; über bewaffneten Kampf, Knast und die Linke* ((Hamburg: Konkret, 2nd ed., 1999), 57.

57 "Es war nicht alles schlecht—Gnade für die 68er," *Der Spiegel* (Oct. 10, 1967). The transcript from the multi-day discussion was turned into a book, Irmela Hannover & Cord Schnibben, eds., *I can't get no—ein paar 68er treffen sich und rechnen ab* (Cologne: Kipenheuer & Witsch, 2007).

> value, that is families, mothers and children—that was all abolished.[58]

Her view is skewed, and hyperbolic to be sure,[59] but points to the fact that, whereas the 68ers saw their antics as provocation and fun, it is not uncommon for today's critics to trace contemporary social problems to the wild politics of that era. One core problem with this general critique is the assumption that the politics of the 68ers was homogeneous. As we have seen on almost every issue, there were deep divisions, on the question of violence, on the family, the state, the nation, on Trotsky vs. Stalin vs. Bakunin, hedonism vs. austerity and a host of other issues.

Blaming the 68ers for social problems almost a half-century later quite simply accords the graying radicals too much credit. The problem was not that the 68ers changed German society, but rather luckily, they failed to achieve most of what they set out to accomplish. In contrast to other revolutions in European history, the student movement was, in the apt phrase of Conor Cruise O'Brien, which serves as an epitaph to this chapter, a "pastoral ballad on a revolutionary theme.[60] In other words it was a song about a revolution, an imitation, a reflection, also a manipulated and steered attempt at a revolution. Effective historical revolutions, even rebellions, (the more fitting term for 1968), were preceded by years of grass roots organizing, rather than a spontaneous eruption of protest. The Civil Rights Movement of the 1950s and 1960s in America was preceded by decades of careful planning and organizing in civic society among African-American leaders. When the time came for the ideas and methods to have their day, those leaders were ready

---

58 Ibid., "Bürgerlich bis in die Knochen," 74. When one adds up the number of sins of the 68ers from all the critics the list is very long: environmental fundamentalism, unaffordable pensions, welfare fraud, bureaucracy, the EU, anti-patriotism, laziness, mediocrity etc.

59 Herman, whose real name is Eva Bischof, and her partner Frank Eckhardt, are building a colony with hundreds of German right-wing radicals and conspiracy theorists on the Canadian island of isolated Cape Breton. She is an example of the conflicted way that 1968 has affected German politics.

60 Stephen Greenblatt, "Wondrous, Fragile, Tedious Berkeley," *New York Review of Books* (Feb. 6, 2014), 13.

with an organized base all across the country. By contrast, the Occupy Wall Street and the Arab Spring were examples of protest against power, but were almost entirely lacking in organization and a sophisticated plan for reform. The same was true for the activists of the 60s everywhere. They had strong voices but had not built any kind of civic organizations on the ground, nor were they prepared to undertake the hard political work that constitutes the reality of governance. Not until the Green Party first cleared the 5% hurdle and entered the Bundestag in 1983 did they begin to make that transition.

To borrow some terms from physics, social movements sometimes appear to the observer as particles and sometimes as waves. To its participants, 1968 looked like an inexorable wave, but to historians looking back, the German youth revolt and the terrorism that followed look, from today's perspective, more like random particles going in every possible direction rather than proceeding towards any identifiable end point. But then, as the Cheshire cat said to Alice, if you don't know where you are going, any road will get you there.

II.
West German Generations and the *Gewaltfrage*:
The Conflict of the Sixty-Eighters and the Forty-Fivers

A. Dirk Moses and Elliot Neaman

Introduction

Die Gewaltfrage—the question of violence—haunted West Germans in the 1960s despite the fact that the country was at peace. As might be expected, the memories and consequences of the World War II remained palpable. Over five million German soldiers had fallen between 1939 and 1945, more than half of them in the final year of hostilities, while tens of thousands of women suffered horrific sexual abuse at the hands of Soviet occupation forces. Over 500,000 civilians were killed in allied bombing and, of the 14 million Germans expelled from central and eastern Europe, 1.71 million perished.[1] Hundreds of thousands of other Germans, namely Jews and those classified as Jews by the Nazis, had fled the country in the 1930s or been murdered soon thereafter. Millions of Jews in other parts of Europe had less chance of refuge; they were exploited, starved, shot, or gassed in their millions by a wide range of German organizations, ranging from the SS, the *Wehrmacht*, the railways, and civilian occupation authorities.[2]

---

1 Hans Ulrich Wehler, *Deutsche Gesellschaftsgeschichte, 1914-1949*, 4 vols. (Munich, 2003), 4: 942-44; Michael Geyer, "The Place of the Second World War in German Memory and History," *New German Critique*, no. 71 (Spring-Summer, 1997); Atina Grossmann, "A Question of Silence: The Rape of German Women by Soviet Occupation Soldiers," in *Women and War in the Twentieth Century*, ed. Nicole Ann Dombrowski (New York, 1999), 122-85.

2 Ulrich Herbert, ed., *National Socialist Extermination* Policies (New York: Berghahn Books, 2000).

What is more, violence had been a continuous presence in the lives older Germans who endured the first global conflagration of 1914-1918 and subsequent street fighting of the Weimar Republic. Even members of the celebrated "sixty-eighter" generation, born roughly between 1938 and 1948, possessed childhood memories of cowering in bomb shelters or marching in refugees' columns; those without such experiences grew up in ruined town and cities, with devastated families, and amid the national shame for the Holocaust. Not surprisingly, pacifism was a popular political current after the war.[3]

Yet if peace had finally come to continental Europe after two world wars, the tension between the west and communist countries, decolonization, and the subsequent Vietnam War meant that violence was always more than a memory. The mortal struggle of national liberation movements with European counterinsurgency, as well as the prospect of nuclear Armageddon appeared each evening on television screens. For West German intellectuals of all generations, these pictures were not only interpreted through the lens of the Cold War, as they were elsewhere. Images of the Nazi/fascist past were linked with contemporary events like the Vietnam War (would communism triumph as it almost had in Germany in the early 1930s, conservative feared? Or would capitalist elites unleash global war yet again, leftists worried?) because these intellectuals suffered from the "Weimar Syndrome," the acute anxiety that the Bonn Republic might suffer the fate of the first, ill-fated German experiment in democracy.[4] "Bonn is not Weimar," the Swiss journalist F. R. Alleman assured Germans in 1956, confirming what was uppermost in people's minds. Twelve years later, in the wake of the right-wing electoral success and student mobilization, the political scientist Karl Dietrich Bracher (born 1922) was also moved to ask

3 Andrew Oppenheimer, "West German Pacifism and the Ambivalence of Human Solidarity, 1945-1968," *Peace and Change* 29, nos. 3-4 (2004): 353-389

4 A. Dirk Moses, "The Weimar Syndrome in the Federal Republic of Germany: Carl Schmitt and the Forty-Fiver Generation of Intellectuals," in *Leben, Tod und Entscheidung: Studien zur Geistesgeschichte der Weimarer Republik*, ed. Holger Zaborowski und Stephan Loos (Berlin: Duncker und Humblot, 2003), 187-207.

whether Bonn was in fact Weimar after all.[5] Who was to blame for 1933, asked intellectuals, and are they carrying out their evil work today? In a discourse of crisis structured in this manner, different factions of the intelligentsia defined one another as standing in the tradition responsible for the destruction of German democracy in the past. The syndrome thus tended to escalate debates because opponents always fulfilled the threatening clichés of the other.[6] By framing contemporary public dramas in terms of Weimar politics, it contributed to the hysteria and paranoia of postwar West German politics. Ironically, then, the passionate effort of Bonn intellectuals to ensure that the turmoil of the 1920s would not ruin the Federal Republic meant that some of the spirit of those years—including the question of the legitimacy of political violence to defend democracy against the perceived enemies of democracy—was imported into the political discourse of the 1960s and 1970s of and about the student movement.

Thanks to the terrorism of the Red Army Faction (RAF), political violence in the Federal Republic is often associated, however obliquely, with the student movement and New Left, that is, with "'68." Instead of participating in the Weimar Syndrome by asserting that '68 was either the enemy or savior of West German democracy, we propose to historicize this contentious period by observing how the events of the day were interpreted by intellectuals as acts in a drama whose script was provided by German history itself. This essay, an exercise in the political history of ideas, examines the question of political violence in the "red decade" after 1967 among the sixty-eighters and their older counterparts, the forty-fiver generation of intellectuals, born roughly between 1922-1932.[7] The ideological and political conflicts around '68, we will see, reflected many of the themes of generational tension elsewhere in the world, but were overlaid with specifically German concerns: the legitimacy of violence to defend democracy. Political action in Germany, then,

---

5 Karl Dietrich Bracher, "Wird Bonn doch Weimar?" *Der Spiegel*, 13 March 1967, 60ff.

6 J.G.A. Pocock, "Verbalizing a Political Act: Toward a Politics of Speech," in *Language and Politics*, ed. Michael Shapiro (Oxford, 1984), 38f.

7 A. Dirk Moses, "The Forty-Fivers: A Generation Between Fascism and Democracy," *German Politics and Society* 17 (1999): 95-127.

was characterized by "melancholic repetition," never solely future-oriented, but framed by traumatic memories that defined the temporal horizon in terms of historically-embedded moral imperatives.[8]

The New Left, the Student Movement, and the *Gewaltfrage*

If the German student movement took its cues, its tactics, and rhetoric from the youth culture of the United States, its members also saw themselves as inheritors of European social radicalism. This dual influence meant they struggled with the question of the extent to which extent social change could be accomplished by peaceful, legal protest, or by subversive, revolutionary tactics. But the "question of violence" (*die Gewaltfrage*) was not solely self-generated or driven only by a dynamic internal to the student movement. It developed in relation to considerable state and right-wing violence, as well as to anxieties about the course of West German politics. For the students interpreted the Grand Coalition of 1966-1969 as a reenactment of Weimar and themselves as anti-fascists who would not make the same mistakes as when the Weimar Left underestimated the threat of Hitler's movement. Two texts were very important in situating the years 1966-1969 within the Weimar context of 1930-1933, delivering a concept *authoritarianism* against which to agitate: Max Horkheimer's *Autoritärer Staat* and Adorno (and others') *The Authoritarian Personality*. The Grand Coalition appeared as a reincarnation of the last years of the Weimar democracy, as broad coalitions operated on the basis of emergency decrees that eventually gave Hitler the opening he needed to transform the system into an explicit dictatorship. It also appeared to confirm Carl Schmitt's analysis of parliamentary democracy as the triumph of interest groups masquerading as representatives of the peoples' interests. The fact that Karl Schiller the finance minister from the SPD also succeeded in forging bodies of co-determination between the employers' associations and the unions, was seen as another sign of the ultimate integrative power of the capitalist state to close down

8 Martin Jay, 'When Did the Holocaust End? Reflections on Historical Objectivity', in his *Refractions of Violence* (London and New York, 2003).

opposition and exclude possibilities of other social and economic models. The students also saw confirmation of Adorno's "authoritarian personality" in the hostile attitude of the West German population to their politics. In particular they viewed the Springer media empire as an incubator for the fascist personality—a resentful middle class with ego-weak characteristics such as the love of order, hierarchies and subordination to power. The rising popularity of the far-right NPD only added to the students fears as did the looming passage of the emergency laws (*Notstandsgesetze*).

Student opposition to the emergency laws was linked with opposition to US foreign policy, and its war in Vietnam in particular: both were attacking democracy and socialism. This opposition reached a boiling point in Germany in 1967-68 with street demonstrations, strikes, sit-ins, the fatal shooting of a student on 2 June 1967 and an ultimately the attempted assassination of the leader of the Berlin chapter of the SDS, Rudi Dutschke on 11 April 1968 which set of a convulsion of violent protests against the German state and other institutions, the police, the university and mass media, all viewed by the students as conspiring to destroy German democracy.

The radicalization of the student movement was presaged by a growing split, beginning in the mid-1950s, between the venerable Social Democratic party and its youth organization, the Students for a Democratic Society (SDS). Herbert Wehner and other party leaders led the SPD away from doctrinal communism towards reform socialism and away from nationalism towards liberal internationalism, looking to the United States as the protector and guarantor of West German sovereignty. Many of the leaders of the SDS disliked the growing anti-communism of the SPD and were suspicious of NATO and the United States. When the U.S. became involved in the conflict in Indochina after 1954, the suspicion that United States foreign policy was neither leading the free world, nor embodying the principles of the United Nations, but rather reflected neo-colonial aspirations, only seemed to confirm their darkest fears. The SPD also became increasingly irritated with the attitude of the young cadres in the late 1950s over the question of how to deal with the East German State (GDR). In May 1960, the left wing of the SDS split from the SDP, while moderates and the right wing of the organization formed the Social-Democratic University Association (SHB). The SDS announced the split on 8 May 1960, the fifteenth anniversary of the capitulation of Germany in World War II.[9]

Two strains developed in the burgeoning student radical movement after the SDS broke with the SPD in 1960/61, one "anti-authoritarian" the other "classical" Marxist.[10] The former was inspired by situationism and was centered in Munich around a group called "Subversive Aktion," while in other major centers, Frankfurt, Bochum, Hamburg, and Berlin classical, or more precisely Marxist-Leninism and later Reform (Frankfurt School) Marxism constituted the ideological core of the movement. Rudi Dutschke began as a proponent of the anarchic version of radical politics associated with the Munich subversives, but he later moved in the direction of a non-sectarian, heterodox Marxism, based on Luxemburgian revisionism. Dutschke's genius was to be able to combine many elements together, as the German media elevated him to celebrity status from mid-1967 onward.[11]

Like the situationist movement in general, the German group, founded in 1957, saw itself as the inheritors of the Dadaist innovation that equated the artist to an avant-garde revolutionary. The German chapter of the Situationist International, called SPUR, was based on the name of the journal founded in 1960 as the German organ of the Situationist International (SI). [12] The artist Dieter Kunzelmann, who joined in 1960, became the most prolific theoretician of the movement. In his view, the working class was no longer a revolutionary subject, but rather had become the passive object of manipulation in an age of Cold War and restorative tendencies in Western Europe. The remaining revolutionary subject was the artist

9 Ibid., 374.

10 See Jens Hager, ed., *Die Rebellen von Berlin. Studenenpolitik an der freien Universität* (Cologne/Berlin, 1967), 50-51.

11 See Ulrich Chaussey, *Die Drei Leben des Rudi Dutschke* (Frankfurt, 1989), on Subversive Aktion, 37ff. On Dutschke's brand of Marxism, see Bernd Rabehl, *Rudi Dutschke, Revolutionär im geteilten Deutschland* (Dresden, 2002).

12 Lothar Fischer et. al, *Gruppe SPUR, 1958-1965* (Regensburg, 1986).

him or herself, who through experiments in living and public provocation (therefore the title "provos" for its members) could hope to build the basis for future revolutionary movements. In the place of organized mass movements, led by the Marxist vanguard, the situationists embraced the notion that small groups could use targeted violence to attack the bourgeois order.[13] Kunzelmann passed onto the SDS an eclectic mix of surrealism, Dadaism, psychoanalysis and German philosophy, in the main derived from the Frankfurt School.

Kunzelmann imported the peace-love-drugs culture of San Francisco encapsulated in his famous reply to what he would do about the war in Southeast Asia: "What do I care about Vietnam, when I have orgasm difficulties."[14] By contrast, by 1967 Dutschke was married and considered Kunzelmann's emphasis on sexual freedom a distraction for the movement ("pseudo-sexualization"[15]). But German situationism was not just playful Bohemianism, since it also anticipated both the theory and praxis of the extreme radical wing of the student movement. Kunzelmann himself organized a terrorist group in the mid-1960s called the "Tupamaros West-Berlin" whose most spectacular and troubling act of violence was a bombing of a Jewish synagogue in Berlin on the carefully chosen date of 9 November 1969. The Tupmaros called for attacks on judges, and lawyers and destruction of American, Jewish and Israeli property in Germany, and were thus the direct predecessors to and inspiration for the later *Red Army Fraction* (RAF).[16]

Around early 1965, Dutschke and his friend, another former citizen of East Germany Bernd Rabehl decided to join the SDS, partly because of their distrust of the links developing between the SDS and FDJ. For them, both East and West Germany were occupied by an imperialist superpower and therefore "co-existence" would simply stabilize a status quo that perpetuated Germany's subjugation. They favored instead a *Deustchlandpolitik* that would

13 See Dieter Kunzelmann, *Leisten Sie Keinen Widerstand* (Berlin, 1998).

14 Ibid., 51-73.

15 Rudi Dutschke, *Die Revolte*, (Hamburg, 1983), 169.

16 See Wolfgang Kraushaar, *Die Bombe im Jüdischen Gemeindehaus* (Hamburg, 2005). See also his *Die RAF und der linke Terrorismus* (Hamburg, 2006).

ratchet up, not decrease confrontation between East and West. The logic of this position can only be understood against the background of how the Cold War conflicts over de-colonization were interpreted in the mid-1960s.

Dutschke captured the essence of the student's movement's fascination with Third World revolutionary movements by pointing to the parallels he saw between neo-colonialism and a divided Germany. Just as Georg Lukacs had tried to explain the problem of a gradually de-radicalized proletariat in Western Europe after World War I as the result of the reification of consciousness (in *History and Class Consciousness*), Dutschke interpreted the lack of opposition to modern imperialism in the 1960s along the same lines and relegated to the extra-parliamentary opposition the task of opposing neo-colonialism as a new revolutionary subject. In the Cold War, Germany was just as much the object of imperialism as Vietnam.[17] A contemporary poem nicely captured this widespread perception:

> Vietnam is Germany
> Her fate is our fate
> The bombs for her freedom
> Are bombs for our freedom[18]

These lines, written by Erich Fried, a German-Jewish exile and Holocaust survivor, introduces a curious inversion. The American bombs being dropped on the North Vietnamese, to make them "free" could not help but bring forth in a postwar Germans' imagination the trauma of allied bombs that destroyed German cities to make them free. In a world turned upside down by US imperialism, the Germans and Vietnamese alike are akin to Jews facing extermination. That a leftist thinker like Fried could not see the nationalist-revolutionary implications of that analogy was only possible because the self-identification with the victims of the holocaust was actually part of the international student movement, often led by

17 See Rudi Dutschke, "Die Widersprüche des Spätkapitalismus, die antiautoritären Studenten und ihr Verhältnis zur Dritten Welt," in Bergman et. al. *Rebellion der Studenten*, 33-57. See also his interview with Günther Gaus from 1970, in Rudi Dutschke, *Mein langer Marsch*, esp. 51.

18 Cited by Ingo Juchler, *Rebellische Subjektivität und Internationalismus* (Marburg, 1989), 8.

Jews, outsiders and minorities. In France particularly, for many leaders of 1968 (Cohn-Bendit, Glücksmann, Finkelkraut), the French state had not only not owned up to its fascist-Vichy past, but had perpetuated another holocaust in Algeria. When Cohn-Bendit, a son of Berlin Jews was expelled from France in 1968, thousands of Parisian students took to the street shouting "*Nous somme tous des juifs allemands.*"[19] By equating the anti-imperial struggle with the Holocaust, Bonn was not so much Weimar, but rather a subordinate player in a neo-fascist axis that circled the globe.

The Students' Confrontation with the German State

In following the tactics of the Berkeley Free Speech movement and the SNCC (student Non-Violent Coordinating Committee), the German radicals adopted their methods as well: Sit-ins, strikes, peaceful demonstrations, poster actions, etc. The Berlin students developed a method of sending small groups of students (provos) through crowded shopping streets attracting attention through political clownery, like holding out tins to collect money for "warm underwear for the police."[20] The police responded by invoking Article 3 of Germany's *Basic Law* and sent undercover policemen into the crowds to arrest the students.[21] There was persistent tension among the provos and the "classical" Marxists. The latter frowned upon what it viewed as undisciplined spontaneous actions, like throwing eggs at the Amerika-Haus and attacking the American flag, as happened after an anti-Vietnam demonstration on 5 February 1966 or a happening in front of the popular Berlin café Kranzler on 10 December 1967, where two paper-mâché puppets of Lyndon

19 Wolfgang Kraushaar, *1968 als Mythos, Chiffre und Zäsur* (Hamburg, 2000), 329.

20 See Bernard Larrson, *Berlin—Hauptstadt der Republik—Fotographien aus einer geteilten Stadt 1961–1968* (Göttingen, 1968).

21 See Jens Hager, *Die Rebellen von Berlin*, (Cologne, 1967), 50 ff. The Basic Law, Article 3, paragraph 1 states that "all persons shall be equal before the law." The police asserted (with dubious legal reasoning) that the students were placing themselves above the law.

Johnson and Walter Ulbricht were fed to the flames. Actions of this type were designed to incite and provoke the authorities, not much more, but they edged ever further into the gray areas of illegality.

Inside the SDS, the question of violence was debated repeatedly before the death of Benno Ohnesorg. Not unlike the splits that occurred inside the SNCC, after the election of Stokely Carmichael as chairman in 1966, some SDS activists questioned the effectiveness of relying solely on non-violence tactics. Acts of provocation that only destroyed objects, or simulated violence, were the first actions in more confrontation direction that led to a loss of support among moderates and "bourgeois" liberals, but also led to recriminations from other SDSers.

In early 1966, German student demonstrations against the Vietnam war began in earnest. The students called the winter of 1965/1966 the "Vietnam Semester."[22] Bernd Rabehl and Rudi Dutschke had formed a small group called "*Anschlag*" (attack) that used the SDS name in placards during demonstrations. During the night of 3 and 4 February, they and a small group of SDSlers carried out an illegal "*Plakataktion*" blanketing Berlin with posters calling Chancellor Ernard and the Bonn coalition a band of murderers for supporting the war in Vietnam and the repression of colonial peoples.[23] The old guard at the SDS was extremely unhappy with the *provos* and tried to have them thrown out of the SDS, but ultimately they could not gain enough votes to carry out such a disciplinary action. After a sit-down strike on 9 February, modeled on Berkeley, students marched to the *Amerika Haus*, pelted it with eggs and ripped own the American flag. Berlin's mayor, Willy Brandt, and other dignitaries, rushed to apologize to the American authorities. Inside the SDS, a fiery internal discussion ensued, in which Fritz Haug, an orthodox Marxist professor of philosophy, and editor of the influential journal *Das Argument*, inveighed against Dutschke for trying to push the working class prematurely into a revolutionary state. The discussion was a key moment that showed fissures within the SDS on the issue of violence. Haug invoked Marx's thesis

22 Uwe Bergmann, et. al. *Rebellion der Studenen* (Frankfurt, 1968), 18.

23 See Jürgen Miermeister and Jochen Staadt, *Provokationen: die Studenten und Jugendrevolte in ihren Flugblättern* (Darmstadt, 1980), 82.

against Putschism, and Dutschke responded with Lukaçs' theories from the early 1920s on the failure of the Russian Revolution to abolish the state. According to Dutschke's interpretation of Lukaçs, the working class, while objectively the subject of history was objectively stuck in encrusted class relations and so the revolutionary agent, the student movement, has to lead the workers into a new mode of consciousness. Rabehl, who had written a doctoral dissertation on the Paris Commune as reflected in Soviet historiography, also argued against Dutschke that the situation in 1966 was neither pre- nor post revolutionary as had been the case in 1920.[24]

Global politics and the German past merged on 2 June 1967 when the Shah of Persia, Mohammad Reza Pahlavi, and his wife Farah Diba arrived at the Schöneberger City Hall to present an exquisite carpet to the Mayor, Heinrich Albertz. The Shah was of particular significance to the students because of the perceived centrality of his role in the Cold War as a puppet of the United States and as an example of a Third World tyrant "of the Free World" who lived in splendor while his people starved.[25] Outside of the City Hall, Pro-Iranian students (probably organized by the Persian secret police) faced off against anti-Shah demonstrators.[26] The *Jubelperser* (cheering Persians) suddenly brandished long, wooden clubs and flailed wildly at the students while the police watched passively for ten minutes before intervening. The students vowed to return that evening, when the Shah and his wife were to attend a performance of Mozart's Magic *Flute* at the Opera House. On the Bismarckstrasse the demonstrations became even more bloody as eight hundred police started clubbing the students without any warning. At around

---

24 Interview with Bernd Rabehl, Berlin, 27 August 2006. On the three different strands inside the New Left in relation to the seizure of power, (Neo-Marxists, Anti-Authoritarians, and Radical Socialists), see Wighard Härdtl, "Strategie der neuen Linken zur Machtergreifung," in Heinrich Barth, ed., *Die Studentische Protestbewegung* (Mainz, 1971), 95-123.

25 A bestseller at the time popularized these ideas: Bahman Nirumand, *Persien, Modell eines Entwicklungslandes oder Die Diktatur der Freien Welt*, (Hamburg,1967).

26 The presence of the Iranian secret police was widely reported, see Berlin—Knüppel frei," *Der Spiegel*, 12 June 1967, 41.

8:20 p.m. Karl-Heinz Kurras, a criminal inspector, shot Benno Ohnesorg, as he was trying to flee the demonstration.[27]

Had one of the ringleaders been shot, perhaps in the act of throwing a brick, the Springer Press would have poured out indignant rage and the students would have been put on the defensive. As it was, the *Bildzeitung* was hardly reticent. The headlines the next day read, "Who produces terror must be prepared for a harsh response." But Ohnesorg was an entirely different case. He came from Hanover, was twenty-six years old, recently married and was then studying modern languages and philology at Braunschweig. He was a pacifist, described by friends as an independent type who would not join any student groups, though he did attend some events put on by the Evangelical Students Association. In hindsight, Ohnesorg's death provided a perfect grounding mythology for the student movement. Thousands watched as his casket was transported from West Berlin to Hannover, through East Germany, where the SED had made a special exception to the transit rules in order to embarrass the West German government. Like Americans who remember where they were when they heard the news of the death of John or Robert Kennedy, the shooting of Ohnesorg remained etched upon the collective memory of the generation of 1968.

The events of 2 June 1967 reverberated throughout the nation, but the center of gravity was located in Berlin. As the political scientist Richard Löwenthal and others noted at the time, the fact that the wall had been built in Berlin drew politically interested students—the FU had the most politics majors in the nation, nine hundred and seventeen to be precise. Second, the special Berlin Model of co-determination actually increased, not decreased potential tensions. Third, the island character of the city and the Cold War pressures made the Berlin citizenry particularly sensitive, sometimes even panicky about the rebellious and seeming anarchic behavior of students, so many of whom came from outside the city.[28]

---

27 Kurras was an East German Stasi asset. See Elliot Neaman, *Free Radicals*, op. cit, 68-74.

28 "Die aufsässigen Studenten von Berlin," *Der Spiegel*, 5 June 1967, 48-50.

Die *Gewaltfrage* and the Split inside the SDS

From the point of view of the students, the German state and the police were acting in concert to suppress their legitimate desire for social change. And like in the Weimar years, the state did in fact put pressure on leftwing political dissent, responding to street demonstrations with phony invocations of the Basic law, clubs, dogs, and high-pressure water hoses. Unlike in Weimar, however, there was no organized rightwing street violence that offered some kind of comparison. Violence was thus both a political reality, driven by escalating confrontations between the authorities and the students, and a theoretical discourse to justify the necessity of violence as a means to effect social change.

Both aspects were on clear display when Herbert Marcuse visited the FU in July to give four talks before a packed audience of student radicals. The leadership of the SDS heralded Marcuse as the preeminent theoretician of the student movement because he offered not only a post-Marxist analysis of late capitalism and consumer society, but seemed to accept, with some reservations, the guru role offered to him by the students.[29] The students were particularly attracted to Marcuse's contention that late industrial capitalism opened up the possibilities for an entirely new kind of human being who could transcend animal aggressive instincts in the building of a new society. Marcus's main topic was the "End of Utopia," which he interpreted as the opposite of realism. Realists believed that social problems were inevitable, while modernist utopians could point to the advances of material productive forces as proof that concerted social action could lead to a free society. If one succumbed to the realists, one might as well concede the "end of history."[30] His second talk, "The Problem of Violence in the Opposition," was crucial. Here he pointed to the civil disobedience movement in the United States as an example for the German students, even though he never explained who were the equivalent agents of

29 See Bernd Rabehl, *Am Ende der Utopie* (Berlin, 1988), 238-42.

30 Herbert Marcuse, *Five Lectures: Psychoanalysis, Politics and Utopia*, trans. Jeremy J. Shapiro and Shierry M. Weber. (Boston, 1970), 62.

socially oppressed African Americans in Germany. Marcuse saw violence as legitimate when it countered what he considered to be the illegitimate use of violence by the state (as in, for example, Martin Luther King's opposition to the war in Vietnam). Marcuse's final lecture on this topic, "The problem of Violence and the Radical Opposition," was a decisive influence on Dutschke's thinking on this issue.[31]

Dutschke's development in fact highlighted the acute tensions that soon arose inside the SDS and the student movement in general over the question of political violence. Dutschke was directly blamed for the violent turn of the protests that occurred in front of the Moabit courthouse in the fall of 1967 as a student agitator, Fritz Teufel, sat in custody awaiting trial on charges of inciting a riot.[32] Dutschke suggested storming the courthouse and invoked the burning of the Supreme Court in Vienna by workers on 15 July 1927, implying that the students may wish to follow their example. Everyone, he said "should think about what it means for him or herself."[33] Bernd Rabehl began to break with Dutschke at this point and made contact with the Berlin police because he did not want to see the student opposition spiral out of control.[34]

Worry about Democracy

The SDS had established a Study Group on Vietnam and held a series of popular conferences on the war, beginning in May 1966. The national leaders at the time, Helmut Schauer and Hartmut Dabrowski were able to follow up on the success of these events by getting the largest of the German unions, the IG Metall to finance another conference at the end of October 1966 in Frankfurt. The topic, "Democracy at Risk" (*Notstand der Demokratie*), was aimed at

---

31 See "Diskussion zu 'Das Problem der Gewalt in der Opposition' vom 10-13 Juli 1967 in Berlin," in Rudi Dutschke, *Die Revolte* (Hamburg, 1977), 183-205. The most important influence, besides Lukacs, whose essay on "Legalität und Illegalität" Dutschke often quoted.

32 Chaussey, *Die Drei Leben des Rudi Dutschke* (Frankfurt, 1989) 168.

33 "Studenten; der lange Marsch," *Der Spiegel*, 11 December 1967, 52.

34 Gretchen Dutschke-Klotz, *Wir hatten ein schönes barbarisches Leben* (Cologne, 1996),183.

the emergency laws that were being discussed at the time between the potential partners of the Grand Coalition, the SPD, CDU, CSU, and FDP. The laws would curtail some civil liberties and give the police wider powers to infiltrate subversive political groups and clamp down on violent acts by protesters. More importantly, the laws would give a special commission, made up of representatives from the *Bundestag* and the states, the right to declare war by a simple majority in the case of a threat of external danger ("*Zustand der äusseren Gefahr*"). Critics warned that this undemocratic procedure was analogous to the almost unanimous granting of war credits to the Kaiser in 1914 and the Reichstag's support for Hitler in may of 1933.[35] The ideas behind the emergency laws had been discussed since 1958, but through the early 1960s the conservatives had not been able to pass them. Both the unions and the students feared that the price of power for the SPD would be agreeing to the emergency laws. In fact, after much tumult and controversy, they were finally enacted on 30 May 1968, requiring a two-thirds majority to amend the German constitution. The fears that the laws would be used to undermine Germany's parliamentary system proved of course to be unfounded.

The German "1968"

Youth social protest was a global phenomenon in 1968. Historically, the German "1968" as a movement can be dated from 1966 to 1969, though the "hot period" lasted only from the acquittal of Kurras in December 1967 to the mass protests following Rudi Dutschke's assassination on 11 April 1968. After those protests died down, the *Bewegung* was without a leader who could orchestrate public protest that commanded media attention. Throughout the fall of 1968 and through 1969, the student opposition splintered into cells and diverse grouplets and organized student groups at the universities quarreled about tactics and strategies. There were still many large demonstrations throughout 1969, but they seemed more and more

35 See Dietrich Thränhardt, *Geschichte der Bundesrepublik* (Frankfurt, 1986), 175ff. See also Rudolf Augstein, "Notstand durch Gesetz?" *Der Spiegel*, 6 November 1967.

like repeat performances and then historical enactments. One can date the end of APO with fair precision with the beginning of the SPD/FDP coalition in 1969. In general terms, one could argue that "1968" was coexistent with APO and therefore with the Grand Coalition from December 1966 to October 1969. But at the start, from 1966 to mid-1967, the active members of the radical student groups were small in number. Even in Berlin, the SDS only held two seats in the nine seat executive council of the General Students Association (*AstA*). By the beginning of 1968, however, Dutschke's call alone could bring six or seven thousand students onto the streets of Berlin. That was a potent weapon in a city whose leaders were jittery about the moral authority of the youth and in fact imbued with general guilt about the use of military and police force against the left from the Weimar period and specifically in relation to the events of 2 June 1967.

Dutschke realized the power of the student movement and exploited it with deftness. But in hindsight, including his own, his plans were megalomaniacal. He believed that the student movement alone had the power to confront NATO and change what he perceived to be the German government's acquiescence in the US's global imperial strategy. His geopolitical vision included re-unification of Germany, followed by a Council Republic (*Räterepublik*) along the lines of the early Soviets, before Lenin crushed them in 1918. Dutschke's other model was the French commune of 1870. He foresaw a breaking down of the barriers between worker and intellectual, the disappearance of crime and a reduction of the work week. When asked (by H.M. Enzensberger) whether or not the allies would not impose a blockade in the event that Berlin became a Council Republic, Dutschke replied that just as with the Paris Commune, the workers and students would organize to break it.[36]

Dutschke was so convinced of the possibility of revolution at this time that he even became involved in a bizarre plot to blow up ships in the Hamburg harbor carrying weapons for the US war effort in Vietnam. The explosives were actually delivered to Dutschke's

36 All of these ideas can be found in a discussion between Dutschke, Rabehl, Enzensberger and Semmler in "Ein Gespräch über die Zukunft," *Kursbuch* 14 (October, 1967).

apartment in Berlin, thanks to an eccentric Milanese millionaire and radical publisher, Giangiacomo Feltrinelli. Dutschke hid the explosives for several days, even transporting them in his infant son, Che's baby carriage, before finally abandoning the plot as too risky.[37]

Violence against the Students

During the winter months of 1968, Dutschke's role as supra-leader of the movement became increasingly evident. He traveled the country incessantly, giving speeches and organizing student demonstrations. He also made the cover of Germany's major magazines, even receiving money for his efforts, all of which led to a counter-movement against him inside the SDS, but more ominously, created an image in the public's eye of a Lenin-like figure emerging to lead the students. There was an air of hysteria surrounding Dutschke which became evident on 21 February at a pro-American demonstration held in front of the Schöneberger City Hall, during which a young man who resembled Dutschke was kicked to the ground and almost trampled to death. Harking back to the "people's justice" atmosphere of Weimar, posters called Dutschke the "public enemy" a 'Jewish pig" and other obscenities.[38]

The assassination attempt on Dutschke confirmed the worst fears of the students, that the combined power of the anti-student Springer press and proto-fascist sympathies of middle class Germans would eventually result in murder of one of their own. The martyrdom of Dutschke seemed apocalyptic: he was born on Easter Day, he was shot during Easter week (*Gründonnerstag*) and often invoked Jesus as an inspiration.[39] The political violence also had a world-historical parallel. On 4 April 1968 Martin Luther King was gunned down in Memphis by James Earl Ray, a loner and petty criminal. Joseph Bachman, Dutschke's assailant, likewise a loner and down on his luck, had read about King and wondered to himself

37 See Chaussey, *Die Drei Leben des Rudi Dutschke*, 179-180.

38 Jürgen Miermeister, *Rudi Dutschke* (Hamburg, 1986), 92-94.

39 Jürgen Miermeister has noted the many parallels between Jesus and Dutschke's messianism, see his *Rudi Dutschke*, 38-39.

why the American civil rights leader, a pacifist, was killed, while the German student leader who promulgated violence, was free to draw thousands of young people onto German streets.

Up until Dutschke's shooting, the student movement did not possess a coherent organization or worldview. The small student groups were good at setting into motion waves of political action, but they weren't well equipped to harness the energy and create lasting institutions. Since the Federal Republic could boast, by any measure, a very wealthy economy, the students much less interested than traditional socialists about issues like inequality. They did not want a better standard of living, but a different kind of living, beyond industrial society. The political spectrum was correspondingly wide, reaching from libertarian anarchists to hippies to Trotskyites to Stalinist die-hards.

The events of Easter 1968 finally gave the students a sense of unity of purpose and provided them with a single object for their anger and frustration, thus solidifying the movement. But Dutschke would soon go into exile, and his parting also signaled the begin of the end of the movement. The *Gewaltfrage* as theory was put, as it were, into suspended animation. The possibilities to use it remained, and were of course used in the 1970s by small underground groups, but the question for most, when and to what extent it was legitimate to employ, was never resolved: could German democracy and society be saved with the application of calibrated doses of provocation and violence, or did one have to smash the system and start all over again?

The Forty-Fivers and the Sixty-Eighters

These events and the question of violence after 1966 revived traumatic memories for all Germans because they interpreted it in terms of the "Weimar Syndrome." As might be expected, this syndrome affected older Germans who had experienced the Weimar years as adults more than it did younger Germans. The leftist and liberal members of the generation between them, the forty fivers, who were children during the Weimar years, maintained remarkable sympathy for the student movement, even after the *Gewaltfrage* was posed, but there were limits to their tolerance, as we shall see. At some point, even they could not escape the Weimar Syndrome.

Ludwig von Friedeburg (born 1923) made clear where he and Habermas, who were in close communication with the SDS leadership in Frankfurt and West Berlin, stood. He called them the "democratically engaged minority," and at the SPD congress in 1968 Horst Ehmke hailed the students as "the generation for which we have been waiting".[40] Leftist and some liberal forty-fivers saw in the sixty-eighters images of themselves and the opportunity to realize those ambitions that had been thwarted since 1945.

By the winter of 1967/68, this support became more difficult when the humanities and social science departments in many German universities were taken over by students who proclaimed the inauguration of the "critical university," as in Berlin, or the "political university" as in Frankfurt.[41] Some of the occupiers were simply enthusiastic reformers who sought to integrate the learning process more closely with their most pressing political concerns, as Habermas, Hofmann, and others had recommended. Others were more radical and, according to one historian, adopted a "guerrilla strategy," wanting to "set up bases at the universities that would offer a collective' opportunity to discover and develop long-term social-revolutionary strategies for the cities."[42]

At the SDS conference in Hanover on 9 June 1967—one week after Ohnesorg's death—Habermas used the infelicitous term "leftist fascism" to characterize the mentality and strategy of actionism.[43] His reaction underscored the common posture of all forty-fivers to revolutionary rhetoric, whether of the left or the right. Their

---

40 Horst Ehmke, "Die Generation, auf die wir gewartet haben [1968]," in his *Politik der praktischen Vernunft* (Frankfurt, 1969), 187-207.

41 See the documentation in Wolfgang Kraushaar, ed., *Frankfurter Schule und Studentenbewegung. Von der Flaschenpost zum Molotowkocktail, 1945 bis 1995*, 3 Vols. (Hamburg, 1998); Detlev Claussen and Regine Dermitzel, eds., *Universität und Widerstand. Versuch einer Politischen Universität in Frankfurt* (Frankfurt, 1968).

42 Rolf Wiggershaus, *The Frankfurt School: Its History, Theories, and Political Significance*, trans. Michael Robertson (Cambridge, Mass., 1994), 632f.

43 Jürgen Habermas, "Diskussionsbeiträge," in his *Protestbewegung und Hochschulreform* (Frankfurt, 1969), 148. He later regretted and withdrew the term.

commitment was to the Federal Republic as a project of reform, either radical or conservative; having witnessed it in their youth, blind actionism was an anathema. Thus novelist Günter Grass condemned the violence and confrontational posture of the SDS, saying that "The slogans 'ban the SDS' and 'Expropriate Springer' are written in the same authoritarian ink."[44] Marxist political scientist Peter von Oertzen, in taking issue with Habermas' controversial term and through distancing the students from fascism, had to admit that one had to regret "the actionism of the radical wing of the rebelling students, and one needed to criticize most harshly their partly irrational character, lack of tactical wisdom, their strategic aimlessness, and often bitter intolerance."[45] And in his criticism of the conservative reaction to the students' call for the democratization of society, the pedagogue Hartmut von Hentig had to refer disparagingly to the left's program as "either breathtakingly naïve or ideologically strained."[46] Ralf Dahrendorf famously crossed swords with the SDS leader Rudi Dutschke on the roof of a van before thousands of students in Freiburg in 1967, putting his case against the New Left, utopianism of any sort, or criticism of representative democracy.[47]

Nonetheless, despite the violence and revolutionary rhetorical of key student leaders, leftist intellectuals continued to support their aims insofar as they coincided with their own. West Berlin professors and writers were more worried about the escalation of the street clashes, and especially by what they called the "pogrom atmosphere" among the population and the police described above. "The disturbance of the youth is justified," they wrote in an open

44 Günter Grass, "Gewalt ist wieder Gesellschaftsfähig," *Der Spiegel*, 6 May 1968, 57.

45 Peter von Oertzen, "Was ist eigentlich Linksfaschismus?" *Süddeutsche Zeitung*, 13/14 January 1968.

46 Hartmut von Hentig, "Das Sache und die Demokratie," *Die Neue Sammlung* 9 (1969): 121; idem, "Die grosse Beschwichtigung," *Merkur* 22 (1968): 385-400.

47 Ralf Dahrendorf, "Aktive und passive Öffentlichkeit," *Merkur* 21 (December 1967): 1109-22; idem, "Sozialismus oder Liberalismus," *Die Zeit*, 21 November 1969, 59f.

declaration in *Die Zeit* that was probably penned by Habermas, because the parliaments were not discussing the pressing issues like Vietnam.[48]

Such support was not surprising. What was significant was that many liberals also affirmed the movement after 1968 despite the radicalization. Figures like political scientist Kurt Sontheimer, Bracher, and political theorist Alexander Schwan who are today thought of as anti-student neo-conservatives were among these liberals. Typical was Horst Krüger's reaction. While highly critical of the radical wing of the student movement, he argued that one should not reduce the protest movement to this dimension. On the whole, the protest movement was effecting a liberalization of society, and the sooner some of its members abandoned revolutionary activity and devoted themselves to concrete matters, like anti-authoritarian kindergartens, reformed doctors and legal practices and so on, the better. "The fork in the road [*Kreuzweg*] between romanticism and reality, between anarchy and social engagement, is still open."[49] Writing in 1969, Bracher had no doubt that the danger to the republic still came from the right. He remained disturbed by the passive character of the population regarding the state, and the "frighteningly little" identification with its democratic institutions. "Here also lie the constructive aspects of the current 'disturbances' insofar as they are directed towards inner reform and the recognition of the GDR."[50]

Even the chief editor at the *Norddeutscher Rundfunk* and later anti-leftist editor of the conservative *Frankfurter Allgemeine Zeitung* Joachim Fest (1926-2006) ran this argument. "Their [the students']

48 "Appel an den Berliner Senat," *Die Zeit*, 8 March 1962, 6. The signatories included Wolfgang Abendroth, Theodor W. Adorno, Richard F. Behrendt, Dieter Claessens, Wolfram Fischer, Otto Flechtheim, Ludwig von Friedeburg, Günter Grass, Jürgen Habermas, Werner Hofmann, Walter Jens, Walter Killy, Alexander Kluge, Christian Graf von Krockow, Werner Maihofer, Fritz Raddatz, Hans Werner Richter, Wolfgang Schnurre, Jakob Taubes, Harald Weinrich.

49 Horst Krüger, "Wohin treibt die Protestbewegung?," *Merkur* 23 (September 1969): 883-86.

50 Karl Dietrich Bracher, "Die zweite Demokratie," *Die Zeit*, 12 December 1969, 54-7.

legitimate need for suggestive future options have been neither recognized nor addressed for twenty years."[51] Unbridled utopianism, revolutionary rhetoric and violence were the fruit of such neglect. The student movement's inability to articulate coherently its demands and utopian vision merely reflected the muteness of the establishment. The one-sidedness of both parties, Fest suggested, put the republic in danger, but the real problem was the German prejudice against the left. "Not in student annoyance, in their lack of respect and call to action, but in the authoritarian reaction against it, lies also well-founded what will be essentially the real test for the Federal Republic in the near future."[52] Sociologist M. Rainer Lepsius made precisely the same point.[53]

Kurt Sontheimer was even harder on the establishment. The threat continued to come from the right, he argued in 1968 because the conservative establishment could not distance itself satisfactorily from the far right, sharing as it did an ensemble of dubious concepts and categories. To be sure, the APO had some anti-parliamentary streams, but it presented no danger and was in fact a salutary challenge to the regime.[54] Like Fest, he insisted that the real danger to the republic did not come from a revolutionary but essentially isolated and impotent group of students but rather from the latent authoritarian, indeed fascist sentiments they may evoke in the population. The electoral success of the rightwing National Party of Germany (NPD) should be a lesson to politicians that only through the true grounding of democracy in public institutions would the country be rendered immune from such threats in the

51 Joachim Fest, "Das Dilemma des studentischen Romantizismus," in *Revolution gegen den Staat? Die ausserparlamentarische Opposition-neue Linke*, ed. Hans Dollinger (Bern, 1968), 225.

52 Ibid., 239, 232.

53 M. Rainer Lepsius, "Unruhe als Studentenpflicht?" *Stimmen der Zeit*, no. 180 (1967): 299-310.

54 Kurt Sontheimer, "Antidemokratisches Denken in der Bundesrepublik," in his *Antidemokratisches Denken in der Weimarer Republik. Die politischen Ideen des deutschen Nationalismus zwischen 1918 und 1933* (1968), 317-47.

future.[55] The alarmist "Cassandra calls" of conservative professors that students were paralyzing the universities were understandable, he agreed, for it was true that some of them had resolved to use the campuses as launching pads for revolution. But the professors had to realize that the student push for a direct, plebiscitary input into university decision-making represented a frustrated reaction to stalled university reform.[56]

There were of course forty-fivers who opposed the students from the outset. Two of the most significant interventions were Erwin Scheuch's *Die Wiedertäufer der Wohlstandsgesellschaft* (The Anabaptists of the Affluent Society) and Wilhelm Hennis' *Die deutsche Unruhe* (The German Disturbance). Their main argument expressed the Weimar Syndrome: the students and New Left had imported the intellectual currents of the 1920s, namely that truth was beyond academic proof and scrutiny, into the 1960s. This was the ideology in which the crimes of the twentieth century had been committed, and it was typical of youth movements that possess a pre-critical desire for total explanation in the manner of theology or philosophies of history. Scheuch went so far as to lend academic credibility to the popular canard that linked the leftwing students to rightwing Nazi students from the 1930s by employing the term "*linke Leute von Rechts*" (left people from the right). Not for nothing did he think that the students reincarnated the Anabaptist religious chiliasm of the radical Reformation[57]

With the sixty-eighters he contrasted members of his own generation who were replacing the reconstruction generation whose work it viewed "mostly with critical distance." The main conflict between the generations, however, was not between the sixty-eighters and the reconstruction generation, but between the sixty-eighters

55 Kurt Sontheimer, "Gefahr von rechts—Gefahr von links," in *Der Überdruss an der Demokratie: Neue Linke und alte Rechte—Unterschiede und Gemeinsamkeiten*, ed. Kurt Sontheimer et al (Cologne, 1970), 1-43.

56 Kurt Sontheimer, "Die Demokratisierung der Universität," in *Reform als Alternative. Hochschullehrer antworten auf die Herausforderung der Studenten*, ed. Alexander Schwan (Cologne, 1969), 63-73.

57 Erwin Scheuch, "Zur Einleitung," in *Die Wiedertäufer der Wohlstandsgesellschaft. Eine kritische Untersuchung der 'Neuen Linken' und ihrer Dogmen*, ed. Erwin Scheuch (Cologne, 1967), 7-13.

and what Scheuch called his own "middle generation." The latter were appalled by the ideological protest of the New Left unlike some members of the older generation such as the Marxists Ernst Bloch and Wolfgang Abendroth who were sympathic to the students. Why did the forty-fivers find the emphasis on political spirit and orientation (*Gesinnung*) so disturbing?

This generation remembers its elementary experiences that in modernity all the great crimes were committed by people and groups who asserted that the content of their politics was an ideology and that their spirit and orientation could not be questioned. The *Gesinnungskriminelle* of politics is the typical arsonist and murderer of great magnitude of this century.[58]

The social democratic philosopher Hermann Lübbe agreed. He thought that the student generation of the 1920s and the culture of the World War I experience had been replicated in the 1960s and 1970s by a "world wide student-intellectual partisan cult." It represented a "flight from reality" indicative of those who had been unable to stabilize their identities due to the pace of the modernization process. As a result, they exhibited a sectarian worldview well known since the nineteenth-century as "partisan romanticism." In short, the students were the apostles of the counter-enlightenment because they "rediscovered the old political 'truths' that not only decisive arguments but violence also cuts the Gordian Knot, clarifies situations, and simplifies everything."[59] This was the argument about the "second student movement" (the first being that of the turn of the century that fed into rightwing student radicalism in the Weimar Republic) made popular by Rudolf Krämer-Badoni.[60] The radical wing of the student movement represented precisely the totalitarian agent that many of the liberals and conservatives who had studied with the neo-Hegelian philosopher Joachim Ritter in Münster feared: a social group that identified its own interests as universal and which justified itself by appeal to a philosophy of history.

58 Ibid., 11.

59 Hermann Lübbe, "Das Elend der Universitäten [1970]," in his *Hochschulreform und Gegenaufklärung* (Freiburg, 1972), 62-4.

60 Rudolf Krämer-Badoni, "Die zweite Jugendbewegung," *Aus Politik und Zeitgeschichte* 44 (1967): 3-16.

The antidote was to protect the state from a totalitarian seizure of power.

The SDS-Nazi analogy was popular in these circles. Moderate students were entreated to resist the attempts of the SDS to democratize and politicize scholarship, which one commentator argued were akin to Goebbels' attempts to control university life in the Third Reich.[61] The journalist Giselher Schmidt published a book in 1969, *Hitler's and Mao's Sons*, in which he equated the anti-parliamentary stance of Germany's neo-Nazis and the New Left, although admitting that the latter was at least honest about its program.[62] The philosopher Ernst Topitsch, who had spend the 1950s and 1960s campaigning against conservative clericalism, argued that the students' claim to a privileged insight into truth was just the latest in a long line of threats to academic freedom that went back through the Nazis to the Church.[63] These provocative analogies drew a sharp response from leftists and some liberals. Peter Glotz thought the comparison "unbearably tasteless,"[64] while the historian Helga Grebing (born 1930) wrote a book that aimed to invalidate the equation of left- and rightwing radicalism.[65]

Conservatives failed to criticize the violence of the state, of which they implicitly approved. Typical was the conservative Roman Catholic historian, Konrad Repgen (born 1923), who, in condemning student violence, did not mention the attempted assassination of Dutschke in April 1968, or the press campaign against the student leader to which the shooting on a Berlin street was obviously related, as the subsequent statements of the perpetrator indicated.[66] Liberal critics pointed out that conservatives had nothing

61 Karl Willy Beer, "Die Demokratie in Gefahr," *Die Politische Meinung* 13 (1968): 3-6.

62 Giselher Schmidt, *Hitlers und Maos Söhne* (Frankfurt, 1969), 17.

63 Ernst Topitsch, *Die Freiheit der Wissenschaft und politische Auftrag der Universität*, 2nd ed. (Neuwied, 1969).

64 Peter Glotz, "Die bündischen Professoren," *Süddeutsche Zeitung*, 18 November 1970, 8.

65 Helga Grebing, *Linksradikalismus gleich Rechtsradikalismus. Eine falsche Gleichung* (Stuttgart, 1971).

66 Konrad Repgen, "Staatskrise?" *Hochland* 60 (1967/8): 474-77. See the letter from Josef Bachman to Dutschke, 15 January, 1969 in Rudi Dutschke, *Mein langer Marsch* (Hamburg, 1980), 134.

to say about the pressing problems that outraged the consciousness of younger Germans, above all the eight month silence of the Berlin city government about the shooting of Ohnesorg, and establishment's exaggerated outrage about a few thrown rocks and protests.[67]

Terrorism and Critical Theory

If the forty-fivers were divided about the meaning of the student movement, they did not fight among themselves in the 1960s. The Weimar Syndrome did not have them in its thrall. During the 1970s, however, when what even liberals as well as conservatives called the campus-based "nihilistic counterculture" developed along with its perceived poison fruit—leftist terrorism—the familiar crisis mentality began to spread to forty-fiver intellectuals, as well.

Their debates were accordingly acrimonious. Liberals who had first expressed sympathy for the students now joined conservatives in denouncing the Critical Theory and the supposed violent effects of the Frankfurt School. Bracher complained that the "Habermas-wave" had been "eagerly adopted and vulgarized," by young radicals, who had collapsed knowledge into interest, and society into the state.[68] Hans Maier thought that the youth movement's "vulgar brand of actionistic Marxism" was becoming increasingly embarrassing for Adorno and Habermas.[69] Writing in 1976, the philosopher Nickolas Lobkowicz agreed that Habermas's influential *Knowledge and Human Interests*,[70] whose central thesis he recognized the critical theorist himself as having by then largely abandoned, had nevertheless "become, in varying degrees of vulgariza-

---

67 Hans Schwab-Felish, "Versuch einer Replik," *Merkur* 23 (February 1969): 121-4.

68 Karl Dietrich Bracher, *Schlüsselwörter in der Geschichte* (Düsseldorf, 1978), 28.

69 Hans Maier, "Reform in der Demokratie," in Schwan, *Reform as Alternative*, 26.

70 *Der Spiegel* described his influence in the following manner: "No work by a German philosopher over the past decade has had found as much international resonance...": in "Immer Diskutieren," *Der Spiegel*, 28 March 1973, 141.

tion, an article of faith for many self-styled critical academic politicians and theoreticians."[71] The socialist critique, Bracher continued, "culminated in a sociologically and psychologically founded emancipation protest against society *as such*, against its values and taboos, and ultimately as political criticism of the system generally."[72] The problem of left-wing extremism, the philosopher Robert Spaemann declared, did not issue from *any* political theory, but one that was unable to justify authority short of the ideal speech situation.[73]

Hermann Lübbe, too, argued against the conflation of the theoretical and social grounding of norms, maintaining that it contained the basic structure of totalitarian domination and terrorism. Grounding norms on the basis "of the most compelling argument" did not lead necessarily to extremism, he implied. Its "political meaning," however, when combined with what he called the "terroristic imperative"—the identity of the empirical subject (an individual or a party) with the transcendental—was that a group with the "terrorist imperative" considered itself in possession of norms that were more "real" (i.e., true and just) than the norms that actually obtained. The inevitable consequence was the transition of the terrorist imperative into terrorist action. Lübbe did not go so far as to name which individuals or groups were possessed by the "terrorist imperative" (other than the terrorists themselves, of course), but his use of the Habermasian vocabulary in the context of the public attack on the Frankfurt School in the Fall of 1977 would have left his readers with a clear picture of whom he had in mind.[74] Prominent conservative politicians like Franz Joseph Strauss and Hans Filbinger (the latter being disgraced by revelations of his activities as

71 Nikolaus Lobkowicz, "Erkenntnisleitende Interessen," in *Die politische Herausforderung der Wissenschaft. Gegen eine ideologisch verplante Forschung*, ed. Kurt Hubner et al (Hamburg, 1976), 55.

72 Karl Dietrich Bracher, *The Age of Ideologies. A History of Political Thought in the Twentieth-Century* (New York, 1984), 213.

73 Robert Spaemann, "Die Utopie des guten Herrschers," *Zur Kritik der politischen Utopie* (Stuttgart, 1977), 135.

74 Hermann Lübbe, "Freiheit und Terror," *Merkur* 31 (September 1977): 819-29.

a Nazi judge, partly on the basis of misinformation fed to the German media by the STASI[75]), publicly laid the blame for terrorism at the feet of the Frankfurt School, who, they claimed, were the terrorists' "spiritual fathers."

Sontheimer, who had defended the students, now came to the same conclusion as Lübbe. Characterizing the Bonn Republic in terms of "structural" or "objective violence" logically implied a utopian state of equality, the unrealizability of which could lead to terrorism. [76] The analogy had unnecessarily accentuated nagging doubts about the system and had thereby destabilized its institutions. Leftwing theory that had its origins in the systemic social crisis only served to worsen it.[77]

For these liberals and conservatives, living proof of the fruit of the "cultural revolution" was the leftist milieu on the campuses.[78] During the notorious fall of 1977 when numerous terrorist attacks provoked a mood of hysteria among middle class Germans and the state took extraordinary security measures that were interpreted by many as a resurrection of authoritarianism, the campuses were targeted as the breeding ground of the so-called terrorist "sympathizers." The social democratic politician Peter Glotz estimated that about fifteen to twenty percent of students (about 140, 000 to 170, 000) agreed with the student author of a notorious article who admitted he had experienced "clandestine joy" at the recent assassination of the Federal prosecutor Siegfried Buback.[79] This shared joy was evidence enough for Sontheimer and others that the left as a whole was responsible for the terrorist disaster.[80]

---

75 See Günter Bohnsack and Herbert Brehmer, *Auftrag Irreführung* (Hamburg, 1992), 59.

76 Kurt Sontheimer, "Gewalt und Terror in der Politik," *Neue Rundschau* 1 (1977): 1-12.

77 Kurt Sontheimer, *Das Elend unserer Intellektuellen. Linke Theorie in der Bundesrepublik* (Hamburg, 1976), 278, 289.

78 Jeremy Varon, *Bringing the War Home: the Weather Underground, the Red Army Faction, and Revolutionary Violence in the Sixties and Seventies* (Berkeley: University of California Press, 2004).

79 Peter Glotz, "'Jeder fünfte denkt etwa so wie Mescalero,'" *Der Spiegel*, 3 October 1977, 54.

80 Kurt Sontheimer, "Um eine Basis der Gemeinsamkeit," *Süddeutsche Zeitung*, 26/7 November 1977.

Habermas naturally rejected Sontheimer's implicit Weimar analogy only to substitute it with one of his own. The official ban on employing radicals was akin to Bismarck's anti-socialist laws a century later. Once again, the only progressive element in the republic, its intellectuals, was being demonized. Old authoritarian traditions were rearing their ugly heads. The real threat was not the left but an establishment that was able to use terrorism to identify an internal enemy (i.e., the left) and thereby stifle any critique. "Only a state that makes the fascist self-understanding of Carl Schmitt its own, needs internal enemies that it can fight, as is the case with foreign enemies during war." [81]

He reminded everyone that he and other leftist intellectuals had been among the first to criticize what Adorno called "student activism." He himself had refereed to "leftist fascism" because the ideology of radical voluntarism and violence reminded him of the German conservative revolutionary professors of his youth, Carl Schmitt and Martin Heidegger. This was his generational experience speaking. The conservative argument that the Frankfurt School was somehow "objectively responsible" for the terrorism was the kind of argument Stalinists used in another context. Invoking the specter of Weimar, he suggested that Strauss wanted to impose "Franco's legacy in the Federal Republic."[82]

The reflex to identify one's own tradition with the victims of Nazism appeared unavoidable. Hans Buchheim (born 1922), the political scientist and contemporary historian at the *Institut für Zeitgeschichte* in Munich who had written early books on the Nazi regime, reversed the meaning of the Weimar Syndrome. He went so far as to argue that the older generation (the forty-fivers and older Germans) were being condemned by the sixty-eighters in terms of the same group-think as Jews were in the 1930s and 1940s.[83]

81 Jürgen Habermas, "Verteuflung kritischen Denkens," *Süddeutsche Zeitung*, 26/7 November 1977.

82 Jürgen Habermas, "Probe für Volksjustiz," *Der Spiegel*, 10 October 1977, 32.

83 Hans Buchheim, "Der Protest aus falsch bewältigter Vergangenheit," *Frankfurter Allgemeine Zeitung*, 6 March 1968, 2.

Conclusion

The notorious "German Autumn" of 1977 with its terrorist killings and police reaction marked the highpoint of intellectual and political polarization in the Federal Republic. Hereafter, the question of political violence subsided as much of the '68er milieu found a political vehicle in the new Green party, although anarchist and squatter scenes lived on in many German towns and cities. Massive demonstrations against the stationing of US missiles were a feature of the peace movement in the early 1980, but public protest was the legitimate exercise of a democratic right, not a paranoid expression of political violence. The Weimar Syndrome seemed to lessen as the different fractions of the intelligentsia realized that changes in government did not spell the end of democracy, however defined. The political alignments of the "Historians' Dispute" of the mid-1980s, in which liberal intellectuals like Bracher supported Habermas, showed they had other concerns. Now many intellectuals worried that Helmut Kohl's stated intention to renationalize German politics entailed a reversion to the cultural politics of the 1950s rather than of the 1920 and 1930s.[84] Memory of the Holocaust and "overcoming the Nazi past" became a central question rather than *die Gewaltfrage* and West German democracy.[85] From 1982 to 1998 the student radicals accomplished the "long march through the institutions" that would create a new elite in the media, the universities and with the Greens, at the highest branches of the German government.[86] If in the 1960s the students had seen themselves as

84 See Elliot Neaman, *A Dubious Past; Ernst Jünger and the Politics of Literature after Nazism* (Berkeley, 1999), Ch. 7.

85 A. Dirk Moses, *German Intellectuals and the Nazi Past in Postwar Germany: Structure and Stigma in German Memory* (Cambridge: Cambridge University Press, 2007).

86 Rudi Dutschke would not have recognized this process as his "long march," by which he meant subverting, not joining the elite. Tony Judt is correct in his assessment that Dutschke managed to combine in this phrase both Mao and Trotsky, since the contemporary Trotskyite strategy was "enterism," that is, the infiltration of institutions such as trade unions and universities and subverting them from the inside. See his *Postwar; The History of Europe Since 1945* (New York, 2005), 407.

"Hitler's children," that is brought into the world by Nazified mothers and fathers, by the 1980s their opposition to the institutions of West Germany lessened as their own influence grew.[87] The anti-authoritarians had in their own way become a new kind of authority—and in that dialectical process had finally overcome the Weimar Syndrome.

87 In 1998, the fourteenth *Bundestag* under Gerhard Schroeder had 332 members from the 1968 generation (out of a total of 669). They were far more likely to be working at the universities, or in the sphere of art, literature or media, than in business, administration or the military. See Heinz Bude, on the "Prominenzphase" of the sixty-eighters, in *Das Altern einer Generation* (Frankfurt, 1995), 95ff.

Part Four:
The Book Matters

These three review essays will not be read, I hope, as conventional, disposable reviews; but rather as miniature essays in intellectual history, that use recent scholarship to reopen questions that run through this entire volume: exile and fascism, the politics of ideas, and the afterlives of 1968. The first essay, on Jewish-Israeli intellectual historian Avihu Zakai's *The Pen Confronts the Sword*, returns to the world of exiled German intellectuals—Mann, Cassirer, Auerbach, Adorno, Horkheimer—and asks how they tried to understand the collapse of German "high culture" into barbarism. In different ways, all five wrestled with the same question that animates much of my own work: how can concepts like Enlightenment, myth, culture, art, and rationality coexist with Auschwitz, total war, and mass mobilization? Zakai's focus on apocalyptic and eschatological motifs allows me to explore their differing answers, and to show how their attempts to "confront the sword" from exile still shape our debates about liberalism, myth, and the possibility (or impossibility) of progress after 1945. The second essay engages German philosopher Johannes Fritsche's Hist*orical Destiny and National Socialism* in Heidegger's *Being and Time*, which I regard as one of the sharpest attempts to tie Heidegger's philosophical vocabulary to the radical conservative milieu of Weimar and to his later embrace of National Socialism. Against those who still want to cordon off *Being and Time* from Heidegger's politics, Fritsche's philological and contextual reading shows how terms like fate, destiny, resoluteness, and Volk were already saturated with right-wing meanings. My discussion of his book connects directly to earlier chapters on Ernst Jünger, the Conservative Revolution, and the long debate about whether we can—or should—salvage "pure" philosophy from compromised political contexts. The third essay, on Australian cultural historian Ben Mercer's *Student Revolt in 1968: France, Italy, and West Germany*, returns us to the terrain of my own *Free Radicals* and to the arguments I make in this volume about 1968, left-wing radicalism, and the mythologies of democratization. Mercer's careful comparative study of student movements reinforces my skepticism about the 68ers' self-image as democratic saviors, while also showing how university reform, mass higher education, and new political languages transformed European societies in ways that went well beyond any single cohort's intentions. By placing Mercer's work alongside Zakai and Fritsche, I underline a central claim of these *Selected Writings*: that intellectual history is not only about original "primary" texts, but also about the books we write about them—how each new wave of scholarship reframes the relationship between ideas, institutions, and political conflict, and thus keeps the larger conversation about fascism, Enlightenment, and revolt very much alive.

I.
Avihu Zakai:
The Pen Confronts the Sword:
Exiled German Scholars Confront Nazism

Albany: State University of New York, 2018

On May 29, 1945 the famous German writer Thomas Mann, living in American exile, offered a public lecture at the Library of Congress on the topic "Germany and the Germans." The German army had capitulated to the Allies exactly three weeks before his talk. Mann reflected on the catastrophe of twelve years of National Socialism by refusing to separate out a "good" and a "bad" Germany, and instead forthrightly identified himself as part of entire German culture, large parts of which had "turned into evil." Arguing from history, he traced the problems of German culture back to Martin Luther and a tradition of "inwardness," which celebrated inner experience at the cost of denigrating external political freedoms. The Germans, he proposed, never experienced anything equivalent to the French Revolution, which, despite its excesses, had created a spirit of civic consciousness sadly lacking east of the Rhine. Instead, educated Germans in the nineteenth and early twentieth centuries had become intoxicated with various forms of romanticism that predisposed them psychologically to morbid cultivation of the self. Observers noted, even at the time, that Mann was engaging in both a historical and a highly personal exercise in reevaluating his own past, since he had written, at the end of World War I, a widely circulated essay he later regretted, proudly identifying himself as a "nonpolitical man," which celebrated Germany's inward, authoritarian culture, in contrast to what he viewed as the superficial, democratic, moralistic "civilization" of England and France.

The Pen Confronts the Sword deals with five German scholars, Thomas Mann, Ernst Cassirer, Erich Auerbach, Theodor Adorno and Max Horkheimer, all Jewish except Mann, who fled the Third Reich and spent much of their time and energy in exile examining the question of how German culture and society could have descended so quickly from high civilization to the dregs of barbarism. The four main chapters of the book are self-contained and can be read as distinct treatments of the five authors covered (Horkheimer and Adorno are examined together in the fourth chapter). Although Zakai repeatedly draws connections between the five authors, it would have been useful to have an introductory discussion on the larger topic of how the "pen confronts the sword" in other historical contexts. After all, the struggle between intellectuals and political power is as old as Plato, whose *Republic* was a not-too-subtle condemnation of the Athenian democracy that had put his beloved teacher Socrates to death. Hundreds of German intellectuals ended up fleeing from the Nazi state, organizing and weaponizing their pens as part of various anti-fascist initiatives. We don't hear enough in the book about how these five writers fit into that larger effort.

In his opening chapter on Thomas Mann, Zakai focusses on apocalyptic and eschatological themes in Mann's great postwar novel *Dr. Faustus*, which Mann began in 1942, when the Nazi empire was at its height, and was published in 1947. Mann's re-telling of the famous medieval story retains the original emphasis on temptation, pride, the devil's bargain and loss of humanity, while mirroring, through the figure of the genius composer Adrian Leverkühn, the pact with the devil that Germans made with National Socialism. Zakai is an expert on the history of apocalyptic thinking in various theological guises and his dissection of Leverkühn's satanic revelations and eventual collapse are striking, original and throw much light on Mann's exhaustive (and sometimes exhausting) confrontation with the tortured history of German's descent into self-destruction and unfathomable postwar guilt in the aftermath of the Holocaust.

By contrast Ernst Cassirer (1874-1945), born into a Jewish family in Breslau (modern southwest Poland), did not have to re-evaluate his politics when he went into exile. He had always been a staunch defender of enlightened rationalism and supported the left-liberal German Democratic Party (DDP) during the Weimar period. The DDP was staunchly liberal, and was led by august figures such as the sociologist Max Weber (until his untimely death in 1920) and the Jewish foreign Minister Walther Rathenau (who was murdered by right-wing thugs in 1922). German Jews voted for the DDP more than for any other, and was therefore slurred by its opponents as "the party of Jews and professors." When the Nazis seized power in 1933 Cassirer fled into exile in Sweden, then sought a safer haven in the United States, eventually receiving a professorship at Columbia University in New York, where he died in 1945 just weeks before the war ended. Zakai concentrates on his last, posthumously published book *The Myth of the State* (1946) and places this work in the context of Cassirer's struggle to make sense of how the Nazi state came into being and by which kinds of ideas was it driven. Zakai aptly sums up the development of Cassirer's thinking as one of "disillusionment," as the philosopher transformed himself from begin an advocate for liberal progress and the human potential for self-awakening in a Neo-Kantian spirit (particularly in his major work *The Philosophy of the Enlightenment* (1932) to a much more pessimistic view of history in *The Myth of the State*. In this last work, Cassirer views history as a series of traumatic, interminable crises and turning points, not along any recognizable path of progress but rather as a struggle between reason and myth (*logos* and *mythos* in Plato's sense).

Cassirer locates the origins of National Socialism, like Mann, in the unfortunate romantic turn in German nineteenth-century thought towards the re- mythologizing the state, as exemplified best by Hegel's political philosophy.

Though Zakai does not delve deeply into this, Cassirer here anticipated the postwar debates on the origins of totalitarianism, which would be carried out by thinkers such as Karl Popper, Carl. J. Friedrich and Hannah Arendt. Cassirer also identifies hero-worship, in the sense of heroic leadership, identified by Thomas Carlyle in the middle of the nineteenth century, as a temptation that too many German intellectuals fell for, as the Wilhelmine state grew powerful around the turn of the twentieth century.

Zakai depicts Cassirer as a believer in the Enlightenment to his last dying day, but one deeply chastened and shaken by the experience of exile and the destruction of German culture. From his post as professor of philosophy in Hamburg in the 1920s, Cassirer worked closely with the famous Jewish art historian and cultural theorist Aby Warburg, who assembled a vast library dedicated to the art and culture of the Renaissance. Zakai rightly emphasizes Cassirer's interpretation of what in America we would call intellectual history as cultural humanism, rather than as *Geisteswissenschaft* (cultural science), which was key distinction for maintaining and then rebuilding a humanistic foundation on which Cassirer believed a post-Nazi recovery of German culture could be established. Cassirer did not believe that human beings were determined by the culture they were born into, but rather had the ability to assimilate the richness of all cultural traditions, philosophies, religions, forms of spirituality etc. This explains Cassirer's own loyalty both to his Jewish past and a kind of proto-pagan cosmopolitanism. It also explains Cassirer's objections both in general to the fatalism of Martin Heidegger's existentialist philosophy, and specifically to the völkisch elements in Heidegger's master work *Being and Time* (1927), that Cassirer early on recognized as politically suspect (and now definitively confirmed with the publication of Heidegger's *Black Notebooks*). Unfortunately Zakai skips rather quickly over the famous 1929 debate in Davos between Cassirer and Heidegger, which illuminated so clearly the former's tenacious hold on Enlightenment values, even in the midst of the coming shipwreck for German culture.

Next in line is Erich Auerbach, born in Berlin in 1892, the son of a prosperous Prussian merchant. He grew up identifying both as a Jew and a Prussian, calling himself a "Prussian of the Jewish faith." His only son Clemens received a Christian name. A gifted philologist of romance languages, his Jewishness hindered an academic career, even during the early Weimar period, but Auerbach made a name for himself with his work on Dante, whose *Divine Comedy* was revered among religious scholars, and so he eventually earned an academic post. In his work on Dante, Auerbach took a strikingly original and somewhat paradoxical stance, arguing that imaginatively, the late medieval Italian poet initiated the modern form of the novel. On the basis of that pioneering work, Auerbach was called in 1929 to the University of Marburg for a chair in Romance philology, a year before Heidegger left. Again, Zakai's book misses a chance to dwell longer on Heidegger, since Auerbach, like Cassirer, recognized early on how ideologically dangerous the trendy existentialism of the Wizard of Messkirch. "Heidegger is. terrible fellow," he wrote later, though he grudgingly admitted that at least he had "substance."

In 1935 Auerbach was released by the Nazis from the University of Marburg and fled into exile to Turkey, where he received an academic appointment, due to the help of Leo Spitzer, an influential Austrian literary critic. He found Istanbul to be a "rough" city and the university's library lacked even the most basic scholarly collections. His dean gave, as his reason for not acquiring more books, that they "burned too easily." Auerbach contributed to his own polymath legend by speculating that *Mimesis*, his magnum opus, written between 1942 and 1945, which covers the entire history of Western literature from the Old Testament to modernism, may have originated out of necessity, since in exile he lacked access to access to a specialized library. The idea that *Mimesis* sprang from Auerbach's head unaided by external sources is a nice story, but probably is not factual. In truth there were many good private and public libraries in and around Istanbul, as well as many well-stocked archives in monasteries, whose manuscripts of the Church Fathers he used copiously in *Mimesis*. The chapter on Auerbach, co-written with David Weinstein, offers the thesis, not particularly original, but carried out with rigor and erudition, that the book-less scholar in exile was trying to reconstitute the entire tradition of Western humanism that the Nazis were busy destroying. There remains a bit of a mystery about Auerbach's relationship with Judaism. He may have been very ambivalent and one wonders, for example, why he turned down Martin Buber's request to write an introduction to the Hebrew edition of *Mimesis*.

One can construct a narrative that *Mimesis* is a long, subterranean meditation on the Holocaust, in the sense that it inextricably ties the Old Testament to modern European culture, but if so, Auberbach hid the traces carefully. Zakai gives us many good reasons to read *Mimesis* as a commentary on how the National Socialists tried to erase not only Jews from history, but also Jewish thought, but the fact remains that in exile in America at least, Auerbach didn't talk or publish much about his politics or discuss his experiences during the war. In the end, he left it up to each reader to decide what epiphenomenal messages were to be read into his writings.

The social theorists Theodor Adorno and Max Horkheimer (Frankfurt School) wrote together a long essay during the war called *The Dialect of Enlightenment.* It was circulated among friends in 1944 under the title *Philosophical Fragments* and even in its published version with the new title, it remains indeed a fragmentary work. Zakai rightly calls it the "darkest" and most pessimistic of all the texts he considers in comparing Adorno and Horkheimer to Mann, Cassirer, and Auerbach. Much of it was written in 1942 at the height of the Nazi empire and the book is profoundly pessimistic about the possibility of human liberation and progress. Leaving behind the Marxist hope for social amelioration of their youth, Adorno and Horkheimer laid out a grim analysis of how the modern forces of industrial production had led to myriad forms of social domination and ultimately the counter-revolution of fascism in the twentieth century. The European Enlightenment is exposed, in their book, as a "myth," since the advance of reason and science do not lead to human liberation, but rather the opposite, mass societies characterized by industrial standardization of all aspects of society, the economy, culture and ideas. In other words, a new kind of barbarism. The liberal state turns out to be a chimera and modern states are all fascistic in one way or another. As the

Slovenian post-Marxist/Lacanian philosopher Slavoj Žižek put it in an interview, the whole project in *The Dialectic of Enlightenment* is "let's paint the ultimate outcome of the administered world as unavoidable, as catastrophe, for this is the only way to effectively counteract it."

In 1949 Horkheimer and Adorno returned to Frankfurt and began work in many new areas, particularly the social sciences, whose empirical methods they had assimilated in American exile. Adorno continued his pioneering work in aesthetics and musicology. The *Dialectic of Enlightenment* was viewed as a period piece, but in the mid-1960s radical German students (and other radical thinkers, like Žižek) Rediscovered it and repurposed arguments from the book to attack the Bonn Republic as proto-fascist and the postwar global market economy as an oppressive behemoth that could only be countered with massive opposition. Horkheimer and Adorno had to plea with the students to read the work in its historical context, but it was too late to put the genie back in the bottle. They both became disenchanted with the increasing radicalization the student movement, which reminded them too much of the extreme positions, both right and left, taken by many students in the 1920s and 1930s. Zakai goes over fairly familiar territory in his analysis of *Dialect of Enlightenment.* Undoubtedly he is right to claim that while they were writing this work Horkheimer and Adorno sided with the "black writers of the bourgeoisie," i.e. Nietzsche and de Sade. But it is important to remember, as noted above, that they distanced themselves from the pessimism of this book in their later years. He is also correct in emphasizing the importance of the last chapter of the *Dialectic* on anti-Semitism and how Horkheimer and Adorno revised Marx's controversial dictum that mankind needed to be emancipated from Judaism to the tenet that all of mankind needed to be emancipated from the enlightenment's myth of power. Not everyone will agree, however, that "Only Horkheimer and Adorn o offer a solution to the Jewish question as true heirs of Marx" (305). There may indeed be a mythological basis to faith in the Enlightenment and human progress, but as Zakai's engaging, learned and in many ways profound discourse on these five writers attests, without that faith, the alternative for mankind is dark indeed.

II.
Johannes Fritsche:
Historical Destiny and National Socialism in Heidegger's Being and Time

Fritsche's book is the best analysis of Heidegger's *Being & Time* to come along in a long time. It appears against the backdrop of continuing ignorance or willful ignoring of the ideological worldview of Heidegger's closes intellectual allies in the Weimar Republic. Rüdiger's Safranski's intellectual biography of Heidegger is a good example. The book is subtitled "between Good and Evil," and argues that National Socialism grew out of Heidegger's philosophy, but was also a violation of its central idea. Authentic Dasein can be resolute about anything, from vegetarianism to Hitlerism, but according to Safranski, Heidegger had up until 1931 guarded philosophy from being used as a *Weltanschauung*, indeed from any practical orientation. This best-seller in Germany tried to refashion the master's own postwar conscience-juggling by reducing the period of the rectorship (1933-34) to a short-lived mistake of a political simpleton.

At least other apologists came up with more subtle face-saving devices. Derrida, it will be remembered, discovered in the absence of quotation marks around the word "Geist" in the infamous rector's speech (May, 1933) the return of a spiritual, non-biological, non-racist anti-totalitarian discourse. Heidegger's mistake was not joining the Nazi party, but falling prey to spiritual metaphysics!

As a third variant of the trivialization of Heidegger's embrace of Nazism, Herbertus Dreyfus and his students in philosophy departments across the United States offered us Heidegger as a new age guru for unlocking human potential, and make profit too! (some of Dreyfus's graduate students found jobs as consultants in big corporations, paid to figure out the "mood" of the company). Charles Guignon tells us that Dasein lives in a horizon of multiple traditions and pasts, and takes a stand on the future, moving into a plethora of possibilities. A Heideggerian in 1933 might become a Nazi, but she was not philosophically predestined to do so. Today, she might work with the homeless and join the Greens. Or a large corporation.

In contrast to these distotions, a considerable body of work has been published since the 1980s that should have put the Heidegger case to rest, but is apparently still powerless to root out the dragon teeth. The archival research carried out by Victor Farias and Hugo Ott, and the interpretive scholarship of Otto Pöggeler, Hans Sluga, Richard Wolin, Tom Rockmore and others have demonstrated beyond a shadow of a doubt that Heidegger's involvement with Nazism was anything but a fleeting mistake. He engaged himself with unbounded energy in coordinating the University of Freiburg according to Nazi educational policies, he supported the laws that removed Jews from tenured positions and he remained a Nazi party member until 1945. The only recourse that Heidegger's apologists have, therefore, is to continue to argue that all this activity was unessential to the lasting value of Heidegger's philosophical accomplishments. They argue that it would be analogous to discount Plato and Platonism because of his ill-fated attempt to put his philosophy into practice at the court of the tyrant Dionysus of Syracuse.

Most of Heidegger's critics have focused on his actions—his eccentric relationship to his students, whom he took skiing and hiking in the Black Forest, his bizarre peasant attire, his fractured relationship with Jewish students and colleagues, his decisions made as rector of the university, his policies about "labor, knowledge and military service," etc. But what about the connection between his philosophy and these actions? Already in Karl Jasper's report to the university commission established in the fall of 1945 to evaluate Heidegger's fitness as a future teacher, the problems associated with the content and style of the philosophy was articulated. Jasper's knew Heidegger very well as a colleague and friend. He reported to the commission that Heidegger appeared to him to be a "nihilist and the mystagogue-cum-sorcerer," and that his philosophy was "fundamentally unfree, dictatorial and uncommunicative." Similarly, Hans Jonas reported that after hearing the rector's speech, he realized that Heidegger threw himself into the "new destiny" of National Socialism, based exactly on the concept of resolve (Entschlossenheit) contained in Being and Time.

More inaccurate would be to say that critics have never seen the link clearly between Heidegger's philosophy and his actions in 1933-34, but Johannes Fritsche's book goes much further. It is arguably the most important analysis of the deep conceptual connections between Being and Time and the decision to support Nazism, and also of the linguistic choices that Heidegger made, using language borrowed (though often in improved form) from the arsenal of radical conservative ideas which were prevalent during the Weimar Republic. Heidegger made the impression on his young students at Freiburg that he was about to free German philosophy from the fetters of neo-Kantianism and other encrusted vestiges of German Idealism. His famous debate with Ernst Cassirer in 1929 cemented his reputation as a philosophical radical. Fritsche's book enables us to solve the seeming contradiction that Heidegger saw himself as making a radical break with the past, but could throw in his lot with a deeply reactionary regime.

Fritsche's training as a classical philologist shine as he stops to focus our attention on the multiple nuances and meanings of some central terms in Heidegger's vocabulary: anticipation, resoluteness, repetition, response, disavowal, fate, community, society. In contrast to Heidegger's own often idiosyncratic etymological exercises, in which every Greek concept turns out to support some aspect of Heidegger's own philosophy, Fritsche situates in concrete intellectual terms, Heidegger's ideological affinities. Take for example the famous passage from Section Seventy-four of *Being and Time*. There Heidegger writes:

> If fateful Dasein, as Being-in-the-World, exists essentially in Being with Others, its historicizing is a co-historicizing and is determinative for it as destiny. This is how we designate the historicizing of the community (*Gemeinschaft*), of the people (*Volkes*). Destiny is not something that puts itself together out of individual fates, any more than Being-with-one-another can be conceived as the occurring together of several Subjects. Our fates have already been guided in advance, in our Being with one another in the same world and in our resoluteness for definite possibilities. Only in communicating and in struggling does the power of destiny become free (*Being and Time*, Macquarrie & Robinson edition, 436).

In this rich and revealing passage, a number of crucial political ideas flow together in a powerful statement about Germany's world-historical situation, as seen by Heidegger in 1927. As Fritsche points out, the meaning of the words fate, destiny, community, Volk and determination (or providence) were known by everyone in the 1910s and 1920s to belong to the politically equivocal vocabulary of the political right-wing assault on liberalism and socialism. Both Liberals and socialists affirmed capitalism. Liberals argued that capitalism was based on enlightened self-interest and would eventually guarantee a free society and rising standards of living. Socialists affirmed capitalism as a doomed stage in the history of productive forces that would eventually be superseded by a socialist economy. Against both these visions, or (a third variant, capitalism with a strong welfare state component), rightists argued that not reason or class conflict determined history, but rather the cultural history of a community thrown together by fate with a common past and future. Capitalism and modern technology are planetary forces that destroy individual cultures and thus constitute a measure of decline. Philosophy's role is to "communicate and struggle," that is, change the attitudes and mentality of modern decadent, atomized individuals, open to them the reality of the cultural traditions of the people, so they will abandon faceless, bureaucratic "society" and return, collectively, to the "freedom" of community.

Fritsche stresses the importance of a number of key terms that Heidegger used to buttress his ideological attack on the seeming chaos of modern society and to support his call for a return to the Volk community. The word *Entschlossenheit*, for example, which is at the root of an entire discourse about decisionism as a political philosophy in the Weimar republic, does not just mean determination, or resoluteness, in its active form, but also contains the idea of "opening up," the opposite of *schliessen*, to close, in its passive form (*entschlossen*). In the same sense that a Christian may be open to the idea of grace, the right wing in Weimar was open to the voice of the people, and a young philosophy student reading Heidegger in 1927 could be resolved to break out of bourgeois subjectivity (note the derisive use if the term Subjectivity in the passage above), and opens herself up the Volk community. Similarly the verb "*erwidern*" means to "respond to" something, but in German there is a difference whether one uses the accusative or the dative as the object of the sentence. In *Being and Time*, Dasein responds to the possibilities of the past by projecting itself authentically into the future with resoluteness. Some critics have taken this to mean that authentic Dasein possesses an infinite number of ways of being in the world, of responding to the various cultures, models and traditions of the past. This would be the dative sense of respond—one makes a rejoinder to the past, choosing among its various models and possibilities. But Fritsche shows quite convincingly that when Heidegger writes "*Dasein erwidert die Möglichkeiten*," using the accusative, he clearly meant that Dasein responds to the possibilities posed by history in an antagonistic way, the way an army counterattacks, or a player in a sports game responds to the opponent. And the enemy in this case was obviously modernity.

Fritsche applies the philological knife to a number of other Heideggerian terms, including *Auslesen*, *aufrufen*, *Destruktion*, *Ursprung*, *Entspringen*, *Erbschaft*, every one of which can be located in a radical conservative discourse decrying the plunging fall of Dasein out of authentic *Gemeinschaft* into the anonymous, false and dangerous Gesellschaft. If Fritsche had contented himself with these clever grammar lessons on the German language, the book would help us understand Heidegger's vocabulary better, but some would argue he had merely used Heidegger's own philological techniques against the master, thus validating the philosophy in spite of the critic's intentions. But Fritsche does much more than this, carrying out a number of fascinating comparisons to the works of three Weimar thinkers and a politician: Max Scheler, Georg Lukacs, Paul Tillich and Adolf Hitler.

The comparison of *Being and Time* to Hitler's *Mein Kampf* may seem like a stretch, but in fact results in some of the most compelling pages in this book. Fritsche is very good at focusing on some specific questions when comparing two texts and thus avoids grand generalizations which could easily be invalidated through counterexamples. In this case, he asks about the way Hitler understood his "destiny" in the struggle to understand his mission to save the German nation. Fritsche interprets *Mein Kampf* as a kind of *Bildungsroman*, noting that Hitler consciously entitled the second chapter of the book "*Wiener Lehr- und Leidensjahre*" (Years of Studying and Suffering in Vienna) in an obvious allusion to Goethe's *Wilhelm Meisters Lehrjahre.* But in contrast to the eighteenth-century *Bildungsroman,* in which the protagonist transcends the abstract freedom of individuality and finds ethical life in the greater community, Hitler viewed the communities of his time as under siege and the ethical models presented by society as degenerate. He thanks fate for being born in a small town, where he knew healthy communal life, already under threat from Slavic influences, and then fate gave him the opportunity to experience the big city of Vienna, where he came to understand nation, race, people and the state and eventually the huge threat to the German *Gemeinschaft* posed by the Jews. In becoming a revolutionary, Hitler constantly alludes to the example from past German history that he learned as a schoolboy, and how in discovering what fate had set in store for him, he realized the relevance of the past for escaping from a bad present and molding a vibrant future for the German people. The reaction of the German people to the call of fate is crucial for Hitler, because in that "turning point," those who listen to the call will understand the need to restore the purity of the German race. The "turning point" in Hitler's understanding is almost identical to what Heidegger concept of historicity, in which Dasein responds to the call of fate to call up forgotten ways of being and push aside the unauthentic everydayness of the "they" (das Man).

Fritsche establishes an interesting matrix of left, liberal and rightwing thought in a series of comparisons between Heidegger and three other Weimar intellectuals, Paul Tillich, Max Scheler and Georg Lukaçs. The case of Scheler is particularly enlightening, because his espousal, during World War I, of a return to the "love-community" of early Christianity and a rejection of the commercial ethos of capitalism and individualism echoed Heidegger's decisionism motif in *Being and Time,* encouraging bourgeois subjects to take a stand on the crisis confronting German society. But as National Socialism emerged in the 1920s as a viable political force, Scheler changed course and moved ideologically closer to the Christian Socialism of Tillich, viewing Nazism as a threat to religious and existentialist values. Scheler's intellectual development puts into sharp relief the conscious choice Heidegger made by employing rightwing vocabulary.

Lukaçs and Heidegger also shared, on the surface, some philosophical similarities. In his polemics against Social Democracy, Lukaçs fought against modern socialists whose reified consciousness accepted the evolution of capitalism as a natural order, and hoped to reform it, rather than take an existentialist stand for the proletariat, and by the use of violence, if necessary, overthrow the existing order. The terms crisis, decision and even fate shows up in Lukaçs's writings, but Fritsche argues that Lukaç's concept of historicity was opposite to Heidegger's: the Proletariat leads the way into a new order of society, not a repetition of the past.

A number of objections might be raised about the general argument of the book. Fritsche tends to homogenize "right wing thought" as if all the radical conservative thinkers of the Weimar period thought of themselves as united by common assumptions and traditions. Just comparing the Prussian socialism of, say, Oswald Spengler or the more extreme National Bolshevism of Ernst Niekisch, with the militant Catholic Hobbesian tenor of Carl Schmitt, will disabuse anyone of such a generalization. Fritsche's own political predilections run like a red thread throughout the text, especially in the uncritical assumption that all socialist thinkers were necessarily progressive. Fritsche needs to distinguish more sharply between liberal social thinkers, who were extremely rare in Germany before 1945, and Messianic Marxists who often shared with the right wing the position that bourgeois civilization was cracking and just needed the right kind of push to bring the entire edifice to the ground so that something new could be built.

In most cases Fritsche's philosophical and political judgments are sharp and nuanced. The most impressive aspect of the book is the original combination a subtle philosophical analysis with a deep historical understanding of the intellectual environment in which Heidegger's ideas matured. Many defenders of Heidegger today point to the groundbreaking achievement that he turned Husserl's rather static phenomenological examination of the "facts" of consciousness into a rich exploration of the multiple worlds of meaning that show up for human beings in everyday interaction, with each other, and with nature. But Fritsche shows that thinkers like

Scheler were onto the same theoretical expansion of phenomenology, without the dubious political overtones. It will be remembered that Habermas made a similar point in *The Philosophical Discourse of Modernity*, where he includes American pragmatists like Mead and Pierce, as well as Wittgenstein, Austin and Gadamer as examples of a hermeneutical critique of metaphysics that renders Heidegger's approach much less original than the Heideggerians wish to claim.[1] No one will be able to read Fritsche's book and remain complacent about Heidegger's politics. As many have suspected, but only a few have been able to show with such acumen, the phenomenology in *Being and Time* can scarcely be saved by screening the nuggets of gold and throwing away the dirt. Heidegger's famous "turn" came about not only because he thought Dasein was still too trapped in a philosophy of Cartesian subjectivity, but also because he may have come to realize how deeply he had been fooled by National Socialism. That he never properly admitted this was a great human failing, but how much did Heidegger's politics really change? At least his personal crisis, including a nervous breakdown in 1946, led to the more fruitful linguistic turn that had such an enormous impact on twentieth-century philosophy. Now one can only wish that Fritsche, or someone with the same exegetical talents, will examine the writings of late Heidegger, in particular his essays on technology, art, and the World Picture, the Nietzsche and Hölderlin lectures and his final refuge in poetry, and flesh out the connections to post-modern cultural pessimism and our current age.

1 Jürgen Habermas, *Der philosophische Diskurs der Moderne*, (Frankfurt/Main: Suhrkamp, 1985), 164.

III.
Ben Mercer:
Student Revolt in 1968:
France, Italy, and West Germany

Cambridge UP, 301 pp.

Like most academic studies of the student movements of the 1960s, Australian historian Ben Mercer weaves together a multinational narrative. Student movements of the 1960s erupted in both Latin and North America, Europe (both east and west), Asia and even the Middle East. Mercer takes as his focus an important core of the action, concentrating on the three European states that were prominent, France, Italy and West Germany.

The main thesis is not strikingly original, but provides a solid structure for the book. Mercer argues that the student movements in Europe were part of larger "cultural relations" of the period, and "wider social transformations, and that "democratization" meant different things to different social groups of the era. In Mercer's view, the global aspect of the 1960s has corollaries to social movements of the long nineteenth century, as described by Eric Hobsbawm. He also pays attentions to the "myth" of the 1960s as it was transformed by the 68ers themselves into a collective memory of accomplishments and triumphs that do not always bear out historical scrutiny. Like the long nineteenth century, the year 1968 of the title of the book is a stand-in for many different kinds of social movements, that began in the 1950s with anti-nuclear-weapons protests and didn't end until the dissolution with various underground and armed groups becoming anti-state terrorist organizations. The book is meticulously researched and Mercer has read large swaths of the scholarly literature on the topic, though not all, understandably, since scholarly works on the 1960s has become enormous over the years since.

The book is not divided into three separate national narratives, but rather general categories, the relationship between institutions of education and the larger culture, the self-understanding of the politics of revolt by students themselves in the 1960s, and finally the changing structure of European universities of the period. This methodology makes sense because it allows Mercer to weave together the synchronic themes and attitudes that tied together student activists in very different cultural settings.

Mercer deftly guides the reader through the various debates about, and crises of higher education in the 1960s, which was seen optimistically by some observers as the democratization of opportunity for new middle class students, but also pessimistically by critics as opening up the floodgates to unprepared and lesser talented young people forced into mass institutions, not unlike modern industrialized factories. At issue was the tension between higher education as a means of self-fulfillment and expanding democracy against the needs of modern economies for skills-based training in science and technology. An entire new bureaucracy made up of education administrators, economists, sociologists and public foundations developed in the 1960s, advocating for a "new civilization" predicated on open access to the universities. But the hopes of many technocrats were disappointed when students, particularly female students, remained dedicated to disciplines in the arts and humanities, not sciences or engineering. The students as a whole however, absorbed the utopian aspirations of the promises of fundamental social change on the horizon and then went on to push for more radical transformations of the university and the larger society in a neo-Marxist, rather than a technocratic direction. A point Mercer could have made was that nothing similar happened in Europe of the 1960s and 1970s compared to the era's main alternative to Marxism, namely a "Whole Earth Access" version of radicalism, put forward by someone like the Californian visionary and futurist Stewart Brand, who predicated and predicted massive social change by means of computers and other new technologies.

Mercer argues convincingly that the tensions described above between a vision of the future based on self-realization, on the old model of *Bildung*, against the technocratic vision of the new university model to serve as a fulcrum for the modern industrial economy played out among sociologists. The French intellectuals Pierre Bourdieu and Raymond Aron played a large role in this debate and thematically in this book. France, Germany and Italy all had similar clashes of ideas and institutions in this regard, which Mercer tracks with a solid grasp of the sources.

The students of the 1960s also brought high academic culture into the mainstream, by walking around, literally, with the newly popular pocket books in their jean pockets, carrying titles of many neo-Marxist authors whose work began in the 1920s and 1930s, and then in exile, such as the philosopher/sociologists Georg Lukács, Herbert Marcuse, Walter Benjamin, Max Horkheimer and Theodor Adorno. Mercer is right to be skeptical about whether the radical students actually read these sometimes relatively abstruse texts, but the impact on the general culture as "commodification" of radical sixties ideas, was significant. The sections in the book (mainly Chapters 3 and 4) on the era's business, democratization and undermining of the business through widespread copying of pirate texts, "Books for All," is very informative, since Mercer also covers the conservative backlash against paperback books as a "desacralization of culture. But even more intriguing, as Mercer describes it, was the students' own desacralization, since books *in toto* came to be seen as products of high culture and therefore suspicious.

In the second section of the book Mercer concentrates on the actual political manifestations of the student revolt, that played out differently in Italy, France and Germany, but had common themes. At play was the contention by the radical students that the parliamentary democracies established after World War II in Western Europe were in fact facades for a re-assertion of autocratic or even fascist governments. Most of the student leaders described in this part of the book were of course delusional, both in their diagnosis of the political situation but also in the claim that they alone could save democracy. Mercer does excellent scholarly service here in tracing the splits and confrontations between various student organizations in confronting the issues of the day, but one wishes he would have been more critical of the authoritarian nature itself of the student groups, instead of concluding that they fell apart only because of disappointment over their "marginalization (p. 129).

In the "Crisis of Representation" laid out in chapter 6, Mercer delves into the minutiae of demands for reforms during the period around 1967-68 of the institution of the university itself. Here Mercer does point to the autocratic tendency of many radical student groups as manipulative, theatrical and prone to create new hierarchies through splits and mutual recriminations. He also highlights the hypocrisy inside the movement. One German student leader kept a suit and tie in his office, to but then discard it when he went on to the campus for an official meeting with the rector, in order to show his bona fides as a radical.

One of the lasting consequences of the student movement of the 1960s is what Mercer accurately calls the "informalization of speech," meaning the rejection of codes of deference to professors, which had a lasting impact on the wider culture. Many students stopped using the formal pronoun for "you." The students refused to treat the professors, who even today, at least in Germany, use a separate door to enter the classroom, as gods who always deserved respect. One result was a brutalization of language, calling authority figures pigs, for example, but also the creation of a kind of crypto-language, wherein a complex lexicon, mostly taken from neo-Marxism, gave the students the illusion that they were in possession of higher truths. Mercer is right to focus on these forms of pseudo-sophistication and aggressive over-simplification of complicated ideas. Another effect on the wider culture was the proliferation of graffiti slogans sprayed on urban walls and the trend of scabrous comic books (zines). Mercer also includes an enlightening discussion of the way that the politicization of speech empowered but also embittered female students, who endured condescension and marginalization from their male colleagues.

The third section of the book follows various confrontations on university campuses between the students and the administrative authorities, primarily over the issue of free speech. The students bristled at the arcane laws that did not allow them to organize, assemble and express themselves in manner reflecting the changes in democratization at a wider societal level. They won many of those battles in the mid 1960s and then used their power to protest the Vietnam War in the years when the United States escalated engagement under the LBJ administration. This is when the students began to sense their actual power and over-reached, often transferring what Mercer labels as "student power" into the larger public sphere, but thereby creating a backlash among regular citizens, who, even if they did not support the U.S. strategy in Vietnam, also would not endorse the Soviet and East German funded propaganda in the west, that America, rather than communism, was the actual enemy. Mercer does not pay enough attention to these intelligence-services-backed information wars. But he does note, on a few occasions another problem, that the Vietnam War protests also elevated various charismatic student leaders, who began to assert quite un-democratic control over their student followers.

In a final chapter, Mercer gives a detailed exposition of the attempts by various groups to reform the university in very fundamental ways as a "Critical University," meaning the students would have control over the hiring of faculty and the curriculum. Although the administrators conceded some reforms on self-governance, on the whole, the students demands and vision ended in failure.

The book ends with the obvious conclusion, even to most participants and leaders of the sixties student movement, that the endeavor failed to achieve most of its goals. As others have noted, the student protests did change important cultural valences, from language to music, fashion and attitudes, resulting in many lifestyle reorientations in the 1970s and beyond. The European universities also changed as a result of the anti-authoritarian revolt, becoming in many ways more democratic. But the larger transformation was always a pipe-dream.

By way of conclusion, a story is worth telling. On June 2nd, 1967, a student bystander, Benno Ohnesorg, observing a demonstration against the Shah of Iran by radical German students in front of the Berlin Opera, was shot by a city policeman, who later was discovered to be a Stasi informer. At Ohnesorg's funeral, the esteemed sociologist Jürgen Habermas, heir to Frankfurt Critical theory, warned the students of creeping "left-fascism." It is unfortunate that Mercer does not include this key episode in the history of the German student movement in his otherwise remarkably lucid, balanced and critical monograph. He ends the book by observing that in spite of student radicalism, the legacy of 1968 is worth appreciating, because many of the aspirations of the period are worth preserving. "The struggle continues" is the last line of the book. This phrase echoes a slogan from Rudi Dutschke, the most important student leader in Germany until he was almost murdered with three bullets by a right-wing conspiracy nut in April, 1968. Dutschke left Germany but came back in November 1974 to attend the funeral of Holger Meins, a Red Army terrorist who died due to a hunger strike in a German federal prison. Dutschke clenched his fist and uttered, "The Fight Goes On." Yes, one would have liked to ask Dutschke, and now Mercer, but which fight or fights? And how exactly, given the failures of the sixty-eighters

Part Five: Interview with Martin Woessner

Pathways in Intellectual History

Martin Woessner
Let's start at the beginning. How does an ice hockey-playing Canadian kid come to study in Zürich, Berlin, and Berkeley, becoming an intellectual historian in the process? Where and when did your fascination with Ernst Jünger, the German student and protest movements of the 1960s, and the politics of cultural memory begin to take shape?

Elliot Neaman
Thanks, Martin. Great to talk to you. Like everything in life, a lot of it was serendipitous, or even accidental. I was born in 1957 in Vancouver, British Columbia. I did my undergraduate degree at the University of British Columbia. In Canada, you most often go to school where you grow up. It isn't like here. The higher education system used to be fairly egalitarian and there were no elite colleges in those days. I was near the end of my undergraduate career and I had no idea what I wanted to do with my life. I was actually a sociology and anthropology major, and thought I might go off for a year and study aborigines on an island in the South Pacific. As a default, I was going to go to law school, even though I was completely unenthusiastic about that. Then, in my last, I year sat in on a class—I didn't even take it—that changed everything.

I was an auditor in this class of very smart kids who had formed a kind of cult around a very charismatic professor originally from the United States, who had come to UBC with a wave of young intellectuals, young scholars who were fleeing the United States in the 1970s because of the draft. His name was Edward Hundert. I sat in on this class and was immediately fascinated. He did a standard course starting the Enlightenment, then the Romantics and up to the present, which in the late 1970s meant Foucault and poststructuralism. Existentialism was in its last throes.

Hundert was a kind of Western Marxist, but he was very careful not to situate himself politically. As far as I could tell, most of the students were Marxists, a bit critical of the Soviet Union, but definitely anti-capitalist. So that is what I identified with. I remember that Hundert taught us to think of ideas as actions in the world. I was radicalized by the course politically, but I also realized I needed to learn a lot. When it came to intellectual history, I was a kind of blank slate.

Another thinker I took seriously from Hundert's class was Rousseau. Hundert later published a very good book about Bernard Mandeville and public interests; he was a serious student of eighteenth-century French thought. And so, from Rousseau, via Hundert, I took the notion that modern autonomy is a secularized version of Luther's self: free from the dictates of external institutions. Rousseau taught the perfectibility of humans as moral agents, a concept that Kant turned into the principle that we should always serve others, in moral terms, as ends, not means. I thought that autonomy was the most important achievement of modern society. Many years later, my Master's thesis at the Free University of Berlin was about the Young Hegelians and the Concept of Autonomy.

When I studied romanticism as a historical period in depth later, I realized that this period in my life was a romantic search for some kind of supernatural meaning in life. I identified with the Young Hegelians because I think that was a large part of what they were up to when they secularized Hegel. You can put a mystical veil around reason and Hegel was very good at that. I also came to understand later that romanticism isn't a closed historical era, but rather is part of the psychology of people who feel alienated from the world. Young people often go through this escapist phase in life and come out the other end, sober and better able to tackle the real world, but glad they had that experience. I felt that way. The young Nietzsche's writings were entirely romantic, a struggle with the Dionysian, and I was entirely under his spell, until I wasn't. Some people never leave their romantic past behind. Bernie Sanders is in his eighties, and he is still a romantic. There is a story, probably apocryphal, that he tried to join a commune in Vermont in the 1970s, but they wouldn't accept him because he wanted to talk about politics all the time, but not do any physical labor. In Congress he is still doing that. That's romanticism.

But back then, I still didn't know, in practical terms, what were the next steps to study intellectual history. As it happened, there was a guy living upstairs in our rented house, about five years older, who was doing a Master's degree in European medieval studies. He was writing about European feudalism. He looked like a monk, with a long beard, and was quite mysterious. He would go out nights and often not return until the morning. I found out later he was a somnambulist. But he had a room full of books and I was completely fascinated by him.

MW: This was in Vancouver?

EN: This was in Vancouver. This was in 1979. I had to prepare for a test. It was on the history of war, so I went up there and asked him, "Hey, can you help me? I have to take this exam tomorrow. I'm completely unprepared." He started talking, and we ended up chatting until the wee hours of the morning. He did most of the talking. His name was Steve DeMelt—a very strange guy, but I'll save that part of the story for another time.

I told Steve I didn't want to go to law school, but I had no idea what I should do. He said, like an oracle, you should go study in Switzerland. I have no idea, to this day, why he said that. But I knew somebody in Switzerland, so that was a first hook, and I applied to the University of Zürich. To my surprise, I got a letter of acceptance about a month later. I didn't know then that anywhere on the continent, at least in those days, if you had a Bachelor of Arts, you could study there and it cost very little. On top of that, you got student discounts for many things and even free health care. It's really quite an amazing deal and I have always told my smart students who want to study in Europe to take advantage of no tuition (or very little) offered by the continental European welfare state. So off I went to the land of cow bells, maidens in festive skirts, and the gnomes of Zürich. My grandfather footed the bill at first, until I got a job as an English teacher to supplement my income. I began by studying

German at the Goethe Institute in a small town in Southern Germany. I had one of the best summers of my life in Staufen, near the University of Freiburg.

I signed up originally for eight weeks at the Goethe Institute, and then I did another eight weeks—almost the whole summer. Heidegger had died five years earlier, but his spirit was still very much there. And I was very into Sartre, and therefore into Heidegger. I had Sartre's *Being amd Nothingness* in a paperback that Steve had given me, all dog-eared and thoroughly worn. I used to take walks in the Black Forest and think about existentialism. I'd written also a paper for another professor that I took with me, and it was kind of based on Löwith's book *From Hegel to Nietzsche*. I basically recapped that book. There was an academic at the language school there who read it. Even though the footnotes had become lost, he said, "This is Löwith, right? But you have some good ideas on your own, so keep going." His comments gave me some confidence.

MW: Had you studied German in Vancouver?

EN: A little bit. Not much. I landed in Europe with very little German. The teacher of the one course I took happened to be married to a Swiss fellow, so that was one anchor I had in Switzerland. It was all quite coincidental.

In Zürich I signed up for a bunch of lectures and every day I sat in these big lecture halls and listened. At first, I didn't understand that much, but by the sixth month I was pretty fluent. The brain is quite elastic, even at age 23. I read a lot of Nietzsche in those days and I really wanted a whole change in society: beyond good and evil, dance on top of the structures while they crumble, create a whole new set of values—all of that. Capitalism was evil, the system was rigged. I was alienated so I assumed everybody else was alienated, too. [Laughs.] I projected many of my personal gripes onto the whole society. And I wanted to read Marx in the original. That became a central objective. I took courses on Kant and Hegel, and, eventually, the whole idealist tradition. I never understood Schelling and Fichte that well, but I tortured myself through those texts. I felt like I was communicating in code with these masters of the universe, who held the keys to all knowledge. It was all quite intoxicating, this Teutonic profundity.

But Zürich was an odd place to pick to study this stuff, because their German is so different. I immediately had to learn Swiss German. The classes were in high German, of course, but I wanted to fit in with my cohort, so I learned the Swiss dialect as well. And Swiss really is a separate language. Pluck a northern German, say from Hamburg, and plunk him down in in a Swiss city, and he won't understand much of what people are saying.

In a Swiss or German university, the lectures are separate from seminars, so you can just sit there and listen. You are not required to do anything. If you want to get credit for a course, you have to take the seminar and write a paper. But I was able to sit in on lectures by big names, as it turned out, at least in the fields of history and philosophy. Paul Feyerabend, for example, was at Zürich. Four hundred people turned up in massive lecture halls to watch the Feyerabend Show, which was quite theatrical. Feyerabend was very interested in theater—he had actually worked with Brecht in his youth. He would wander back and forth on stage, gesticulating as he gripped a crutch. He was an injured war veteran. I got interested in the history of science through him.

There was a great Hegel scholar there as well, whose seminar had only 12 people. We were like his apostles. And I took courses from a young historian of science with whom I later reconnected, Paul Hoyningen-Huene, who's now a world- famous scholar. So that's how it all started. I had found my path to intellectual history by going German.

MW: That's a good beginning! I remember you saying at one point a long time ago that your mom wasn't so happy you were heading off to learn German, and study all things German. Is that true?

EN: Yeah, it's true. My mom, as a good Jewish mother, wanted me to go to law school. She was very disappointed that I didn't do that. My grandfather, to his credit, was a little baffled by the idea of going to Germany, but, you know, he asked me, "Well, what do the men say?" Meaning the male professors at UBC. "Do they think it's a good idea?" I assured him that they thought it was a very good idea, that there would be a job for me at the end of all this. And he said, "Well, okay, let's try it. Go ahead." But my mom, no, she thought that I was acting out, probably against her. There's a famous scene in our family history of my mother and I sitting next to the pool in my grandfather's apartment building—he'd gotten sick by then and was about to die. At one point, my mom stood up, marched around the pool, Monty Python-style, John Cleese-style, goose-stepping, holding her finger to her upper lip as a mustache, a Hitler mustache, and repeated, "My son is a German. My son is a German. He's decided to become a German."

MW: That was the story I remember you telling.

EN: In class? Yeah, that's great. [Laughs]. I eventually won her over and she even visited me in Berlin.

MW: Did you know then that you wanted to be a professor, or were you just planning to be a Marxist agitator, reading Marx in the original German and debating the finer points of dialectical materialism? At what point did you think, "Oh, this could be a career, or, I could be an intellectual historian"? Was that in Zürich? Because after Zürich, you go to Berlin, right?

EN: I don't know for sure. I think I was keeping my options open. I remember that when I turned 24, I was very freaked out, because I hadn't written the Great American Novel yet, and I was already so old.

MW: So that was an ambition in the background, too?

EN: Yeah, I thought I would write a novel, like *The Great Gatsby*, but about Switzerland. I had this idea to write a story about a bond trader in Zürich, with all kinds of intrigue. I banged out several versions on my portable typewriter, but I realized that literary prose really didn't come naturally to me. I also wrote some short stories, which weren't bad, but unfortunately most of them, I think, are lost. People thought they were pretty good, but I don't think that fiction is my forte.

When I was in Zürich, I remember I submitted an article to *History and Theory* about Karl Popper. It was rejected, but they were encouraging. So I *must* have been thinking about scholarship already then as a vocation. Paul Hoyningen-Huene thought my article was good enough to invite me to attend a Tuesday evening Hegel Club, which met at his apartment in the old part of town every week. That was really exciting. We read Hegel's *Logic*, probably the most difficult text ever written in German philosophy, line by line. We would cover maybe three paragraphs in one evening. Once Hoyningen-Huene got quite upset with me, because I was moving too fast while reading the text. "Slow down, Elliot, slow down." It became a running joke when we reconnected later in life, because I am quite impatient, actually, and he nailed it way back then.

Zürich was interesting for another reason I should mention. Just as I arrived there, a youth revolt broke out. The city had built a brand new, beautiful opera house: glass and steel, very modernist. Young people resented the amount of money that had been spent on it, because they wanted a new Youth Center. That became the rallying cry, "Build Us a Youth Center," where people could meet, put on plays, have music and dancing. The kids began to go out onto the streets, protest, make a lot of noise. They became quite threatening. The city responded with police and water tanks. It was all very exciting for me, a kid from Canada, where nothing like that ever happened. Then the youth leaders upped the ante and demanded an *autonomous* youth center, in other words, without adult supervision. Every Saturday afternoon there were protest marches through the streets of Zürich, staid, conservative, normally very quiet Zürich. Again, it was all very exciting. The pragmatic city fathers gave in eventually and an autonomous youth center was built in a seedy area behind the main train station. Every evening loud meetings were held to discuss operations. Immediately a problem emerged: drug dealers and prostitutes exploited the fact that the police could not enter the compound. Two groups formed in response: the radicals, who wanted to tolerate criminals, and the moderates, who thought the undesirables should be thrown out, so as not to jeopardize the success of the experiment. Even in those days I was wary of the radicals and joined the latter group. And just as we had warned, within six months the place was overrun by bad actors. The city closed everything down. Still, it was a great real-world experience in grass-roots politics.

MW: At what point did you trade Zürich for Berlin?

EN: After two years. I arrived in Zürich, fall of 1980. I studied four semesters. In the summer of 1982 somebody told me, you've got to visit Berlin. When I saw the city, I realized I was living in the wrong place. It was like having been brought up in a small town in rural America and getting on a plane to New York. Berlin was unique, a walled city at the height of the Cold War, spies and all. By contrast, Zürich was a small and sleepy place that barely had been touched, physically, by World War II. Berlin, on the other hand, was still pockmarked by the war. You could see bullet holes everywhere in the walls of old buildings in the center of town. There was also no curfew, so the city lived day and night. If you wanted to avoid the draft as an eighteen-year-old, you simply moved to Berlin. Those were the rules of the occupying forces: no soldiers in Berlin. Even though I grew to love Zürich, and had some amazing friends there, I really had outgrown it, and once I saw Berlin, I knew that was my fate. Also, I wanted to learn proper German. I spoke German with a Swiss accent at first.

MW: Say a little bit more about Berlin in the Cold War era, and obviously the transformation of it that was coming: the 80s were going be a pivotal moment, not just for Berlin, not just for Germany, but for Europe and the wider world. And you were there, right smack in the middle of it all.

EN: Right. You know, as a walled town, one did feel isolated. Crossing the wall into East Germany meant navigating a maze of security and forced currency exchange. Driving to West Germany involved armed guards, outposts, and a strict route from which one couldn't diverge. If you broke any rules there was hell to pay. The wall was a constant presence, you lived with it in the background of your life. The scrawled graffiti was a kind of song in your head that never left: it faded sometimes, but it was always there.

I was busy reading philosophy and history, attending lectures and seminars at the Freie Universität. I got to study under amazing people. Michael Theunissen, Ernst Tugendhat, and Jacob Taubes all taught in the philosophy department, which had its own strangely designed building on campus. In the history department, which was housed in a huge, ugly structure containing the humanities departments, I studied with Ernst Nolte. He became super-famous, because he got involved in the Historians' Debate in the mid-1980s, about whether Germans should let the Nazi past fade into history like all other eras, or should treat it uniquely as part of a collective memory that was too important to be forgotten. Nolte thought it should pass into history, and was accused of relativizing the Holocaust as a result. I started studying with him just before this international cause célèbre broke out.

The Cold War atmosphere was there, behind all this, especially the Historians' Debate, but I didn't think about it too much. I did write a short story that had to do with the wall. It, too, wasn't very good. I remember that we definitely felt that Berlin was unusual as a city and heavy with history, you know. Again, I really didn't think about it at the time, but it was only forty years since the end of the war. Not a long time. I mean, there were people, lots of people, who had been in the crowds, applauding Hitler and marching off to war. A lot of them were still alive. I regret that I didn't interview more people. I didn't think about it then. For me, all of that was so long past, but really it wasn't. It was very much alive.

MW: Yeah, the first and only time I got to Berlin—and stayed in your old apartment there—was in 2000. That was when cranes were everywhere, because they were rebuilding everything. But you could go to districts where there were still those bullet holes in buildings. It just felt like the city was a palimpsest, with so many layers of history—walking to the east side of the city, and back the west side, you saw it everywhere. It was long after the wall had fallen, and yet it still felt like Berlin had all these open wounds, I guess.

EN: Yeah, lots of ghosts. East Berlin was where it really hit you in the face. Because when you went over there, it was kind of grim and scary and depressing, and, you know, the difference between the two—for me, that's where the grip of Marxism started to get very loosened, because I saw what real existing communism was like.

MW: So that's when you started to abandon your radical Marxism? Just living in Berlin?

EN: The seeds were planted. When I came to Berkeley, I still thought of myself as a Marxist, but my many doubts about Marxism as a living philosophy had grown. Like many on the Left in those days, I cognitively rationalized the dissonance between Marxist tenets and "real existing Socialism," as the East German government called it. They had betrayed Marx, I thought at the time. But having seen how people had to live under communism and meeting people from East Berlin, and then debating the people who *defended* that system in West Berlin, I became pretty disillusioned. The reigning Communist Party in East Berlin had a sister party in West Berlin and I knew some of those people: they were rigid, orthodox, and so narrow-minded. I was completely turned off.

MW: They embraced dialectical-materialist Marxism, not Western Marxism?

EN: They argued that the system is seemingly oppressive because of the evils of capitalism and imperialism. East Germany was only defending itself, they would say, and so it's necessary to retrench and build the wall, the anti-fascist wall. That was what the wall was for them. I remember being shocked by that. I was always a Western Marxist in that sense. When I read Martin Jay's *The Dialectical Imagination* I thought, "okay, *that's* my Marxism."

MW: So, you read Martin Jay's book in Berlin?

EN: Already in Zürich. I saw it in the library and just grabbed it and took it home and read it in two days.

MW: And was that what got you to Berkeley? How and when did that transition happen, from Berlin to Berkeley? Didn't you finish an MA in Berlin?

EN: Yes. I was admitted to the graduate program in Berkeley already in 1984, but I waited another year to finish the degree in Berlin. In Germany you get what is called a *Magister*, which you could translate as a Master's, but really, it's somewhere between a BA and a teaching degree if you want to go in that direction. It's a little bit broader than a BA, but it's not a doctorate. It's something in the middle. I didn't need it. I could have gotten into Berkeley—I did get into Berkeley—without it. The only thing that changed was I had to do one less little test when I got to Berkeley. But I decided to stay an extra year because I didn't want to leave Berlin just yet. Also, I thought: I started this, I'm going to finish it.

I was very lucky to have studied with Ernst Nolte at the FU Berlin. That was a big deal, because Ernst Nolte ended up writing me a letter of recommendation. I found out later that the faculty at Berkeley was impressed, since Nolte had become world-famous thanks to the Historians' Debate. When I applied to Cal, I was up against all these kids who had gone to amazing prep schools. And I came from Canada, University of British Columbia. *What was that?* But since I was older and had all this European experience, I got in.

MW: So you had a letter of recommendation from somebody who had become famous for articulating conservative, quite controversial positions about German history, and yet you came to Cal to work with Martin Jay, whom I don't think we would call a conservative, right?

EN: To the credit of the faculty at UC Berkeley, they didn't vet your political positions. They wanted solid scholars, not ideologues.

MW: Did you go to Berkeley specifically to study with Martin Jay?

EN: Not entirely. Before I started applying to doctoral programs, I went to see Edward Hundert, whose course on intellectual history had hooked me on intellectual history so many years before. He said, "Well, apply to Montreal, apply to Toronto." Those were the graduate programs that had good intellectual history, at least German history, whereas UBC really didn't have it at the time. UBC is now a great university; it wasn't that good in those days. It was kind of provincial.

On Hundert's advice, I applied to Toronto, Montreal, and then a bunch of schools in the States. I must have applied to ten. I think I applied to Harvard, Yale, Stanford—all the big ones. Chicago and Berkeley were the two that accepted me. That was it. And then Toronto and Montreal were going to offer me scholarships, but not Berkeley and not Chicago. Hundert said to me, "If you want to make it in academia, you really should go to an American University." It came down to Berkeley or Chicago. I talked to people about both. I remember somebody telling me about Chicago, and they said, "Well, in winter, when you walk out the door of your apartment, the wind is so strong, it'll blow you back into the door." I said, "I think I'll go to Berkeley." [Laughs]

MW: You had had enough Canadian winters.

EN: Yeah—I really didn't know about Berkeley, but of course, the whole idea of going to California, that was attractive.

MW: Let's talk about Berkeley. You arrive in Berkeley what year?

EN: '85.

MW: And what were your first impressions? I mean, Berlin is a city that's famous in its own right, but Berkeley is a city that's famous in its own right, too, with its own historical and cultural memory. On top of that, you were working with Martin Jay, a scholar who was relatively young (b. 1944) but who already had a global reputation. If there is a kind of intellectual-history guild in the States, Jay is one of the more prominent figures in it. And you had classmates—other Jay students—who today are pretty famous intellectual historians. I'm thinking, in particular, of the four with whom you published that *Festschrift* for Jay in 2009: Peter E. Gordon, Warren Breckman, Dirk Moses, and Sam Moyn, people who are standard-bearers for the field. So, what was Berkeley like when you got there? What was campus like? What were the classes like?

EN: Let me back up a bit. In 1984, while I was still living in Berlin. Jay had a year-long academic sabbatical and was living in Paris. I visited him there, in a pretty little house in the suburbs, and he got me very excited about studying at Berkeley. As I said before, I applied twice to Berkeley. I didn't really realize how hard it was to get in. I didn't go in '84. But I applied again and got in in '85. That was lucky, because it wasn't guaranteed. And I was lucky that Marty was doing that sabbatical year in Paris, writing his big book about late twentieth-century French philosophy called *Downcast Eyes*. It had to do with the French suspicion of sight—the critique of ocularcentrism—in favor of the other four senses.

MW: You taught a whole seminar on it!

EN: That's right.

MW: And I was there.

EN: Were you in that?

MW: Yeah.

EN: I remember now.

MW: I have questions about it later, so we'll have to come back to it.

EN: Okay. So, yes, Marty was working on that book. It was a nice coincidence for me that he had written *The Dialectical Imagination*. Once I met him in person, I *did* see myself as a Marty student. In Germany they call mentors "doctor fathers," *Doktorväter*. He was my "doctor father."

When I got to Berkeley, in the summer of 1985, I was blown away by, first of all, just the physical beauty of the Bay Area, but also of the campus. I fell absolutely in love with the place. In the beginning, I viewed Berkeley through European eyes. It had a whole mythos, a mythology wrapped around it: the sixties. But when I started my seminars, I have to say, it was hard. There was a lot of reading to do, and it felt very serious. In Berlin, you wrote your papers when you wanted to and turned them in when you wanted to. Students hung around for twenty semesters or more. It was very different at Berkeley. There were deadlines, and the other students were very bright and hard-working. I didn't feel intimidated, though. In fact, I was a little bit cocky, because I was older and my German was better than theirs. Still, underneath the veneer of self-posturing, I did feel the pressure. Years later, I met up with a fellow student, a wonderful person and scholar named Carolyn Dean, and we laughed about a particular afternoon when we met for lunch on the north side of Berkeley to talk about the work of Jacques Lacan. To show off, I brought a copy of Lacan's edited writings, which I could barely read, and placed the book next to me on the bistro table where she was sure to see it. We both felt intimidated by the other, and we were both cosplaying. Me especially.

MW: The students all expected to become professional historians?

EN: I think so. It was the first time I really had been with peers who were doing the same thing I was interested in and knew their stuff, knew what they were talking about. I hadn't really encountered people like that before. Some of the German students were very accomplished, but they came out of a different world. I automatically felt sort of inferior to them, but that was good for me—like playing chess with people you know are better than you so you can learn from them. As a result, I arrived in Berkeley feeling like I was a big shot. I had been to Germany and I knew my Hegel and Marx. Then I realized that a lot of them did, too.

MW: Warren Breckman and Dirk Moses, people like that?

EN: Yes, though Dirk came a little bit later. But people like Warren, Ross Dickenson, John Abromeit, and Alon Confino did German history. Heath Pearson did economic history. Josh Cole and Carolyn Dean did French stuff. And Stephen Kotkin was one of us: he became a very famous scholar of Stalin's Russia. Peter Gordon came earlier and Sam Moyn a little bit later. There was a division between those who studied French history and those who did German history. We ghettoized a little bit. The Frenchies all hung around with their professors, like Lynn Hunt and Susanna Barrows, and we Germanists clustered around Jay and Gerald Feldman and other teachers, like Gene Brucker and William Bouwsma—all heavy hitters. This was at the height of post-structuralism, so Foucault was very important. We felt like the Frenchies were too indebted to his method, that we were more serious historians. A classic example of the narcissism-of-small-differences.

The other important thing that happened at Berkeley was that I met Martin Malia. He was the other intellectual historian at Cal. He was an intellectual historian and an historian of Russia. He was world-renowned, taught part-time at the Collège de France as well as at Berkeley. And he was a conservative. So I had two Martins and in time was swayed as much by Malia as by Jay. The part of me that moved in a conservative direction had a lot to do with Malia's influence.

MW: That's interesting. Is that where your interest in Ernst Jünger comes from? Because it seems like kind of a leap: at one point your mom is walking around the pool saying, "My son has become a German." Now, all of the sudden you *are* a German. Not only that, but you are reading somebody who was considered *the* voice of the conservative reaction of the 1920s and '30s. How did it happen?

EN: Long story short: I'm studying in Berkeley from '85 until '87. I do it fairly quickly because, first of all, I had the MA from Germany, so I had fewer boxes to tick off. There's an exam at Cal you take after one year to get the Master's credit. I didn't have to do that. And I didn't have to worry about languages because I had German down and I had my French and Italian down, partly because I'm Canadian, but also because I had spent time in France and Italy. I zipped through all that and was done by 1987. I did my orals in '87 with Malia, Marty, Feldman, Brucker, Bouwsma, and [Hubert] Dreyfus, from Philosophy. I was auditing Dreyfus's classes then and started to really get into Heidegger, right around '86, '87. It was through Dreyfus that I met Hans Sluga, John Searle, and some of the other faculty in the Philosophy Department.

MW: So you got West-Coast Heidegger? A very specific, distinct version.

EN: You would know better than I, but that sounds right. My Heidegger was all Dreyfus at that point—and I totally bought into it. I see it now, but at the time I didn't: Dreyfus had turned Heidegger into human-interaction anthropology, right?

MW: Yeah, I think that's true, which makes him more appealing to an American, pragmatist tradition. It gets rid of all the metaphysical baggage that would be there otherwise.

EN: Yep.

MW: But let's get back to Jünger, the subject of your dissertation. You do your oral exams in '87, with all these folks. Do they ask you about Jünger? Or does he come after the oral exams?

EN: After. I had no idea who Jünger was at that point. I went back to Berlin in the spring of 1988 to work on the dissertation, with no clue about what I wanted to write about, which wasn't that unusual. I knew I wanted to do a post-war German topic because I felt like there was something new there. So many people had done the age of Bismarck, cultural despair, things like that. I found that era too well covered. I'm not going to compete with Fritz Stern and Geo Schöneberg, and I find a little paperback of Ernst Jünger's *On the Marble Cliffs*. I remember looking at the back cover, seeing Jünger in this slick, dandyesque outfit, gazing back at the reader with this intriguing squint in his eye, like he was looking through you and off into the distance. I was very curious about who this person was. I took the book home. I don't even think I finished reading the novel that time, but it stuck in my head. And then, about half a year later, I had decided that my topic was going to be German intellectuals who had remained in Germany throughout the war and resurfaced after 1945. Since Marty had done a book about exiles, those who had *left* Germany, I thought, well, what if I do those who *stayed* in Germany? What about the German intellectuals who survived the

Nazi period and had to make a comeback, make names for themselves, after 1945? One of the books I found on the topic was about twelve intellectuals like that: writers, scholars—a mix. One of them was Jünger. And that's when I sort of thought, that's an interesting guy. At the time, Jünger had basically been forgotten; he was not on people's radar screens. But as he approached 100, in the 1990s—

MW: He came back.

EN: He came back. With a vengeance. Literally. But in the late '80s, when I started working on him, people often asked me, "Is that guy still alive?" "Yeah, yeah, he's still alive," I would say.

MW: But initially you envisioned a larger project on inner emigration?

EN: Or rehabilitation. Mastering the past. Literary work under a dictatorship. Things like that. Initially, I planned on covering several of figures: at first six, and then it was three. In the end, only one man was left standing.

MW: Was that because Jünger was the most interesting, or?

EN: Jay suggested I narrow my focus: *Don't bite off too much.* So I had to choose. Jünger intrigued me, which goes back to your question about why I chose a reactionary conservative, or whatever you want to call him, to write about. I was still indebted to the Frankfurt School, so I viewed him from a critical, dialectical perspective. I certainly wasn't won over to reactionary politics, but I realized early on that this guy was a much more complicated figure than those who attacked him as a fascist allowed. The Germans regard literature almost always from a moral perspective: good guys and bad guys, especially with regard to the Third Reich, of course. I have always found that to be myopic. There's something wrong, unfair, with pigeon-holing writers that way.

MW: So when you started working on Jünger, was that the received opinion, that he was just an old Nazi, a relic of the discredited old right? And yet you found all these layers of other things going on in his writings?

EN: Almost all of Jünger's critics were one-sidedly negative. *His politics are bad.* And anybody who defends him is guilty, automatically, of being Nazis themselves.

MW: Guilt by association.

EN: Yeah. Exactly.

MW: In college I remember reading *On the Marble Cliffs* in an English translation, because I thought I had to understand this writer you were writing a book about. If Elliot thinks this guy is important, then clearly, he must be. But *On the Marble Cliffs* was one of the strangest things I had ever read, like *Dungeons & Dragons* meets gothic horror. It had this fantasy element, but it was clearly a parable or an allegory for what was going on with National Socialism, too, and written in this really esoteric, mystical kind of language. How did *that* book convince you that you wanted to learn more about this person? And to add to the strangeness, Jünger did all those experiments with LSD and mescaline—it's as if he's lived nine or ten lives, not just the one.

EN: Right.

MW: So was it the political ambiguity or the esotericism of the writing that attracted you?

EN: A little bit of all that. I don't think it was *The Marble Cliffs* that really drew me in, though. I think it was more the journals. Jünger kept journals his whole life. And at some point I read *Storms of Steel*, which was his first journal. It's really a diary.

MW: And the thing that makes him famous.

EN: Yes, *Storms of Steel* catapulted him to fame as a young man, during the Weimar Republic. With it, I could make a connection to the Frankfurt School. Walter Benjamin took Jünger seriously, for example. I thought this would make for a good dissertation topic. On top of that, Jünger had lived such a long life. And was still alive!

But back to *The Marble Cliffs*. Whatever it is—and it is a strange story, set, like you say, partly in a kind of old gothic, partly mystical, partly fantasy world—I just knew that this, whatever it was, was not fascism. It was clearly a critique of the Nazis, hidden behind an allegory. The more I dug, the more I thought that Jünger really deserved to be taken seriously as a thinker. After all, he was friends with Heidegger, he was friends with Carl Schmitt. He was hanging out with other thinkers we still discuss in detail.

MW: Indeed, you could hang a lot of different stories on this one remarkable life. What was the reaction to your choice of the dissertation topic like? What did Marty think of it? What did Martin Malia think of it? Was he on your dissertation committee?

EN: No, Malia wasn't really involved. Malia didn't really know that stuff. My committee was Jay and Feldman, a German economic historian, but he knew about everything. Marty was very supportive. He realized that this was—at least in the English-speaking world—tracking out into new territory.

MW: Yours was one of the first monographs on Jünger, right?

EN: Marcus Bullock had published a very good book about Jünger in 1992—I became friends with him—called *The Violent Eye*. But it was from a comparative literature perspective. So, no, there weren't many books in English about Jünger. J.P. Stern had published a little book in 1952. And Jünger would get a mention in the *New York Review of Books* here and there, but his career was uncharted territory for the most part.

MW: Once you started writing about Jünger, did people start to pigeonhole you as a conservative, because you were writing about a conservative?

EN: I think people, my friends at Berkeley, might have a little. I remember Peter Hoffenberg, who was a real lefty, telling me that every time that he had an idea having to do with politics, he would run it by me, to see what the other side would think. So I must have emitted that vibe somehow. But I really didn't see myself as a conservative.

It is important to remember the context. I was living in Germany in the late 1980s. I was there when the wall came down. But I returned to Berkeley just as the Gulf War broke out. I taught at Cal for a while, while trying to finish the dissertation. It was around this time that I met Jeffrey Friedman, who was the editor of a new journal called *Critical Review*, a libertarian journal. I really didn't know anything about American libertarianism, but Friedman asked me to write an article about German collectivism. At least that's the title I eventually gave the piece. He wanted to know about how Germans interacted with the Welfare State, about why Germans were so attached to the state. In order to write the article I had to immerse myself in the American-British tradition of libertarianism. And *that* attracted me. I'm still very critical of libertarians, but it opened my mind up to this whole strain in American political thinking that I had reflexively rejected, without knowing a lot about it. I think it was just one more way in which I was leaving my Marxist past behind. I never became a convinced libertarian. But to this day, just as Peter Hoffenberg would run ideas across me to see what the other side might say, whenever I think about a policy, I'll say to myself, "Well, what would a libertarian argue?"

MW: Were you reading Robert Nozick, Murray Bookchin, or any of that kind of stuff?

EN: I read around in all of it, but what I could not accept was the weak state aspect. Open borders, isolationism, things like that—that's just weird and impractical. But free markets and classical liberal principles, I was attracted to those. Locke. Not Marx to the left, or Hobbes to the right. I'm good on that. And on the critique of socialist economics. I was quite influenced by Ludwig von Mises and Friedrich Hayek. And by Aristotle. I used to have long debates with John Ely, who calls himself a left-wing Aristotelian filtered through

Hannah Arendt. We never agreed on much. I prefer to take my Aristotle straight up, thank you very much.

MW: But this brings us back around to Jünger, doesn't it? The recent interest in Jünger's life and work, can't that traced back to libertarians? Russell Berman and others—the *Telos* crowd—seem to be interested in him because of the possible connections between some of his writings and contemporary libertarianism, right?

EN: I think that's true, except that Russell Berman and David Pan and the *Telos* crowd don't think of themselves primarily as libertarians, but what they would call post-liberals. They like to flip Critical Theory against the left, as they did—with cheap tricks—using Carl Schmitt. They are flirting with right-wing populism today in a way I find quite foolish.

MW: On that point we certainly agree. But let's go back to your first encounters with libertarian thought, in the 1990s, after the fall of the Berlin Wall. And maybe you could say more about that world-historical event itself. What was it like to have been in Berlin then?

EN: The fall of the wall was really kind of anticlimactic. I was often driving back and forth between Aachen and Berlin in those days, because my girlfriend lived in Aachen, which is on the western border, near Belgium. I remember I was driving that night, November 9th. I must have been one of the last thousand cars that drove into the city that night. It was nine o'clock or thereabouts. The news had broken that Ossies were jumping on the wall while the guards just stood there, frozen in place, watching. People were drunk and dancing. It was still unclear exactly who was allowed to do what. I remember taking the subway down there near midnight and it was a party scene. The television cranes had already been set up and were filming. But it was a kind of post-historical event in the sense that nothing really happened, say like the Berlin Airlift. Rather, it became real through interpretation. The narrative was constructed afterwards, because it was a long, slow process. The wall didn't fall in a physical sense. That was a metaphor. Many things happened all at once, which had to be constructed by a narrative, by different narratives.

By the next morning, there were holes in the wall where people could drive through. I went home and went to sleep. For the next few weeks, it was irritating. There were people who were flooding into the subways. Everything was chaotic. We West Berliners went on with our lives, while the Ossies wandered around in a kind of daze.

MW: Did they act like tourists? Were they thinking, "Oh, so this is the West we always dreamed about"?

EN: Exactly. They got 200 Marks of "Welcome Money." They bought out everything, because they were used to ration lines. The stores were running out of stuff and you couldn't get anywhere because the subway was overfilled. I just wanted to go on with my daily life. I realized that this was a great historical event, but I followed it like everyone else, on the television, even though it was happening all around me. I didn't run out and interview people and take pictures, even though so many people were doing that already. I didn't collect any pieces of the wall. It took a while for the event to happen—what became the Fall of the Berlin Wall.

MW: And meanwhile, you're working on Ernst Jünger. As the wall is falling.

EN: Yes. I have to tell you an interesting story from this period related to my Jünger research. In a course I took from Nolte about the history of conservative thought, I met a young woman. We were just friends at first, but we flirted with each other. She came over to my apartment for dinner one night and told me that her father was a journalist. And I said, "Oh, really? Which magazine or which newspaper?" She said, "*Der Spiegel.*" There happened to be a copy right next to us. "Show me who your father is," I asked. Her father was the publisher of *Der Spiegel*, Rudolf Augstein.

Long story short. I visited Augstein's daughter in Hamburg. (She is today a very prominent journalist in Germany.) She took me to the twelfth floor, to Rudolf's office, which had a direct hotline to the Chancellor of Germany on his desk. And she allowed me to go into their archives and copy their entire Jünger archive. That was an unbelievably lucky score, because the other archives didn't have what the *Spiegel* had in terms of the breadth of originality of their collection. Every possible newspaper clipping was in there, as well as letters and various primary sources about Jünger. I copied the whole thing. I spent two days there and was allowed to use their copy machines. Because we had become romantically involved by then, I was seen as an extension of the boss's daughter. I packed up all the boxes with these materials, along with sources from the Marbach archive, and sent everything to Berkeley. That was the basis of the dissertation. The boxes arrived half-broken, held together by packing tape. Some guy at the post office luckily helped me. The stuff was falling out. It's amazing that it all arrived intact. The dissertation was a rough draft of what later became the book.

MW: You finished the dissertation and then got a job at the University of San Francisco. Just like that?

EN: Not quite. One year, I was unemployed. I worked as an intern at *Tikkun Magazine*. But that helped me get the job, because it was very important, even back then, to be somehow active in the community or do something for social justice. And *Tikkun* was seen as that kind of magazine.

MW: Did you get that through Berkeley connections?

EN: No, my first wife was flipping through a copy of *Tikkun Magazine.* We had a roommate who was interested in it: Hajo Funke, a visiting scholar from Berlin. He had met and interviewed *Tikkun's* editor, Michael Lerner, so there was a copy *of Tikkun* lying around. My wife at the time noticed that they were looking for interns. She wanted me out of the house, and so she said, "Well, why don't you go and apply for this?" It wasn't paid, and maybe for that reason Michael Lerner was happy to have me. That's how I ended up becoming friends with him and his son, Akiba, who is one of my best friends to this day.

During my year as an unpaid intern at *Tikkun*, I started applying for university positions. I have a binder somewhere with at least sixty rejection letters. The reason I got the job at USF was thanks to a stroke of good fortune. The Renaissance scholar at USF was named Elisabeth Gleason. She was the *grande dame* of the department. She read the article I wrote about German collectivism and must have liked it, because she chose me over people who were much more qualified than I was at the time. I hadn't even finished the dissertation when they hired me in '92. People like Jeffrey Herf had applied, for example, and others who were established scholars already or had at least finished their dissertations. So again, the luck of youth intervened.

MW: But that was a big change for you. Your first time on a Jesuit campus and, I'm guessing, in a Catholic environment. Even though it's just across the bay from Berkeley, there's a rather different feel to the place. What was it like? What were your first impressions of USF, of moving across the bay and teaching different kinds of students? I would imagine your students were quite different from what you were accustomed to, either in Europe or at Berkeley.

EN: I arrived at USF at a time when there was a new dean, Stanley Nel, who didn't come out of the Catholic tradition. He was a math whiz from South Africa, super smart and ambitious. He didn't suffer fools gladly. USF was transitioning from being a rather parochial school, a feeder school from Catholic high schools in the area, for which Catholic values were really important, St. Ignatius and so forth. I knew it was Catholic, obviously, but most important to me was that this school was going somewhere. And frankly, I was happy to have any job. Academic jobs were in short supply. As far as the students went, that was a culture shock, because I had been teaching Berkeley students and all of a sudden, these were very different students. They weren't as interested. They weren't as curious. They weren't as smart, with a few exceptions. [MW laughs]. And so that took a while to adjust to. But the other faculty members were in the same boat. We all had to adjust our expectations. If you didn't, you were fighting an uphill battle.

MW: I was very fortunate because just then, when I came to USF to study, there were many young, very good academics who were doing interesting work: Eduardo Mendieta, in philosophy, for example, and you in history. There was a lot of good energy among the new faculty. USF was a small, out-of-the-way college, yet I remember Habermas visited, and Richard Rorty came up once from Stanford. One of my fondest memories was sophomore year, taking your honors seminar in one of those old, wood-paneled rooms atop Lone Mountain. I think I was one of the younger students there. Everybody seemed older and smarter. You had a reading list that took us through all of the major developments in intellectual history in the twentieth century. Every week was a different book, a different topic, a different subject. There was this sense that intellectual history was kind of the master discipline. Looking back, it was at the tail end of theory wars, right? All of us, as students, wanted to know what poststructuralism was. We wanted to know where Derrida or Foucault came from. We wanted to know how to understand Judith Butler or Richard Rorty, and it was as if intellectual historians had the ability to contextualize all that, to give it a genealogy. My classmates and I lapped that up.

In your seminar, we had to read a book a week, and I remember everyone back then just thought, "Oh my God, really?" But that was the first time I read anything having to do with intellectual history, let alone critical theory, or poststructuralism. We read Jim Miller's biography of Foucault. We read Rorty's *Contingency, Irony, and Solidarity*. All in the same seminar. It was amazing.

EN: Wow, I've forgotten all that.

MW: But if, back then, intellectual history seemed well-positioned to help people navigate all these different developments, it now seems like intellectual history is falling back on its heels. People don't look to intellectual history to try to explain what's going on, whether in the academy or outside it. Intellectual history is on the defensive these days. But back then, I felt like it was really growing and expanding.

EN: You are reminding me now of an era at USF that is gone, I'm afraid. In those days, I complained that USF was a letdown from Berkeley, but compared to today, the students were much more engaged. How many students were in that class?

MW: I think it was like fifteen, maybe twenty.

EN: And you're sure you're not projecting on the others, that they were as interested as you were in this stuff?

MW: No, they were. Maybe because it was an honors seminar. Not everybody was interested in history, but because it was an honors seminar, there were people who were studying art and there were people into literature. It wasn't just history. In the history classes, the students tended to be not as interested in all that.

EN: Now I remember. Honors—it was an honors class. Yes, it is coming back to me. Good memories!

MW: You taught another honors class, a year or two later. And because I had already taken your honors seminar, they wouldn't let me do it again. I had to petition to take it, explaining how it was a totally different syllabus this time. You were teaching Martin Jay's *Downcast Eyes*, which had just come out. I remember you brought Marty to come and talk to the class.

EN: That's right.

MW: I wanted to ask you about that semester, actually. As a true intellectual historian, you had us reading all kinds of stuff: philosophy, literature, social theory, political thought, all across the board. We read so many different things in these seminars, which was really unique. It helped shape my own thinking, giving me this kind of interdisciplinary, ecumenical approach. I remember when you taught the seminar on *Downcast Eyes*, you assigned George Bataille's *Story of the Eye* [EN chuckles] and I think one of the conservative Catholic students complained. Didn't the president of the college call you, and you had to explain why you put pornography on the syllabus?

EN: [Laughing] Yeah. He was nice about it. He just, he said, "Well, could you tell me why we want them to read the book?" And so I launched into this monologue, using big words like ocularcentrism. You could see his eyes glaze over. And he said, "Well, I see, but perhaps next time, you know, you might want to consider the effects that a book like this has on them." But the Jesuits were great, you know, they didn't threaten me in any way, even subtly or anything. There was no cancel culture in those days, either from the right or left. What a great time to be in academia, as compared to today. Anyway, word about this "porno" book got around and apparently it went from hand to hand in the dorms.

MW: I thought it was pretty cool. I remember telling my friends, "Hey, guess what I'm reading for class. Can I read you a passage?" It was a lot of fun.

EN: Well, that was really Marty's lasting influence on me. He has a sense for the outré and subversive aspects—the fun aspects—of intellectual history. You see that in his work on aesthetic theory and on modern art especially. Bataille was a serious thinker, but he transgressed all boundaries. Reading him made intellectual history seem like one was exploring forbidden territory, a kind of cheerfully magic realm of thought. I think that is what Nietzsche meant by the untranslatable term *fröhliche Wissenschaft*: "exhilarating ideas" is what Nietzsche was after, I think. I enjoyed coming up with new themes for all of my seminars. Most professors taught the same thing every year.

MW: Over and over—

EN:—But I would use the new seminars as a way of just of finding stuff that I was interested in. It was learning through teaching. I don't remember teaching intellectual history as a kind of master narrative that could tie a lot of loose ends of the historical discipline together, but I can see how one would read it that way.

MW: Because people needed a context. It felt like everybody was talking about Derrida, but had no idea that any of that came from Heidegger, say. Or everybody would talk about Foucault, but you wouldn't really know anything about the larger history of structuralism or post-structuralism.

EN: Right.

MW: You had us reading H. Stuart Hughes, Dominick LaCapra, Fredric Jameson and other scholars who would give us a sort of narrative account of where the ideas came from and where they ended up. And in your own work on Jünger, you were really interested not just in Jünger, but in his reception, in how a body of work gets packaged or received or disseminated. At the time, it seemed to me that in all the courses my classmates took in English or literature, it was just a matter of applying theory X to book Y. Whereas it seemed like for you, especially in your lectures for the European intellectual history class, there was always a narrative. There was always a story, whether it was a biographical story, about a particular thinker, or a story about a movement, like Dada or decadence or existentialism.

EN: Again, Marty's influence. People say that Marty writes as if he is surveying a field from 30,000 feet.

MW: I always got the sense this was stuff that needed to be understood over time.

EN: Yes, synchronic but also diachronic.

MW: And not just in a theoretical way. But at the time, in the '90s, everything was theory.

EN: That's right.

MW: And I think that's why I was really attracted to intellectual history, because it gave us a sort of narrative about that theory, or it helped us understand that theory.

EN: I said that Marty's method has been described as going up 30,000 feet and looking down and making the connections, in a way that, as you say, other academics don't see their disciplines. Many academics don't try to make the connections in that syncretic way. For example, you observed that Derrida is *not* separate from Heidegger. Heidegger's lectures make explicit that his thought is *not* separate from the entire history of philosophy. That is what Quentin Skinner's whole project is about. I always found the idea that you had to see ideas in historical context as kind of a trite observation. But what he means, really, I think the deep sense of it—and this is also in Marty's work—is that the ideas themselves don't have validity in an abstract sense. Kant's categorical imperative, for example, is not universal. It was conceived at a certain point in time, as part of the European Enlightenment project. Kant thought that his ideas were valid for all times and in all cultures. But for Skinner, there is no such thing as a universal idea. It's always situated. That was definitely part of the training that we got through Marty and his work. Plus, the idea that a concept like the categorical imperative can be dialectally conceived as universally true and particularly situated at the same time. That's when things get interesting.

MW: Yes, the problem of how, or whether, to historicize transcendental ideas. It's at the heart of his recent book *Genesis and Validity* (2022), right? But I want to go back to what you were saying earlier about your first and second books, about how they were connected: you were looking at two constellations, the German intellectual right and the left after 1945. That makes sense, yet there is a big difference, I think, between the Jünger book and *Free Radicals*. There's a difference in style, or maybe at least in tone, between the Jünger book, a kind of critical monograph, and *Free Radicals*, which you suggest could be read as a political thriller. There's a shift toward a more narrative history. You're interested in telling a good story. And there are a lot of good stories to tell when you look at what's happening in the late '60s and early '70s in Germany.

EN: Good point. I think I shifted a little bit away from intellectual history when I wrote *Free Radicals*. I felt freer to write a book that was a combination of different types of history: social, cultural, political, and intellectual. Simon Schama is a model for me. His books synthesize a lot of different facets from a historical period, but the main thing is, he tells a riveting story.

I wanted the German student movement to be read as a family drama of a generation, one that is still around and squabbles a lot about their past. I was trying my hand at being just a regular historian rather than an intellectual historian. The Jünger book was a more traditional intellectual history, and I added the angle of reception history and collective memory. When I was researching it, there were many debates in Germany about how to theorize memory. Konrad Jarausch was a big influence on me then. His book, *Shattered Past,* is all about the way the memory of the war generation was filtered through the debris of the ruins of war. He has thought a lot about the layers of reception and collective memory.

MW: Isn't reception history tied mostly to literature?

EN: Yes.

MW: Hans Robert Jauss and the horizon of expectation?

EN: Yes, Jauss and the so-called Constance School were very important for rethinking literary theory. Jauss was also a fascinating figure because he spent two winters on the Russian front in WWII as a captain in the Waffen-SS, and was probably involved in war crimes. In 1995, almost at the end of his life, it was revealed that he had obfuscated his own past. A man who worked on time and memory, on the work of Marcel Proust, had lied and covered up his own past. Talk about a dubious past! For me, reception history was a good way to package the Jünger story. I had a lot of good material from the archives, especially the *Spiegel* Archive, to work with. I followed my sources.

MW: But I have the sense that, with *Free Radicals*, you were aiming for a more popular kind of history book.

EN: Or just like a regular history book, rather than an intellectual history book. A book about the German radical students couldn't be pure intellectual history anyhow, because they were not original thinkers. They were copying the Frankfurt School or even further back, the nineteenth-century anarchists and early twentieth century Marxists, people like Gramsci. One can't really point to a seminal thinker among the '68ers. Hans-Jürgen Krahl, one of Adorno's star students, was potentially such a figure, but the twenty-seven-year old died tragically in a car accident barely six months after Adorno's death in 1969. The tapes of Krahl's speeches were later transcribed and published.

The reason I wanted to write about the 68ers was that Jünger was a story about the conservative right. I wanted to do a story about the left, and the '68ers fit into that. I'd also had long-running arguments with the '68ers, actual '68ers in Germany, who were taking credit for the democratization of Germany, and I didn't agree with that. My book was the result of those long-standing debates.

MW: I wanted to ask you about that. How much did your experiences living in Germany in the '80s shape your research topics? For example, *Free Radicals* was about events that had occurred not that long before you arrived in Berlin in 1982: the Red Army Faction, the terrorism of the 1970s, all that kind of stuff.

EN: As a self-conceived Marxist in 1982, I was stuck, generationally, a decade behind the 68ers. I'm too young to be a '68er, but too old to be of the more conservative Generation X, which followed the boomers. I've got one foot still in that Sixties generation—I was a little kid in 1968. But the *Zeitgeist* was still there in the '70s, so I remember it personally. The generation that came after us had the reputation of disillusionment: the slacker generation. That's a cliché. But many of the clichés about the boomers, that they are full of themselves and exaggerate their contributions to culture, are kind of true. That comes through in my book anyway.

MW: This gives us a segue to one of the themes in the essays collected in *Selected Writings*, which is your interest in collective memory, or popular narratives, as opposed to, or distinct from, academic history. One thinks of a kind of popular memory of '68, not just in Germany, but also here, in Berkeley, or, indeed, all around the world. Doesn't every generation, in every place, invest in its own self-mythologizing?

EN: At least since 1914. That was the first time you saw the self-conscious creation of a myth around a shared experience. Perhaps the European Romantics were a prefiguration. Wordsworth: "bliss it was in that dawn to be alive."

MW: Is your role as a historian to come in and take the air out of the myths, to puncture the artificiality of collective memory or popular storytelling?

EN: A good question. Unfortunately, I only have this one piece on collective memory in this book and it's still a little rough. I'm actually going to work on it before I publish it. That was written for a forum at a conference in Frankfurt in 1996 on collective memory in the mid 1990s. It had to do with the Balkan wars and the breakup of Yugoslavia. I was in interested in the connection between the way that the violent breakup of Yugoslavia had to do with very strong attachments to certain historical memories among regular people, which didn't come down to the masses through scholarly or academic writings. Instead, there were really deep associations in people's sense of their own identity and history. The Slavs today remember, as if it happened yesterday, a battle on the Field of Blackbirds from 1389, when their army was defeated by an Ottoman sultan, leading to centuries of rule by a foreign power. All peoples have these pivotal memories, even Americans, who are supposed to be ahistorical. I found that fascinating. I started reading and found there is a rich literature on collective memory. Maurice Halbwachs was one of my key sources.

MW: You have another essay in this collection about German debates after 9/11. And you wrote an essay with Dirk Moses, too, about the question of violence in Germany, a replaying of debates the '68ers had, which in fact replicated debates from and about Weimar. It seems the struggle over collective memory is a struggle over how we interpret the past, but as a society, not necessarily as historians debating amongst ourselves. One of the things you show in the essay on German debates about 9/11 is that they had little to do with 9/11, actually. They had much more to do with Vietnam, with American involvement in Vietnam. Was that just because it's all tied to a particular generation, or are we always fighting the previous intellectual battle? We think we're talking about what's going on now, but really, we're talking about the past. In that regard, what should the historian do? Should we be participating in those conversations?

EN: Yes, historians are citizens as well. We think we can help illuminate the discussion, but what I found from my work on collective memory is that we need to understand first how collective memories are distinct from what we might call factual history. The story of ancient Jews who left Egypt and wandered in the desert for forty years is almost certainly ahistorical (where are the archeological traces?), but those constructed memories and how they have been passed down over the centuries are very real.

MW: One of the first classes I took with you was a historiography class, I think it was the second semester of my freshman year. You taught historical methods through a confrontation with the phenomenon of Holocaust revisionism—still relatively insignificant at the time—as a kind of case study. Today, we now call it Holocaust denial, not revisionism. You assigned some prominent Holocaust deniers, like David Irving, and we compared them to established historians like Deborah Lipstadt and Richard J. Evans. You used them to show the difference between good, sober scholarly research, with scholarly ethics and integrity, as opposed to making stuff up and politicizing history with a hidden or not-so-hidden agenda. If historians are pushed today to write for more popular audiences, I wonder whether we end up sacrificing that sober, scholarly, critical distance when we join the debates or the conversations about popular memory. Sometimes it feels as if the debate about popular or collective memory has overtaken historical scholarship. People don't listen to scholars anymore. They listen to YouTubers and podcasters and people like that.

EN: A lot to unpack there.

MW: Yeah, sorry. I kind of overwhelmed you there.

EN: I would start by looking exactly at that phenomenon, which fascinated me back then, that phenomenon of denialism. You have to remember that Holocaust denial back in the '90s was something very few people knew about.

MW: Yeah. I got the sense that it was a fringe thing.

EN: It was fringey, yeah.

MW: And now, it's everywhere.

EN: It's everywhere. And when you bring up YouTube, a good example today of what you are talking about is Darryl Cooper. He is an amateur historian who went on Tucker Carlson's show in 2024 and said that Winston Churchill was the chief villain of WWII because Hitler actually wanted to make peace with England, and if it hadn't been for Churchill, Hitler never would have started the war. As with all these dangerous fantasies, there is a tiny grain of truth in it. Hitler did want to make a deal with England, but of course, the rest of the theory is preposterous. Now Cooper has a popular podcast called *Martyr Made* from which he spouts this nonsense, and has amassed many followers in the MAGA world. In a telling sign of our age of polarization, Churchill has always been a bugaboo for the left, since he was an unapologetic imperialist, but now the right-wing fringe has decided that isolationism is a good thing and people like Churchill are the problem. That is how history as collective memory is abused.

MW: Somewhat similarly, at the time you were working on Jünger, I thought of him as an esoteric German writer, fascinating, but really on the margins. And yet now, with the rise of the New Right and the new authoritarianism, from Orbán, Bukele, and Erdoğan to Putin and Trump, not to mention all the other authoritarian leaders today, he doesn't seem so marginal. Back in the '90s, I *never* thought this kind of right-wing ideology would gain any legitimacy in the public sphere. There was still an "end of history" and "history arcing toward justice" vibe, which continued even up to, and maybe through, the Obama years. And yet now they're all around us.

EN: Everywhere you look. Have you followed this right-wing ideologue, Curtis Yarvin?

MW: I wanted to ask you about him.

EN: Yarvin loves Jünger.

MW: There was a *New Yorker* article about that recently.

EN: That is how far Jünger's influence reaches. In American politics! I never expected that either.

MW: So, given all that, how do we guard against the abuse of collective memory?

EN: First, draw a clear demarcation between source-based rigorous history and how memory in the public sphere becomes a political tool. I think in the same way that today, politics has been weaponized, the economy, culture, law, you name it, history has become one more weapon to use against your partisan foe. The best we can do as professional historians is to track the phenomenon. People think history is just a bunch of facts about the past. If that were true, then we would not be able to distinguish between what the drunken ranter at the bar tells you about why Hitler wasn't such a bad guy after all and any random professor at Berkeley.

Something malevolent has happened to our culture. I don't want to be one of those aging nostalgic guys who thinks everything was better in the past. A lot of things today are better than when I was growing up. But we are guinea pigs in a world in which social media has changed public discourse in very fundamental and mostly negative ways. Make America Great Again could not have happened without Facebook and Twitter, and it is a prime example of the manipulation of collective memory. The "again" in that phrase gives it away.

MW: Yeah, absolutely. Does the historian have to choose between writing for other academics, maybe three or four people, and the masses, or at least the educated public? Do you think there is room for something in-between?

EN: I think academic historians should not change our methods. It ain't broke, so don't fix it. But as public intellectuals, we have to try as best as we can to point out the way in which history gets abused by the culture. In the mobilization against Trump, it is good to see many historians being asked to weigh in. You see many articles these days with titles like "Ten Historians Assess the Trump Presidency," and historians of Weimar Germany are seeing their cell phones light up with calls from journalists. I guess that is a silver lining for the profession.

MW: Yeah.

EN: Back in Nietzsche's day, it was almost the opposite. He was worried about monumental history, which was being taught in the schools. We have the opposite problem, trivial history. [Laughs]

MW: You could say that the 1776 project is an attempt at monumental history, right? To create a grand narrative of American greatness, quote-unquote. And there's no need, no room here, really, for critical history.

EN: That's true.

MW: And quite a few scholars have signed up for this. Wilfred McClay, a very famous, well respected American intellectual historian, is one. He and others have started putting out books that are primarily celebratory, maybe even jingoistic. I think the disturbing thing is that all this is happening while the Trump administration is attacking higher education in an ideological fashion.

EN: And the history books that are being taught in school.

MW: Absolutely. It seems to me that we've always, in our culture, fought over what gets taught as history. That's ground zero: history, or textbooks, especially in Texas. But this is precisely why I think intellectual history is really relevant—to make people aware of the difference between, for example, liberalism, classical liberalism, and Viktor Orbán's illiberalism; to have people know what these terms actually mean.

EN: Absolutely.

MW: Otherwise, you get people like Curtis Yarvin, who step in and become the influencers of the new political parties, supposedly. But we've said enough about him already. I wanted to ask you more about Jünger, and to talk a little bit more about *Free Radicals,* too. But first, there are some essays in the book related to this question of collective memory and narrative history, which reflect what I would say is a post-Hayden White, post-grand narrative moment. There was a turn after Hayden White to think of all historical scholarship as just another form of writing. And of course, Derrida is influential for that as well. It seems to me that you reject all this. You reject the idea that history is just another form of narrative or fictionalizing. Is that safe to say?

EN: I don't talk a lot about it because I'm not a grand theorist. If you want to know about these kinds of questions, no one has done better than Martin Jay, in that book you mentioned earlier, *Genesis and Validity.* The argument is a tour de force, and I'm not going to try and compete with that. He lays out in fine detail the tension between the contingent origin of ideas and universal truth claims. He argues for a dialectical middle ground, neither pure historicism, nor abstract, contextless validity. Exactly what we are discussing here.

As for what I wrote, I think you're referring to a piece that I did include in this collection, at the end of the section on historiography. It's fair to say I don't buy Hayden White, although White was an incredibly deep thinker, and he is not to be dismissed. For him, history is a narrative construction, not a discovery of pre-existing facts. He doesn't think we can easily distinguish, at a metatextual level, between formal coherence and fictional storytelling. All stories are subjective and have ethical and political implications. Now Hayden White is perfectly aware that there are real events, and that they matter, and what's at stake there. Dirk Moses published a wonderful piece in 2005 discussing all of these thorny issues: like how do you defend against Holocaust denial if everything is a constructed narrative? Moses wants to tackle the public role of history—that phrase is in the title of his piece—so he examined collective memory and national trauma, exactly the same things I dealt with in my work on Serbian nationalism. For me, White plays linguistic games in his formulations, and Dirk addresses this.

Leaving all that aside, I would like to defend a certain old-fashioned sense of history as a basic story about the way things actually were, to quote Ranke. To go back there, though, not naively, and not without taking into account all the objections and qualifications and sophisticated ways in which poststructuralism—or whatever you want to call it—and those who are skeptical about the validity of historical narratives have raised. Let's give that its due. It is true that we write history always from a certain perspective.

MW: There's always a language game; there's always a frame.

EN: That brings us to Derrida. But people often forget how well Derrida knew his history of philosophy. He knew very well that one can't just quote Hegel, say, incorrectly, and get away with it. He was very precise in his seminars. And then there is Paul Feyerabend, and how he taught us to be wary of the fact that scientists make up their method after they have found a new paradigm, often acting as if the method had been in place all along. This is all true, but I still think it's important to hang on to a sense of old-fashioned realism so that we can distinguish between truth and falsehoods in the historical record. History was made by human beings who made consequential and contingent decisions in the world. Structures don't determine history. History is not out of our control; people are not puppets of larger forces that make them do what they do. There *is* agency.

MW: I think a lot of this connects to the work you did on Jünger. As you present him in the book and in some of these essays, Jünger was always interested in subjectivity, in holding onto, or trying to understand, subjective experience, even in the face of massive technological change. He was somebody who addressed—and you show this very well—before Heidegger and others really understood it, the turn toward technology. Because of his war experiences, Jünger was already trying to make sense of what happens to the individual subject in a technological age. Even in his later experiments with drug culture, he is somebody who is doing a kind of phenomenology. He's always interested in subjective experience, never willing to leave the subject out of whatever he's doing. There's a kind of mounted defense of the individual subject throughout his career. Is that fair to say?

EN: It's complicated. At one level, that is for sure true. I call Jünger's approach at one point in the book, "Phenomenology Without a Subject." That's where I'm thinking about Jünger's phenomenological method, which, you are correct, he developed in his early war writings. For him, there are forms—*Gestalt* is a really important concept for him—the *form* of the worker, or the *form* of the soldier, for example, which he's trying to describe. He's trying to offer us symbols, as opposed to allegories, to use Benjamin's terms. The allegory sets up a juxtaposition: understanding something by comparing it to something else. Jünger is more interested in the symbol. What does the war mean, in and of itself? And in that sense, there's no subject. But in another sense, it's true, if you read the war diaries, they are very much centered in personalized experience—and how that represents some kind of universal. He's trying to speak for all the other soldiers who went through the same world-historical drama.

MW: Speaking of world-historical drama, the notion of *Posthistoire* bubbles up in Jünger's later World War II diaries, the Paris diaries, for which you wrote the introduction of the translation put out by Columbia University Press. In those diaries, Jünger clearly uses his own subjective experience as an entry point to understanding larger currents in global or world history. As with some of his other writings, he's trying to navigate between a world of mythic meaning, on the one hand, and modern science and technology, on the other. He wants to say that they can coexist, right, that myth can still coexist with science, and that science is, in some sense, still myth?

EN: Jünger is definitely a proponent of *posthistorical* thinking. What is posthistory? I think, for him, it is the idea that we live in a time in which historical events are not connected serially. They're not correlated in a standard chronological pattern in the tradition of Western logic: *A causes B, B causes C.* Why? Well, for all kinds of reasons related to technology and modernity, the rules have broken down. Modernity was the high point of a secular belief in progress, a telos, an objective endpoint where history would culminate. Hegel calls it the Absolute, a universal compendium of all knowledge and self-consciousness of our place at the end of the unfolding of history. Hans Blumenberg's theory of the legitimacy of the modern age is a more recent example of the idea: humanity's self-affirmation, without the need for divine mandates.

For Jünger and the proponents of *posthistoire*, that project of modernity fails because there's no apotheosis. There is no emancipation, no self-realization. In a post-historical world, all kinds of things are happening, but they don't connect to each other, and they're all happening at once. All we have left are the shards and the relics of the past, like debris or traces that pile up on the edge of the seashore (Foucault, interestingly, would use a similar image). Jünger didn't come up with all this by himself, but he's part of that mindset. Like Heidegger, he thinks we have to go back to the redemption of the divine, to mythology. He becomes the editor of a journal, *Antaios*, which studied myths and archetypes.

MW: How does all this relate to the 1990s discussion of the end of history? Especially after the fall of the Berlin Wall, don't you get something similar from Francis Fukuyama and his [Alexandre] Kojève-inspired reading of Hegel, saying that we're now at the end of history? As you say, the idea comes from Heidegger, too. Heidegger said the same thing after World War II: things happen, but nothing has meaning anymore, only a God can save us, all that kind of stuff. Do these ideas explain why Jünger's weird, apocalyptic sci-fi novels are almost always set in the remnants of an empire, or a fallen civilization, where people are trying to hold on to the lost shards of past meaning? And if that's the case, could this be another reason why the libertarians love him today?

EN: Certainly some of his novels. Especially *Eumeswil*, from 1977, where he conceptualizes a world in which memory is stored in what look like computers, or at least machines with historical databases. Somebody is in charge of the memory for the collective and can go back and pull the pieces out, at random, but there is no meaning to any of it. I think post-history explains Jünger's interest in sci-fi, but it is also connected to the fact that, for him, more important than world history was geological history. He sees nature and the cosmos as something in which we play a very, very small part, a very small role. In a professional way, he's fascinated by nature. He was a beetle collector. He loves looking into that world. He knew all his flowers and plants. He had an amazing mastery of zoology and botany and all that. He was an entomologist, and there are many beetles named for him in official taxonomy. For him, *that's* really history. But he wouldn't even call it history. It's nature, spirit, order. It's another realm. We humans had our time. We were kind of interesting little creatures, but the story that he's interested in is that much larger one.

MW: Do you think some of the recent interest in Jünger could be tied to conversations about the Anthropocene? There's a post post-humanist perspective in his work, no?

EN: For sure. He was an environmentalist before there was an environmentalist Green Party. But his concern with the environment was apocalyptic. It was more like the deep ecology movement in

Germany, which has very right-wing aspects to it. Fascism and environmentalism were connected, but I don't want to paint Jünger with that brush, except to say that the politics of geology are not clear cut.

MW: Let's talk a little bit more about Jünger's popularity today. Who, exactly, is interested in reviving or returning to Jünger today? Are they libertarians, conservatives, ecologists, antiquarians? Would you say your book has played a role in the Jünger revival? And where does that revival come from in your opinion?

EN: My book on Jünger was published in 1999, so, relatively early in the English-speaking world. Interest in his work has grown quite a bit since then. As a result, my book gets quoted as a kind of standard overview—not as a biography, but rather as a reception study written from a viewpoint that doesn't take aim at him from the left or is apologetic from the right, which tends to be fairly common in Germany. I find that the scholars who are writing about Jünger today are more open to the non-political aspects of Jünger. They're not as interested anymore in *Was he a fascist? What is his tie to fascism?* Although that will always be part of the mix. I have received letters and emails from people who ask about his esotericism, his drug experiences, his views on nature, his occultism, etc. Many are independent scholars or writers themselves. He very clearly anticipated the apocalyptic consequences of modernity and the destruction of nature. People are interested in that.

MW: What about the new Silicon Valley right, the tech-bro right, the extreme libertarian right: Peter Thiel, Elon Musk, or Curtis Yarvin, whom we mentioned earlier? These are people fantasizing about outer-world colonies, people who say Earth is doomed, that kind of stuff. Is that where Jünger fits into the conversation?

EN: I think in a mood sense. It's hard for me to see how Jünger's writings fit into—

MW: Silicon Valley—

EN:—Andreessen and Thiel and Musk and all their weird techno-utopianism. Jünger might have been fascinated by Musk's idea of going to Mars and all that. But he would have viewed Musk more like Heidegger might have, as a kind of imperialist attempting to control outer space. We already destroyed our planet with technology, and now we want to export that? I think you are on to something, though. The mood is there, the fascination with thinkers like Jünger on the right. Jünger's writing is very hard to staple down. He saw himself as a thinker in "no-man's land"—his exact phrase—and I think that is correct in many respects.

MW: It's always poetic and suggestive.

EN: It's metaphysical-poetic, exactly. I guess you could do a lot with it, whatever you want to do with it. One of the games I think some intellectuals like is thinking that they've cracked the code on Jünger's thought. Very similar to Heidegger, too. As Adorno called it, the jargon of authenticity. In that sense, I think Jünger fits into our moment, this post-humanist, post-modern, post-post-post-moment. When do we get beyond post anyway?

MW: You don't buy the narrative that—and this gets us back to the post-history thing—September 11th put an end to the era of post-modernism and post-history and all of that? That it brought history back? I remember there was a substantial debate about whether or not the end of history had itself ended. Some thought we were back to regular power politics, the clash of civilizations, and with the invasions of Afghanistan and Iraq, there was going to be a new world order.

EN: I think that was a specific reaction to Fukuyama, rather than the European idea of *posthistoire*. *Posthistoire* is not the same as the end of history, I don't think. Fukuyama thinks we ended up basically at liberal capitalism. That narrative thread is coherent. We live with capitalism and markets, and various forms of liberal democracy. There will be some stragglers, he says, but they're all going to catch up eventually, or fall by the wayside.

MW: He uses the not-so-subtle image of the wagon-train.

EN: Yes, the wagon train going through the new frontier. The European *posthistoire* thing is much more apocalyptic. All of history has been shattered. There is no thread, no trail to the new frontier. There's certainly not liberal capitalism that gives us meaning—or if it isn't meaning, at least gives us an anchor in something. People like Jünger, and the European *posthistorie* thinkers, are useful for these tech bros who are playing with the end of democracy, which they think is weak and outdated. They want to be the rulers of the brave new world they have created with their codes. For sure, they can find lots of support in Jünger, who never really made his peace with democracy. Jünger also saw a new world of steel-eyed soldiers and workers being created that would overcome squishy parliamentarian systems. But the difference is that his heart is really back in eighteenth-century France. He was a big admirer of the works of Louis de Rouvroy, duc de Saint-Simon, a seventeenth-eighteenth century French duke who opposed Louis XIV because the Sun King was curtailing the power of the high nobility. That can fit very nicely into something like Yarvin's new monarchism: the sense that only the elites can save us; that the masses are just sheep who follow their masters, the trends, and can be manipulated; that they'll just have to accept this new order. But Jünger would never buy into this, because he wasn't interested in having followers. Like Heidegger, he goes off into the forest all alone. He is an anarch, but not an anarchist. An inner rebel who appears to be a conformist. If you read him, you certainly get the sense that he sees things that other people don't see, and that he's going to invite you into that realm of magic, to pierce the veil of illusions. He was very esoteric and mystical in that sense. He believed in astrology. He thought that there were other worlds there that were more important and deeper than the ones we experience.

MW: How did you get from all that to the '68ers? Was it a leap, going from the anarch to the anarchists?

EN: I wanted to do then the left side of the spectrum after I'd done the right, and I had also had, as I said, these personal experiences with the '68ers, and the way they saw themselves. It was just a topic that I thought could bring together a number of my interests. I thought it was a good story, and I thought it was important to understand the way that the Germans, in particular, take their history so seriously.

One of the important themes in the book is the creation of an artificial revolution, the idea that the '68ers staged a revolution. I have all these metaphors in the book, at the beginning, in the introduction: that 1968 was a created revolution, an artificial revolution, a staged revolution. The difference between the American '68ers and the Europeans, especially the German '68ers, was, I argue (to sort of oversimplify), that the American '68ers wanted the U.S. Constitution, which had important principles, high principles, to live up to its liberatory potential. They wanted to help it become realized. The European intellectuals, the revolutionaries, they wanted to copy revolutions that succeeded. They wanted to figure out why those failed, so that it would be done properly this time. That's why they embraced violence more explicitly than their American counterparts. The revolutions in the past that had succeeded, well they broke a lot of eggs to make the omelette.

MW: And the German '68ers were far more influenced by third-worldist movements...

EN:—And their own history, the French Revolution, the lessons of failed revolutions in 1848 in Germany and 1917 in Russia.

MW:—And Weimar. A lot of this was a replay of anxieties that go back to the collapse of Weimar democracy. The question of violence, in particular.

EN: Yes. And the responsibility of their parents—who they were, as a generation, up against—who had succumbed to fascism. They saw themselves as rescuing, in a way, their parents' failure to stand up to fascism. They wanted to redeem their parents' failures and atone for their guilt and sins. Some of it was re-enacted redemption, but it could be accusative as well: the inability of the parents' generation to mourn the Holocaust. A lot of people have psychoanalyzed the generation of 1968, and some of it is very speculative, but they are on to something.

MW: One of the surprising arcs in the book—because you talk quite a bit about how somebody goes from being a rebel to an enemy of the state—appears in the later chapters, in which you suggest that the reverberations of '68 long outlast '68 itself. What are those reverberations, exactly? Are they lessons in the critique of violence? Are they lessons of moderation? What did *you* take away, writing *Free Radicals*, about the lessons learned? Was it the idea that moderate reform is far better than the Red Army Faction, or Baader-Meinhof, or something like that? Because obviously, in the States, we still have similar arguments about what something like the Free Speech Movement at Berkeley *really* means or *really* entails, about what the legacy of '68 *really* is. Of course, '68ers themselves are the ones who are most heavily invested in this. But it doesn't seem to me that *Free Radicals* is *just* a critique, or *only* a critique, of the spirit of '68 in Germany.

EN: I don't spend a lot of time answering that question, but in the final chapter, I do talk a little bit about these techno-libertarians in Stanford and Berkeley. Stanford had Steve Jobs and all these people who thought that the real liberation was going to happen through the internet, eventually. Power to the people in the world of personal computers. But to answer your question, I definitely do come down on the side that the kind of political revolution that the Europeans have tried over and over again usually ends up a disaster. The cautionary model really is the French Revolution, which ends up in the Terror, and the right kind of revolution is more the American Revolution, which maybe even wasn't really a revolution, but a restoration of the rights of English people. 1776 was incredibly important for the Europeans. That is often denied. "*Oh, the American Revolution had nothing to do with what happened in France.*" That is nonsense. The French revolutionaries were too proud to admit the influence of the uncultured Americans, so they don't quote Thomas Jefferson, but they translated the ideas of the Founding

Fathers and mixed them up with Rousseau and Voltaire to cover their tracks.

I'm more for pragmatism, but also opening up the possibilities that, if it's done in a nonviolent way, societies can create positive revolutionary changes. You just have to watch out for the Janus-headed consequences of all change. The internet was supposed to liberate us by giving the individual a new kind of power. Instead, we ended up with this dystopian nightmare of social media. At least that revolution was sort of peaceful, if you take out the part where mobs can become so easily engaged and enraged. In general, I think that change is usually a problem. It needs to be managed smartly, more than grappled onto. Both the left and the right have this problem.

MW: But it can't be managed by AI, right? Otherwise, we could have had AI do this whole interview.

EN: Right.

MW: The AI bot could have said a few things right, which you may have said, and then maybe said a few more things correctly, which I may have said, but it also would have spouted a whole lot of made-up bullshit that would be totally wrong.

EN: I'm not an expert on AI, but I'll bet you and I both come down on the same page. I think Bert Dreyfus's critique of computers is still valid. I think he would criticize AI the same way. Computers don't live in a "world"—in Heidegger's sense—the way we live in one. Dreyfus's close friend, the philosopher John Searle came up this thought experiment he calls the Chinese Room. My version of that is that AI is like an alien spaceship lands on earth and leaves instructions behind on how to contact them. The computer figures out the code but has no idea what it is saying. Searle calls this the difference between syntax and semantics. AI is like that. It can ape what humans do, but does not live in our world of chronology and spatial orientation. That said, I think other philosophers today are giving us another way to look at computers, which Dreyfus missed. When you go online, you are entering an alternative reality, AR, that is the real AI. All cultures have created mythologic worlds, in which time is experienced differently, sometimes slower, other times faster, and we meet monsters and fairies and strange creatures, and then return changed beings. The alternative world is dangerous and addictive. There lurk plenty of dragons. We come back from it as in a trance, our selves transformed, for good and bad. Today we treat the online world as a drug, which it is, with all the therapeutic talk of addiction and recovery. But we are never going back in time to a world without magic silicon chips. Social media is our Lord of the Rings and we better learn to live in it and in the real world. Our students today are native to this mythology, so it is hard for them to fathom what it was like before we lived a lot of our lives immersed in seductive and enchanting screens.

MW: I tend to agree. Because you can tell when students use AI. I've tried to point this out to them, and they're still not convinced. That's a whole other topic, though. Before we run out of time, I wanted to ask you one more question in relation to *Free Radicals*, maybe bringing its storyline up to the current moment. You say in the book that it was really the responses to 9/11 that got you thinking about going back to write about '68, and the legacy of '68, because a lot of the responses, especially German responses to American militarism after 9/11, were replaying old debates from '68—debates about American involvement in Vietnam, but also about German history. And so I wonder, now that we're in this new moment of the second Trump presidency and an ascendant right-wing authoritarianism, punctuated by, among other things, Putin's invasion of Ukraine, I wonder if you see the legacy of '68 any differently? Are we just having an endless cycle of debates about the same thing? Or is there something new in this moment that should make us rethink how we understand '68, or Weimar?

EN: That's a great question. Let me give you something biographical about the post-9/11 moment. I defended the invasion of Iraq. I saw myself as one of the liberal hawks. I didn't have the reputation of someone like Thomas Friedman, you know—

MW:—There were a fair number. Michael Ignatieff, for example. I wasn't one of them, but there were a lot of people who defended the toppling of Saddam Hussein.

EN: I saw myself as one of them and wrote a few things at the time. I had some editorials published here and there, and in the *San Francisco Chronicle*, which made some of my friends pretty angry. My justification for it at the time was that it's even okay to lie—Plato's Noble Lie, a myth that serves the greater good—as G. W. Bush did to get us in there, because fighting fascism is always a good thing. The articles I wrote then that were critical of the Germans had to do with the idea that they really were fighting all these other wars, intergenerational ones, that had nothing to do with what was going on Iraq. When I look back upon it, though, I was obviously wrong about Iraq. I fess up to that. I think a lot of it was mistakes that were made, which didn't have to have been made. It could have turned out differently. But it's pretty clear that the people who were horrified by the lies that got us in there, and the ways in which the administration absolutely did not understand the culture there, they were right. I was wrong about that, and was too optimistic that we could rebuild a society like we did in Germany after 1945. The Germans had a history of middle-class stability and democratic practices that the Iraqis obviously did not. Nevertheless, I think one shouldn't count the whole exercise as a total disaster. There is a functioning, if weak and corrupt democracy in Iraq right now. It's better than what they had under Hussein, who was one of the most bloodthirsty dictators of the late twentieth century. The Middle East has changed because of that war, some of it for the good. I hope that contextualizes where those articles came from. Your other question was about today.

MW: Yes, and about what is a rollback, really, of the post-World War II order, especially in Europe, but with Trump, in the United States, too.

EN: So my neocon muscle reflexes are getting triggered again, because I really think Ukraine is like the Spanish Civil War of our day. Selling out Ukraine is like Munich, 1938, with all the usual caveats about historical comparisons noted. I'm horrified by the way that neither the left nor the right can find the courage to support Ukraine, especially when *no* American soldiers are involved in this, and the Ukrainians are doing *all* the fighting against our foe in the China-Russia-Iran axis. Their soldiers are putting *their* lives on the line for their freedom and ultimately ours in the West. And the money we spend on that war goes mostly to American defense contractors. Trump calling Zelensky a dictator and cozying up to Putin is disgraceful and will be judged harshly by later historians. I'm burnt by the Iraq experience, but I'm ready to go to the mat for Ukraine in any way that I can—as a public intellectual, at least.

MW: That leads us to my final question: What's next? You've gathered these essays together, and then? Are you thinking about any other projects?

EN: Not yet. For now, I'm focused on these selected writings. But I hope it is not my swan song. I have a few more verses left in me to sing.

MW: You did talk about wanting to write the Great American novel.

EN: I did.

MW: There's still time.

EN: Not as much as there used to be. But thank you for the encouragement. And for this discussion. It was very meaningful to me and I hope useful for others.

10 July 2025
San Rafael, California

The Best of Scholars and Scholarship in the Humanities

The series showcases the best of the humanities, as collected in essays and other texts by leading scholars. Drawing upon recognized experts across the human sciences, this landmark series brings together scholarly contributions on time-tested humanistic themes. Volumes are comprised of new and/or republished chapters, comment pieces, and interviews by specialists in their fields, grouped around areas of public interest. Throughout, this series remains above the political and media fray, yet without detachment from either area; examines issues critically, but without engaging in polemics or *ad hominem* attacks; and surveys new and challenging ideas, where robustly evidenced, while refusing to chase superficial trends. In keeping with the much-maligned Enlightenment tradition, in short, this series brings intellectual light where there has too often been *both* too much heat *and* the darkness of ignorance. Each book in the series provides real and demonstrable contributions to humanistic knowledge, with all volumes curated to stand the test of time.

International Advisory Board:

